THERE
IS
MORE
TO
THE
STORY

By
MISTRESS T

Cover art by Drew Young

Cover design by Srdjan Filipovic

Back cover author photo by Photobin Photography

Typesetting by Kerry Ellis

Copyedit by Johnny Kolodziejczak

Last chapter and back cover text written in collaboration with Jesse Donaldson

A CIP record for this book is available from the Library of Congress Cataloging-in-Publication Data

ISBN: 978-1-9995551-0-8

This book is dedicated to:

Sandra for the encouragement, Des & MB for the support and editing, and Jesse who literally shoved me and the book across the finish line.

To my dearest friends — those who appear in the book and those who don't, but who have been here for years supporting me through it all.

Lastly, this book is dedicated to my mother, father and brother. I threw them under the bus to tell my truth, but family is complicated, people are imperfect and I love them with all my heart.

Contents

CHAPTER 1

Do You Mind?

"**D**o you mind?"

He asked from behind me, cock in hand, stroking. By the dim glow of the TV I could make out his size: *large*. But I already knew that. Mom loved to brag about her boyfriend.

Even at thirteen I could recognize the face of a man boiling with excitement and sexual tension, but I didn't care, didn't feel threatened, didn't really feel much of anything. Shrugging, I returned to my show. What was on TV? It wasn't porn; he was masturbating to me.

I had already become numb to sexually inappropriate situations, so I wasn't surprised when my mother didn't break up with him for it. She simply ensured that we weren't left alone together anymore. After all, she had been dangling me in front of him from the start by showing him a picture of me in lacey lingerie that barely concealed my budding breasts.

I couldn't have known then that I'd eventually make a career out of countless men masturbating to their fantasies about me.

Few choose the path I've taken. Of those who try, not many achieve significant success or stick with it. Becoming one of the most successful and well-known FemDom fetish porn stars takes a certain mix of ingredients. For me, it started with training my young self to override my natural disgust at inappropriate or unpleasant sexual situations. My mother added intense encouragement to be independent and constantly told me, "You can do whatever you want to do." Stir in several years in the business world developing sales and marketing skills and *bingo!*—the result is a skilled and driven woman uniquely prepared to do whatever was necessary to succeed in a business most people wouldn't have the ovaries to do.

It's not that simple, of course. As with most things, there's more to the story. If you've come for the salacious bits, you won't be disappointed, but my tale can't be told like a Penthouse letter. The making of Mistress T is just as interesting as the crazy things that have happened to me while being Mistress T.

The story starts before I do.

CHAPTER 2

Gone With the Wind

My mother came from a long line of drunks and philanderers, the result of an accidental pregnancy when her parents were sixteen. She was the first of six kids.

Keeping with family tradition, she too got knocked up at sixteen. The father was a no-good so-and-so who also happened to give her crabs. She gave the baby up for adoption and met my father soon after. He was from a family with a better reputation, and she was told he was too good for her, so she married him. She was nineteen. He was in love with her, finding her feisty spirit endearing and getting a kick out of her foul mouth. Oh, and what a mouth she had.

My father enjoyed telling me about my birth—how my mother cursed so fiercely that the nurse said, "My, what a big mouth on such a little woman!" My mother told her to fuck off and continued her tirade.

And so I entered the world—to a soundtrack of screaming and cursing.

I was my parents' second and last-born child. My older brother was a toddler when I arrived, but there was already a wedge between him and my mother. I made it worse. An odd drama was already playing out that even after all these years I still can't fully comprehend. My mother felt that the grandmothers on both sides of the family "stole" my brother from her and turned him against her. She favoured me, which caused my grandmothers to favour my brother even more; a feedback loop of dysfunction.

My mother went through the motions of motherhood often self-medicated with prescription pills and emotionally distant. Although our basic needs were always met, both of my parents had a hands-off approach to parenting, feeding my independent nature and aversion to authority.

My brother directed all of his childhood resentment towards me, blaming me, I suppose, for the lack of connection with our mother. I was his tool for getting the attention from mom he desperately wanted but had no other way of getting. I lost count of the bloody noses and split lips, the number of times he painfully held me down, sat on my chest until I couldn't breathe, spat in my face or put his dirty socks in my mouth. I would scream and scream until mom would finally break it up. This pattern of violence repeated ceaselessly until my brother hit puberty and everyone feared for my safety.

My parents enrolled me in martial arts training so that I could learn to protect myself. They felt helpless about protecting me from my brother's increasing hatred. The message was clear: I had to take care of myself because I couldn't depend on anyone else, even my own parents, to protect me from danger.

After my first class I walked up to my life-long abuser, punched him in the face and ran. As I looked back, he crumpled to the floor. I thought that things would change then because he'd know that he couldn't push me around anymore. I was wrong.

He was two years older, entering puberty, and I was small for my age. I liked to think that I loved him too much to hurt him, but I knew that realistically in the end he would always find a way to get back at me. I feared him, feared his revenge, *that* much. Even though I went on to win medals in fighting competitions, I never hit him again.

We lived in a tiny house in a quiet, rural Nova Scotia community with only a small Baptist church and a community hall big enough for the occasional potluck gathering. Both served as opportunities for gossip, the preferred local pastime. This was farm country: cows, sheep, chickens, vegetable gardens, apple trees. The kind of place with haying season and no more than a dozen trick-or-treaters; if someone's dog got loose, everyone knew whose it was.

My grandparents lived across the road from us on a small, typical farm. I spent a lot of time there observing my gruff grandfather toiling away while my well-spoken and charming grandmother cooked, made preserves, tended the garden and spent countless hours on the phone gossiping with her friends.

My grandmother was the sort of woman who would have lived a radically different life had she been born fifty years later. Sharp, driven, articulate, social—what might she have become had the opportunity risen? She and my grandfather were poorly matched, bickering constantly about everything. She took it upon herself to ensure that I at least knew proper table manners and social etiquette, even if no one else enforced them; that I had good posture and *some* idea of how to act like a lady. Most importantly, she was careful to ensure that I knew how to speak properly and tirelessly supported me in public speaking competitions.

All through my childhood I enjoyed performing in front of crowds: at school or church, even in front of family members. An exhibitionist from the start. I was competitive, but more than anything I craved the rush of being on stage and performing. In my teens, I privately tutored other students in Shakespeare by acting out the various roles so that they could better understand the story.

That's why I was so good at lying to my father about my mother's transgressions: it was, ultimately, all a performance.

The first time I covered for my mother I was eleven. Mom and I went for a drive with Lester to get ice cream. He'd been a family friend my whole life, but we had never gone anywhere with him. He mostly came around to visit my father, so this little adventure was a big treat for me. After ice cream we went to Lester's place, where he put *Gone With the Wind* on and explained that my mother was going to help him with his sore shoulder.

In the bedroom.

Gone With the Wind is a mightily long, boring film for an eleven-year-old to watch while contemplating what might be happening behind a closed bedroom door.

I'll never forget the first time I was used as cover; the unwilling enabler of a tragic lie. I was sick to my core, too young to comprehend the anxiety melting my insides. I blamed it on the ice cream as I sat on the toilet fighting a sudden bout of diarrhea, straining to hear the activity in the bedroom but not wanting to hear at the same time. I tried to be quiet, worrying the flushing of the toilet might disturb them. I wanted to be a good girl, to not be a bother.

But that relentless fucking movie went on forever.

Afterward, Lester was clearly ashamed, his skittish eyes avoiding mine. I never knew exactly what happened in that bedroom, which is odd because shortly after my mother spared few details when recounting the stories of her affairs.

After the Lester incident my mother took her first job outside of our home, working across the road doing farm labour. She had a summer fling with another farm hand, and I knew *all* about it. They worked extra hard in the morning to finish their work early, buying time to smoke hash and have a quickie in the barn in the afternoon.

She temporarily moved in with her sister to help with her new baby, and I spent part of the time there with her. I would walk her to the local tavern and walk home alone. She didn't come back to the house those nights until the wee hours. We shared a bed in the spare room, and I would lie awake waiting for her to return and whisper her conquests of fucking the bartender and barflies in their cars in the parking lot into my ear. My vivid imagination painted pictures of my mother's orgasms, straddling some guy in the reclined front seat of a car, steaming up the windows, both panting like dogs.

The images disgusted me, but I loved being her confidant. I forced an encouraging smile while suppressing my urge to throw up. She hadn't shown much interest in mothering, but now that I was old enough to have *these* conversations, she was glad to have me as a friend. Brightening, she told me about her exploits, connecting with me in a way that she never could before. It was a life raft in which I could have some kind of relationship with her. To refuse to listen to her exploits or keep her secrets was to threaten the fragile shred of a relationship I had with the most important person in my life. So I pretended to be her best friend, pretended to be happy to hear her stories. I encouraged her to enjoy herself. I gave her what she wanted so that I could get the love I needed. Then I would go home to my father and act like everything was fine.

Through her venting about my father I began to see Mom as the victim in their relationship, as though his shortcomings, passivity and aloofness were some great abuse.

She and I were a team united against the enemy, even though he wasn't *my* enemy. He loved me and tried to be a good father to me. In a way I suppose he thought he was being a good husband too, but after 17 years autopilot was fully engaged. Patterns and habits had been formed; he was going through the motions without any thought. If Mom was a prisoner of boredom and regret, Dad was her jailor. A caged animal, she was only attempting to break free in her own confused way.

CHAPTER 3

A Christmas Story, of All Things

How will history remember my father—as the poor cheated-on husband? Maybe. But history never gets all the facts straight. There were vague rumours of his own infidelity all those years that Mom stayed at home while he did plumbing jobs that produced little actual money. The great tragedy is that my father was deeply in love with her, and she didn't return those feelings. He didn't know how to express himself and couldn't give her what she wanted, but he loved her, and she eventually crushed his heart into a thousand pieces that could never be glued back together.

When Mom started to stray and behave like a rebellious teenager, Dad tried to take a hard line. He lectured and tried to punish her. It was no use, though; she was bulletproof by then with nothing to lose. She simply didn't care. She slept on the sofa and went silent, while Dad tried to be tough. He had always been taught that men don't cry; if things were emotionally difficult, you worked harder until you couldn't feel anything. That old-school farmer mentality, the one that said life was hard and men needed to be even harder to survive, had not prepared him for the realities of a twentieth-century marriage.

Mom got a job working at a restaurant on the nearby military base. How anyone thought that was going to end well is beyond me; she had a seemingly endless supply of men to flirt with. And that's when she met twenty-something-year-old Gary, the bold masturbator and pedophile.

I'm not quite sure if Gary was a pedophile or just a creep, but when he asked me if I minded him masturbating a few feet away from me, that was definitely grooming. While the law would consider him a pedophile, there are many examples throughout history and other cultures where a thirteen-year-old is considered an adult, at least in the sexual way. But that's a whole other discussion, I suppose.

The thing about Gary is he never laid a hand on me, and I probably would have broken it if he had; a lot of suppressed rage toward my mother's lovers churned under the surface, and I dare not think what might have happened if one of them had actually tried to touch me in a sexual way. Of course it's easy to think that now and sound tough, but I had spent enough time pinned beneath my brother to know that fighting off a stronger attacker was easier said than done.

That suppressed rage boiled toward my mother as well, and it has been a contributor to my success as well as a key factor in what would nearly be my final undoing. Shakespeare once wrote, "What is it else, a madness most discreet, a choking gall and a preserving sweet." He was talking about love in *Romeo and Juliet*, meaning that love can be both a deadly poison and a healing potion, as likely to kill you as it is to save you. So was my anger toward my mother. That suppressed fire fuelled my ambition, but it also numbed my other emotions. To not feel fully is walking death.

Gary became my mother's boyfriend—or at least more of a steady arrangement. They even started writing a children's book together. That was her cover anyway, as it's what she told my father she was doing with him. This was the most painfully absurd part of the story, the part where my father looks like a complete fool. Where I lied to his face over and over. The start of his undoing.

Imagine us all sitting at the breakfast table: Mom with the toast and butter, Dad with his tea, me rolling cigarettes to sell at school for lunch money. My brother absent, having moved in by this point with my grandparents to get away from my mother. As was often the case, my father asks my mother when she would be home from work that night. She gives a vague answer; Dad's eyes well up. Mom does not make eye contact, pushing the crusts of her toast around her plate. My jaw clenches tightly as the tension builds. She leaves, and my father pleads with me, begs for the truth: "Is she sleeping with Gary?" I treat the question as absurd; Gary is gross, and of course no—she would never.

Gary *was* gross: he enjoyed pretending that he didn't know what time I was arriving at his place to wait for my mother to get off from work. He'd be conveniently getting out of the shower and—gosh—just couldn't seem to keep a grip on that towel, giving me more than a quick glimpse at his half-hard monster cock.

That children's book they were trying to write—a Christmas story, of all things—ended up being the catalyst that changed everything, though. Funny enough.

For me to explain why, we need to travel back in time again to before I was born but after my parents had started dating. Early in their relationship, my mother had an affair with another family friend, Jim. He was their insurance man and a bold, dynamic character. Loud, opinionated, confident. Jim was also married, and their affair was exposed—I don't know how—but my father overlooked it, the affair ended, and life went on. It was the early 1970s, and perhaps free love made people a little more forgiving of such transgressions? Jim had a couple of kids with his wife and moved to Halifax, a couple hours away. My parents had us. When I was four years old, my mother made a trip to the city with me to get tubes in my ears, and she met up with Jim. Jim begged my mother to leave Dad for her, but she stayed and did what she thought was right.

Now, back to Mom and Gary writing that stupid children's book. The only person in the whole world Mom knew who might have enough business sense to help get a book published was Jim. So off to the big city Mom and Gary went, to ask Jim for help.

They met at one of his big fancy offices. Mom had never

seen anything like it in person: high-end furniture, lush plants, a breathtaking view. As soon as she and Jim made eye contact after all those years, they both knew. For her, no doubt it was the atmosphere—his sharp suit, the smell of financial success that makes poor women swoon—and for him, it was a sexual firecracker from his past, some much-needed excitement. Or it was love. Whatever.

By now Jim was on his second marriage, a marriage of convenience, to a homely conservative woman with money. Jim appeared to be doing well, and if he wasn't, he certainly put on a good show. Nice car, expensive watch, an air of superiority and success. Mom felt like a country bumpkin in her best skintight jeans and plain cotton top. It showed off her ass and tits, but it also showed her naivety. Perhaps that had its own special appeal.

Whatever it was, Jim started taking her on extravagant buying trips. She would come home with dozens of new outfits: smart blazers, blouses and dress pants; beautiful objects, lingerie, jewelry, nice shoes. They stayed in luxury hotels and ate at the best restaurants. Her own personal *Pretty Woman* experience. All the while Jim was going behind his wife's back, and Mom was cheating on her husband *and* her boyfriend.

And where was I in the midst of all this? Exploring my budding sexuality, right around my fifteenth birthday. My father was slowly unraveling and I was happy to have distractions outside of my stressful family life, so I didn't come home that summer. Instead, I stayed in a girlfriend's camper in her backyard, where I lost my virginity.

CHAPTER 4

Pull Your Pants Up

Why do we say we've "lost" our virginity? Is it something to be misplaced that might be found eventually? The implication that having it in your possession is better might be even stranger. Sex was a big focus in my life for years before I was ready to take the plunge myself. Hormones did what hormones do: they roared through my body, releasing chemicals in my brain and awakening my nipples and vulva to touch. Showering took on new meaning, and cleaning myself felt different. I started to have heavy discharges and made a mess of my underwear; it would soak right through to my pants. My mother took me to the doctor to ensure everything was normal. To be on the safe side, he gave me cream for a yeast imbalance even though he didn't think I had one.

"Insert the cream using this applicator," he told me, holding a tube similar to a tampon. I hadn't started my period yet, so I didn't have any experience with tampons. I struggled with it while my mother stood outside the bathroom door offering assistance. I wanted to figure it out on my own, but the vagina is a mysterious place. It's placed in such a way that you can't get a decent look at your own without a mirror. I bent over in front of the mirror on the door trying to figure out where this tube was supposed to fit. I tried to pry it into my clitoris, and then my urethra, complaining to my mother that it wasn't going to fit. She assured me that it would—maybe I just wasn't in the right spot? I finally explored the confusing mess of flesh between my "little man in a boat" and my anus. Ta-da! It slid in easily, and it felt *good*. Wow!

The next night when it was time to insert the cream again I laid a towel on the floor, reclined and inserted the applicator, then removed it—in and out, in and out, while complaining through the door that I was having a hard time with it again. An obvious lie, of course; I loved it. I did that every night for a week and set off for more exploration from there. Soon I couldn't keep my hands out of my pants. I masturbated compulsively, constantly. One time, in the middle of the afternoon, I snuck into bed and started to play with myself. I heard my mother call me from the kitchen, wanting me to help make dinner. I didn't answer, hoping that she'd give up. A minute later, my bedroom door swung open. I froze, my face flushing even more than it had already been.

"Why are you in bed?" she asked, confused. I told her I was taking a nap. "Well, get up and come help me. It's too late to be napping anyway." My mother stood there, waiting for me to get out of bed. I realized she wasn't going to budge until I did. Reluctantly, I tossed aside the covers that had been pulled up to my chin, revealing that my pants were down.

With a raised eyebrow, she asked me, "Why are your pants down?"

"I was hot," I explained, "and was in the middle of taking my pants off to be more comfortable."

She shook her head at her strange child and turned back toward the kitchen. "Well, pull your pants up, wash your hands and come help me with dinner."

Why, you might ask, would I be shy about masturbation with a mother who was so gratuitously sexual? Because that was one of the few things she *didn't* do, having heard that people who played with themselves would grow hair on their palms. My mother may actually have been so impulsive sexually *because* she did not masturbate.

So it was around that age that I finally got my period and started to crave sex. I kissed a couple of boys, and it was thrilling. It felt like an electrified wire ran from my lips straight down to my nipples and vagina. I would lay in bed soaking wet between my legs, vibrating with lust.

One of these boys was my first oral sex lover. We weren't dating, and since I wanted my official first time to be with someone I cared for, we only had oral sex. But "only" is a great understatement; his mouth on my vagina was the best feeling I'd ever known in my life—by a long shot.

Soon after that, I started a more significant relationship with another boy and decided to go all the way. I went on the pill, and my mother took me shopping for lingerie: a black lace and satin teddy from our local small-town department store. An uninspiring chain store featuring cheap factory-made merchandise, lit with cynical fluorescent bulbs and spiritless muzak serenading its comatosed customers. My rendezvous with the boy was in a camper in my friend's yard. It wasn't glamorous and, to be honest, it was hardly memorable. But it was sweet. We cared for each other, and we stayed together for ten months, which is *forever* when you're fifteen years old.

It ended dramatically, as many relationships do at that age. I cheated on him with his friend shortly after we discussed opening up our relationship. Turns out that wasn't what he had in mind when we briefly discussed being with other people, and he was deeply hurt. I awoke to him holding a knife to my throat. He was so emotional, so angry, so sad. He wanted to kill me and then himself. The whole situation was particularly confusing for me; my mother had been cheating on my father for years, and he had never reacted like this. I don't remember now how the tension diffused, but luckily it did. I called his father to come fetch him, and that was that.

The next day, I wrote my Grade 10 final exams in a daze, and my mother finally left my father. As she dropped me off at school that morning, she explained that she was moving away to Halifax to be with Jim. I had known she was going to do it, as she'd told me her plan to leave my father. Hell, I had even encouraged her. She promised to come back for me at the end of the summer, once she got settled.

"Right," was all I could manage as I stepped out of the car. It still felt jarring even though I knew it was coming.

CHAPTER 5

After She Left

Later that day I went to the top of a local waterfall and considered jumping. Plenty of people had jumped from it, splashing into the water to cool off in the summertime. As long as you avoided the rocks, the fall wouldn't kill you. But that day I was actually thinking of aiming for them.

I stood there for a long time trying to work up the courage to kill myself. In the end, I lay down and slept, right there at the top of the waterfall. I was too tired, emotionally exhausted in a way that went right through me. Some people came along and helped me out of the woods. I could barely walk and couldn't speak. They drove me home, and I lay around numb for days watching my father come and go with his rifle in hand. He, too, was working up the courage to kill himself. He was also working up the courage not to, if that makes sense.

Those last few months before my mother's final departure as she drifted further away from my father, he begged her to stay. He showered her with presents. He knelt on the floor with his head in her lap, crying. He even had a nervous breakdown. His doctor gave him pills to numb the pain, reduce the anxiety and try to save him from suicide.

Mom, meanwhile, was stone cold. For her, it was release from prison: twenty-one years with a man she didn't really love and maybe didn't even like. A hard life of poverty, cooking and cleaning for an ungrateful husband, child-rearing without his help. I was sixteen, and in her eyes she had done the right thing and stayed until I was old enough to fend for myself. She regularly reminded me that I was the reason she stayed in an unhappy marriage. Frankly, it would have been kinder to leave years earlier instead of putting us all through the trauma of those last few years.

I stayed behind in our house, in the aftermath of her destruction, while she went off to start her new life. I knew that soon enough I would be leaving Dad too. For him this was a period of the deepest depression, and it was too much for me to deal with. I found escape in drinking and fucking the pain away. That summer I had twelve different lovers: some just once, some several times. I didn't care about my reputation; I would be leaving my small town at the end of the summer to live with Mom in Halifax anyway. I was horny and looking for distraction.

I threw myself into work eagerly. I got hired to look after an optician's store while the owner went golfing. I had zero retail experience—I hadn't even gone in there looking for a job—but he wanted to hire me. It was odd to be offered a job out of the blue, especially one that paid well above minimum wage, when I was just accompanying my mother while she picked out new frames. You would imagine there'd be a catch, that he was a perv who wanted to get into my pants, but no. He was actually a gentleman and kind to me. I was in the midst of one of the hardest times of my life, but he couldn't have known. I came to work, did my job and partied like most normal sixteen-year-olds in that small rural town.

Despite growing up poor, I had money as soon as I was able to earn it. It was easy for me to find work or at least find creative ways to make money. According to astrology—I am both a fire dragon and a Taurus—I have the greatest earning potential and the most financial luck of any zodiac sign, if you believe in that stuff. That optical store job was a great example. Most of my friends couldn't find any work at all in that small town, and I was offered an easy, grown-up job that paid well when I wasn't even looking. All I wanted was to be out of the house.

I couldn't bear to see my father through that summer. It was tremendously sad. I had lied to him so many times, and now it was obvious. Through it all, though, Dad loved me unconditionally. He never made me feel guilty, and that multiplied the shame I felt. So I stayed away, sleeping anywhere I could. The distractions were effective, and despite it being a horrible time, I took my fun and pleasure wherever I could that summer.

CHAPTER 6

O Fortuna

Thor was the most significant part of those summer months. He was a tower of a man: barrel-chested, tall and wide. He could scoop me up and devour my pussy as if I weighed nothing. Thor was a well-loved, charismatic party animal and a passionate, open lover. He respectfully pushed my boundaries from the start, making out with his other lovers when I was around while managing to keep me feeling special and cherished. We weren't in a relationship, and I was sleeping with other people too, so he felt it should all be out in the open.

When he suggested a threesome with his best friend, I trusted his judgment, and I was glad I did. For many months, we all had sex together, and it felt great. They were straight, but they enjoyed the shared experience. They enjoyed watching each other with me. Thor and I were closer, though; he always treated me like gold.

I have wonderful memories of Thor, including a drunken night of fishtailing on dirt roads, his friend smashing mailboxes with a baseball bat from the window of the passenger's seat while "O Fortuna" by Carmina Burana blasted on the stereo. I thought we would die, and I didn't care. I felt more alive than ever. I loved the thrill.

About a month later, though, we *did* get into a car accident. The driver missed a turn, and we hit a ditch. Hard. We went end over end, rolling three times. Ground, sky, ground, sky, ground, sky. Looking at the completely totalled car through hazy eyes, I couldn't fathom how we all survived. I wasn't wearing a seat belt, and this actually saved me from a spinal injury since the back seat only had lap belts. Also, I was drunk, so I didn't stiffen up; I was a ping pong ball. As I crawled out of the window of the upside-down vehicle into the tall grass of the field we landed in, I noticed my sweater on the car, between the two back tires. It had been beside me on the seat right before the accident.

That was a real scare for my family, but it didn't hit home for me until the following week. Exactly seven days after my accident, a childhood friend died in an almost identical wreck. She was in the back seat, as I had been, but died on impact. Standing in the funeral parlour at the viewing, the reality of what could have happened to me finally broke through.

By that time I had moved to the city of Halifax to live with my mother, but I was still going back to my hometown to party with Thor a few times a month. It was only a couple hours away.

All of that ended abruptly when Thor got back together with a girlfriend I knew he still had feelings for. He explained that he wanted to get married and have kids. He was in his mid-twenties; I was sixteen. What we had was fun, but Thor wanted a serious relationship. They lived happily ever after, until they didn't; his marriage eventually fell apart. Such is life.

He and I reconnected 20 years later for one strange night. He took me for a ride on his Harley, we drank whiskey and I told him about my work. He had seen my videos on the Internet, so it wasn't a surprise. He took a picture of me wearing his old leather biker jacket and sent it to his best friend, the one we used to have threesomes with. The friend didn't believe it was real. Thor said I hadn't aged, that I looked the same. Thor hadn't aged quite as well, but he was just as sweet and charismatic as always. I wanted to see if the old magic was still there. It wasn't for me, but I think he had a memorable experience.

CHAPTER 7

Raw

B ack to when I was sixteen, my father moved another woman into the house a couple weeks after I first left for Halifax. I came back for something and let myself in under the assumption that no one was home. I noticed that someone had rearranged the furniture and found her washing the dishes in the kitchen. "What the hell are you doing here?" she snapped, as though the house was hers. She would have recognized me from family photos still hanging on the wall. I walked back to my room to grab a few items and saw her pantyhose on what was once my parents' shared bed. I never knew the full story, though. There were rumours that they had been together for a while before my mother left. I found that hard to believe, having witnessed his heartbreak—but then again, love, sex, marriage and all the feelings that go with them are complicated.

Dad could have been mourning the loss of my mother while seeking comfort from another woman. After all, their marriage had been deteriorating for years, and they rarely had sex. I wish I didn't know this part, to be honest, but we lived in a small house, and my mother shared everything with me anyway. I knew every time they had sex; I couldn't *not* know.

But if there was one time that I wish I didn't know, it would be the last time. It was at the very, very end, right before Mom left. I was surprised to hear them having sex; it had been a long time, and I knew Mom found Dad disgusting by then. Afterward, I heard her go to the bathroom and throw up.

The next day at the breakfast table, my father was glowing. He grinned toothily, "I'm sure you heard your mother and I last night?" His optimism was palpable and chokingly bitter to me. My mother, green and defeated, pushed her toast across her plate.

Later, she explained that she needed money to start her new life. He wouldn't give it to her unless she had sex with him.

Up to this point of the story it probably sounds like my mother was mostly the villain and my father the victim. I've painted them that way. But, you see, life is rarely that black and white. After two decades together, it's impossible to lay the blame solely at one person's feet.

Fifteen years after it was all over, I got a glimpse at the version of my father that my mother had developed so much disdain for. Dad and I were sitting in Tim Horton's. The bright yellow tables and glaring fluorescent lights reflected in his watery eyes while small-town folk in plaid shirts and baseball caps with "Ford" logos drank their double-doubles and gossiped. The thick burned aroma of cheap coffee permeated the air as hits from the 80s wailed out of ceiling speakers. The conversation took an unexpected turn when Dad suddenly asked me if it was true. "Back then, all the rumours... about your mother sleeping with Gary and other men. Is it true?" To hear the name "Gary" pass through my father's mouth after all those years was a punch in the guts. Suddenly, I was a teenager again, covering for Mom. I looked away, preparing to lie habitually. Then I considered that after all this time, surely he *must* know?

I attempted to change the subject: "All of that is water under the bridge. No point in bringing it all up again."

I now looked him in the face and was alarmed at his expression. His eyes wide and piercing, he was grinning and clearly excited to get something off his chest. Alarm bells were sounding off in my belly, as the look on his face did not match the topic. I felt ill, desperate to change the topic. "Can I get you a Timbit?" I asked.

He continued, ignoring my question, ignoring everything I'd said. He asked the question, but he wasn't looking for an answer. The question was a set-up. My stomach flipped, my face flushed and I started to sweat. I was desperate to shut him up, to stop him from saying what he looked so gleeful to say.

Nothing good could come from a conversation about my mother's infidelity. Nothing. "Dad, I really don't want to be having this conversation—"

But he cut me off, big hands on the table, sausage fingers rapidly punctuating the words as his eyes gleamed, smiling sickly, "I don't think she was having sex with anyone else..."

"Dad, stop..." I thrashed uselessly.

"...because I was fucking her pussy so raw she couldn't have been fucking anyone else," he spat out quickly with a spray of spittle, punctuating the words with a high-pitched laugh at the end.

Slamming my fist on the table, I roared, "ENOUGH!" as disgust and anger burst from me like an exploding popcorn kernel. Everyone stopped talking and stared at us. I had never raised my voice at my father, but I have a vivid imagination. It is impossible for me to hear something like that and not see it in such clarity and detail that I might as well be standing right by the bed, eyes level with my father's penis punishing my mother's painfully dry, raw, red vagina. In a flash, an avalanche of inappropriate information flooded my vision, along with the knowledge that my mother was indeed still having loads of sex with other men using that very same pussy—the vagina that I came out of, too.

Why? Why would my father tell me that? Well, I've always been the kind of person others feel comfortable talking to; a natural confidante. The weight of their secrets and confessions on my shoulders could sink a tanker. I am a Dominatrix, and my clients feel comfortable telling me— confessing, if you will—their most intimate feelings. My father, unfortunately, had no such outlet for his vile, desperate words. And at that moment, he could no longer bottle them up.

CHAPTER 8

Go Back Again

I know I've digressed and moved around the timeline, so I'll give you a moment to get your footing—especially since that last bit might've been a bit hard to digest. Then again, I suppose much of what came before that wasn't exactly a fairytale either.

Everything changed when I was sixteen. I moved from my small hometown to the big city of Halifax, from a house into an apartment with my mother, and I was starting Grade 11 at a new school. Mom and Jim—still married to his second wife—launched a new business, an agency that placed nurses in private homes. He wanted to leave said wife, but since they had recently gone bankrupt together, they were bound together for a while longer. Enter my mother: mistress and business partner.

The irony wasn't lost on me. Jim romanced my mother away from her husband and boyfriend with the promise of wealth only to then declare bankruptcy. He did have business sense though, and she wouldn't have been able to start a business without him, so at least there's that.

The new apartment served as a home office. I played secretary, answering the phones if Mom and Jim were fucking.

I could hear Jim screwing my mother in the bedroom as I lied to his wife on the phone. I had become an expert in lying for cheaters. At least the sex was good, from what I heard and from the details my mother shared.

It quickly became apparent that I did not fit in at my new school. The upper-middle class students had been together since kindergarten. I, on the other hand, was the only student who was also a school employee. I worked in the cafeteria at lunch and got paid in food. The lack of friends didn't bother me, as I preferred the company of adults—other cafeteria workers and teachers—anyway.

I made a couple of girlfriends from a different school, and on weekends we dressed up in our mothers' "grown up" clothes and snuck into the bars where sailors drank away their cares. We met countless men from around the world, partied on naval ships and had a great time playing adult. For all my previous promiscuity, fucking sailors didn't appeal to me for some obscure reason. It didn't matter; my girlfriend fucked enough seamen for the both of us.

I noticed an ad in the paper for a job in an upscale menswear store, inside the best luxury hotel in Halifax. I casually mentioned to Jim that I'd love to work there.

"So go talk to them about a job," he suggested.

I couldn't take the idea seriously, but he encouraged me to apply. I dismissed him as insane—why would they hire a 17-year-old female inexperienced country bumpkin? He insisted that I put on one of my mother's suits and go in anyway. Despite being walking human waste, he did teach me one valuable lesson: just go for it. See what happens.

I'd recently started a job that was easy to get, selling t-shirts and boxer shorts door-to-door. Funny when I think about it now: door-to-door sales were like an early form of Amazon or online shopping—the idea of not leaving your home to shop or buy something you want or need.

I was supposed to be working my other job when I went to the hotel. I walked into the lobby lugging a ridiculous hockey bag of items, more product than I could sell in weeks, let alone a day, that I had to leave with the hotel concierge. Quite a sight, I'm sure. I didn't even weigh 100 pounds and was wearing Mom's business clothes and carrying a beat-up bag almost as big as me.

I walked into the posh menswear store and approached the older, smart-looking gentleman behind the counter. Perfectly quaffed, white hair combed neatly, his tie and matching pocket square a dignified pattern, his expensive cologne hanging gently in the air like chimes in a soft breeze. I introduced myself, explaining that I was inquiring about the job listing. Squinting, disbelieving, he looked baffled as he sized me up. He explained, "Well, I am looking for someone to mind the shop while I sail a few days a week, but I'm sorry—I feel a man is better suited for the position." I thanked him politely and left, feeling defeated, but not terribly surprised.

"So, how did it go?" Jim quizzed me when he saw me next. I explained what happened, feeling smug about predicting the outcome. He smirked and said, "You're going to go back again." I thought he was joking, but he wasn't. He asked me to tell him everything that was said and everything that I observed while in the store. When I mentioned the part about sailing, he said that was it.

"You're going to go back in there and ask him a question about sailing. Anything from asking him what kind of sailboat he has to where he likes to go sailing," he instructed. "Get him talking about what he's obviously passionate about. You've got two of these," he pointed to his ears, "and one of these," he gestured to his mouth, "for a reason. Listen for as long as he wants to talk," Jim told me. "Ask a few leading questions if needed, but otherwise keep quiet. Then mention that you're still interested in working there."

I'm not sure who was more surprised when I walked back into that store: the owner or me. I got him talking about sailing, and he rambled on for about an hour. Finally, he apologized that he couldn't hire me and that he still felt a man was a better fit for the job. "I wish you the best of luck in whatever you do next," he said, a closing punctuation mark. Feeling defeated, but having learned something of value about how to interact with people, I left.

The next time Jim saw me he again listened to what happened, this time with a big smile, and said, "Go back one more time." This time he suggested that I offer to work for a week at no cost to the

owner in exchange for the work experience and, if he was pleased—
only if he was pleased—a reference that I could use to apply for
other employment.

It worked, and I spent an interesting week learning about the
world of retail, menswear, sailing and a few other things. The
experience led to a job in a tailor shop and another retail clothing
store in the hotel lobby—the retail job being one of three jobs I had
while trying to get through my final year of high school.

I was seventeen, in Grade 12, and partying on weekends while
working three part-time jobs. One was a Victorian lingerie shop,
which sounds sexier than it was, unless you have a fetish for traditional
flannel nightgowns. I missed classes for work, but my teachers
understood that at least I wasn't skipping class because I was getting
stoned behind the school. They knew I wasn't rich like most of the
other students and I was working hard because I had to. Luckily,
most of my classes came easily to me, especially English. And I
somehow found time to tutor Shakespeare to other students who
were still learning basic English.

CHAPTER 9

Dirtbag

Less than halfway through the school year, I came home one day to find my mother packing a suitcase. She announced that Jim's wife had finally left him, so she was going to his place to spend the night. One night stretched to a week, and then to eternity. She never spent the night at our place again, and I had almost no contact with her for months. As I worked, partied and went to school, I lived in our apartment by myself like a regular adult. At least she continued to pay the rent. Seventeen isn't all that young, I suppose, but I did feel abandoned, so I found comfort in a dangerous man.

Faylin was older; he would never tell me by how much, but I would guess he was pushing thirty. On welfare, with long hair and a rebellious attitude, he was a bad boy, no doubt about it. Shifty, slimy and the way he'd look at people sent out the signal that he was one of those guys that you shouldn't trust in your home. And he didn't pretend to be otherwise. "Why are you even here?" he'd ask me from time to time, smirking, trying to scare me. "You shouldn't be with someone like me." Everything about it felt wrong, but I didn't have a genuine connection with anyone those days, and I was lonely. My weekend friends were party friends. All the other adults from my jobs were people I knew through work and didn't see otherwise. And my mother had left.

For the last few months of Grade 12, I toiled away at work and school, spending what free time I had fucking Faylin in his shitty, squalid apartment. I partied a little less in favour of spending one-on-one time with a dirtbag who viewed me as more of an ATM and sex toy than a human being.

The one good thing about our relationship was that I got to have my first positive sexual experience with another woman, who Faylin introduced me to. I had long suspected that I was bisexual, but I hadn't enjoyed the couple of times I had been with other girls. Aneta was different. She was Polish, had impossibly long blonde hair, the highest cheekbones, the fullest pouty lips and the biggest eyes I'd ever seen. A living porcelain doll, beautiful and so vulnerable. Only fifteen, she lived in a halfway house for troubled teens, having left home over constant conflict with her parents. She had a sweet vulnerability about her. I was enamoured, and our lovemaking was passionate, intense, sensual.

We almost had a threesome one night: Aneta, Faylin and I. He had introduced us to try to make that happen. But I was protective of Aneta, and I knew Faylin was a genuinely bad human being. I stopped the whole thing and asked her to avoid him. She took my advice and soon after met a nice boy and moved back in with her parents. I never heard from her again.

CHAPTER 10

Tattoo

M ost people don't notice my faded, crappy tattoo. I could easily remove it, but I keep it for nostalgic reasons. When I was sixteen, there was a local guy who did cheap tattoos. Though he was still only learning, he was nice, and I was young and stupid, so I decided to get one. We went to his place, and he told me that I wouldn't have to pay if I spent the night with him. He was in a wheelchair and explained that he was paralyzed from the waist down, so his penis didn't work but that he'd love to go down on me. I found him attractive and harmless, so I agreed.

I put on lipstick and kissed a piece of paper. I asked him to tattoo that on my hip to represent "kissed by a woman," a symbol of my bisexuality. Never mind that I hadn't actually kissed a woman yet—I wouldn't meet Aneta for another year—but I was so sure that I would like it that I was ready to mark my body permanently to make the statement.

The weird part was that he asked me to wear his mother's perfume while he did the tattoo. It was Calvin Klein's "Obsession" for women, and it still brings me back to that night every time I smell it.

CHAPTER 11

Studying Hard?

A couple months after I turned eighteen, the school year started coming to an end. I had been failing computer science all year and had made the unwise move of taking only as many classes as I needed to graduate, with no extras. Now I badly needed every credit. The night before the exam I went out to the bar with a girlfriend. The drinking age in Nova Scotia was nineteen, but we had been going there for a year and knew most of the staff by name. I was lamenting to my girlfriend that I would have to go to summer school or repeat the year, as I hadn't passed a single test all year and would definitely fail the computer science exam the next day, when I felt a firm hand on my shoulder. I turned to see my computer science teacher smiling at me. He asked, "Studying hard for that exam tomorrow?"

I nearly died of shock and embarrassment, but he laughed and moved on. I said nothing and buried my head in my arms. Then I decided to make a play; I had to try something. I rushed off to find him. He was drinking with a buddy, and I asked him if I could buy him a drink. He put his arm around me and introduced me to his friend as "his favourite student." That was a surprise. He had never acknowledged my existence beyond a nod when I came to class late, wearing my work clothes, communicating through eye contact that he understood and that I wasn't in trouble.

I explained that I knew I wouldn't pass the exam tomorrow and that I was worried because I needed every credit. He pulled me close and told me to walk into that exam room with my head held high and to write the exam confidently like I knew every answer. He didn't care if I drew happy faces all over it. He told me to waltz out of there like I aced the thing and to not say a word about this to anyone. "I don't need anyone asking me questions when you pass," he said with a wink.

I couldn't believe what I had heard. I thanked him and asked again if I could buy him a drink. He declined, laughed and said that he knew I was underage and that I should go have fun.

I did exactly as he told me, and that is how I passed and graduated from high school. I knew it wasn't earned the right way, so I didn't attend the graduation ceremony or even my prom. It just didn't feel right to me. Plus I was going through hell and wasn't in a celebratory mood because Jim and my mother had resurfaced. They had somehow gotten wind that I was dating a dirtbag and demanded that I break it off with Faylin. They wouldn't listen to me when I tried to explain over and over that I had already planned on ending it but was waiting until we both fully cleared up from the crabs he had given me.

Yes, I said crabs. In the middle of exam season, I discovered that Faylin had been cheating on me—not exactly a big surprise—and had given me pubic lice. I told him it was over, but I wanted us both to be clear of them since I figured he would otherwise spread them further and tell people that *I* was the one who gave them to *him*.

Jim lectured me angrily for hours about what a mess I had made of my life. They weren't going to pay rent on the apartment anymore, and I had a week to find another place or move in with them. My mother sat silently while he yelled at me. I hadn't seen her in months. I missed her, and although I despised him, the idea of living with Mom again was appealing enough that I agreed to move in with them. That week I had a little nervous breakdown. I was terribly ill and couldn't keep food down. I lost nearly ten pounds. The drama of ending things with Faylin, which included him flaunting the girl he was cheating on me with right in front of me, Jim's lectures, which made me feel stupid, and the stress of school ending and moving apartments was all too much.

At my new home, Jim didn't make me feel welcome. Though they had a spare room, he said I should sleep instead in the basement on a fold-out sofa—in the laundry room. He instructed me to fold the bed up into a sofa each morning and to always put all my things away in a dresser; there should be no trace of me when I wasn't there. He was an annoyingly tidy person, so I tried to accept this as his version of neatness rather than an effort to make me feel as unwelcome as possible.

Jim and I fought every day. Usually, it was him lecturing me from up on his soap box, as I referred to it. Mom would sit silently as this went on for hours; it seemed Jim never got tired of lecturing me. In his way, I suppose he had good intentions. He saw potential in me, but I had such a loose upbringing that I was a wild animal to him, one that needed to be broken and tamed. We happened to share a birthday—both stubborn Tauruses butting heads—and I only lasted there a couple of months. "The world is a difficult place," Jim told me as I finally walked out the door one day. "Harder than you know." He made it clear that he expected me back on their doorstep before long, begging for help. But I was determined to prove him wrong.

CHAPTER 12

Bobby Bones

Whether he intended to do so or not, Jim's words put a fire under my stubborn ass, and I worked non-stop at several jobs, eating the cheapest food, spending next to nothing, trying to save every penny. I was sleeping on the sofa in the living room of a crummy apartment with two other girls. They weren't friends, and they were not kind to me, but the rent they charged me was dirt cheap. They partied nearly every night and came home drunk, loud and not caring that I had work early in the morning. They made fun of the clothes I had to wear for one of my crappy jobs, laughed at the 25-cent Mr. Noodles that I ate and mocked any other detail they felt was worth mocking. I'm sure now that it looked ridiculous, the way I was living, but the last thing I ever wanted was to make Jim's prediction a reality.

Sunday night was my one night to go out dancing. On one particular Sunday night, a girlfriend and I stopped at a speakeasy for a game of pool before heading to the club. A prissy, slender brunette woman sat in a nearby decorative barber's chair, making no effort to interact with us, until she overheard us saying we were heading out to dance.

Suddenly, she piped up. "There's nowhere good to go dancing

on Sunday night!" We laughed and said that Sunday was the *best* night to go out in Halifax. The Palace would be packed. She pouted and asked if she could come with us. I didn't like her but agreed to let her come along. We stopped at her place on the way, and it was the cutest little apartment with white carpet, pink wingback chairs and a green-and-white striped sofa with a tree behind it, lit with those little white Christmas lights. There were gorgeous French doors leading to a balcony overlooking the city. I'd never seen such a posh little place!

I learned her name was Bobby Bones, a nickname from her childhood, as she had always been skinny. Bobby and I danced the night away and somehow became instant friends.

The next day she came by the coffee shop where I was working and offered me another job. She worked in a place called "The Party Store" that sold party supplies, and they had an opening. She told me that it paid well enough that I could quit two of my three jobs and work less for the same money. I went for the interview the next day and started working there that week.

When Bobby learned about my living situation, that I was sleeping on the sofa and sharing a place with two girls who didn't like me, she asked if I wanted to move to her sofa and pay her the same amount of rent. It seemed like a dream come true then, but times sure have changed. Moving into a small one-bedroom apartment and sleeping on someone's sofa doesn't look like such a golden opportunity now, but back then I really felt like I'd won the lottery.

Bobby and I lived, worked and went out dancing together for nearly a year. During that time I also took my first vacation and loaned Mom and Jim some money. Yes, that's right. I went to Mexico for a week with a girlfriend—my first time on an airplane and my first time out of the Maritimes—and Mom and Jim actually asked me for money since their business was struggling. I felt both proud to be in a position to help them and vindicated, knowing that I was doing better than Jim expected me to.

Inspired by the trip to Mexico, craving more travel, I decided in the spur of the moment to take a trip to Montreal by myself for a few days. I flew there and started looking for a place to stay. This was before the Internet, so I winged it and ended up at the YMCA. It was the kind of place where the orange-and-brown threadbare carpets hadn't been changed since the 60s. The lights flickered where they were still working, and everything smelled of old cigarette smoke and musty books. The small room had a single bed and a wooden chair. It wasn't charming, but it was exciting to strike out on my own. Feeling like a badass, I went looking for the kind of action you couldn't find in Halifax. I went to St. Catherine's street, which at that time was filled with arcades, peep shows and strip clubs. I went to a couple of peep shows—grubby, dark, sticky-floored booths with coin-activated porn movies—and found the whole thing thrilling.

Next, I headed to a strip club, but they wouldn't let me in without a male companion. As I started to walk away, a group of guys came in and said I could join them. We watched a few sad-looking Asian women take their clothes off. This was my first strip club experience, and I didn't know what to expect, but these guys understood that this wasn't a great place. We moved on to another strip club with an upbeat, festive atmosphere. Beautiful women of a variety of ethnicities were dancing all over the place. The guys bought me a dance, and a beautiful black woman joyfully plopped a little wooden stool between my legs, right in front of my chair, and got started. I looked up at her swaying and stroking herself as she smiled and held eye contact with me the whole time. I thought I would melt into my chair.

Afterward, she and a couple other dancers came over and talked to me, asking why I was there and where I was from. Apparently, it was a bit unusual for a female to be there. They invited me to come back the next night for amateur night and encouraged me to try out. I thought they were crazy. At that time I was going through my butch phase: short conservative hair, boxy, unflattering clothing, minimal makeup. I didn't go back the next night, but I've always wondered how different my life might have been if I did.

CHAPTER 13

Mick

Bobby eventually met a guy and moved in with him, and I got headhunted from the party store to what I thought was a great opportunity. It wasn't. It was a crappy job selling ad space in a tiny weekly newspaper serving an industrial business area. The manager who headhunted me was more interested in sleeping with me, which was fine by me—Armondo was hot. It was a short-lived situation, though. I gave him a heart attack during sex, and another manager took the opportunity to fire me while Armondo was in the hospital.

My next job was working at a call centre, selling carpet-cleaning services for Sears. I was a fearless salesperson with a nice telephone voice; a good fit. At that time working in call centres was a new thing in Halifax, and it paid better than most other jobs for uneducated folks.

The first week we had a staff meeting in the middle of the call centre. Surrounded by dozens of new, light grey, soulless little cubicles and a view from the 20th floor overlooking the city, thirty of us gathered around and were introduced to the owner, Mick. The HR manager joked, "Mick didn't have grey hair when he started the call centre a few months earlier!"

I heard someone whisper that he was only 30 when he had gone fully grey. It certainly made him look older.

Another manager quipped, "It could be the baby, too!"

Mick looked slightly shy and awkward, quick to blush as he was being introduced. When he spoke though, he filled out his crisp, grey suit. He exuded confidence and enthusiasm—as well as optimism with hints of desperation. His ice-blue eyes darted around the room, making eye contact with his staff members as he tried to rally the troops.

"I believe that we can beat our numbers from last week. I've been working hard to win some better markets for you to call into. They're remote and don't get opportunities to have their carpets cleaned professionally. Remember to up-sell furniture cleaning as well!"

He wanted to create the feeling that he was part of the team and not just "the boss." I was vaguely curious about him, but he was so tense it was off-putting.

Over the next few months I dialled for dollars. I was one of the company's top salespeople, but honestly there wasn't much competition. Most of my coworkers were putting in their time to get their base pay and drinking it away in the evenings. We did party a lot, which meant there were many interoffice romances. In other words, everybody was fucking everybody else. It was that kind of environment.

Over time, Mick's motivational speeches become more desperate. There were whispers of the company struggling. Mick appeared increasingly stressed and borderline distraught; he had bitten off more than he could chew. It wasn't long before the announcement came that they were going out of business.

It would be a slow wind down, as they had contracts to fulfill over the next couple of months. Everyone was given a heads-up that they should start looking for other work. Mick looked utterly defeated as he made the announcement: "It was an ambitious idea, opening a call centre of this size. I tried my best—we all did, I'm sure." (He looked doubtful about that.) "I would like to take you all out for a drink this evening as a celebration of what we did learn and accomplish. And to give a nice send-off to those who will be leaving us sooner."

We all went out that day after work and partied on Mick's dime with no restraint. This was Halifax, after-all; a town with more bars per capita than nearly any place in the world. Mix in the navy port, three big universities and a culture of social drinking—yeah, we all knew well how to party.

As the evening wore on, I eventually found myself standing next to Mick at the bar. We'd never had a real conversation before. He looked broken; it was all he could do not to cry. I tried to cheer him up: "Have you ever had a slippery nipple?" I looked at him coyly. He was taken aback, so I didn't let the joke go on too long. "It's a shooter. Let me buy you one. You've been buying the drinks all night."

I was tipsy and could tell by the flush on his cheeks that he was too. I started to flirt with him, simply because I could. I was a hopeless flirt and a bit of a slut, to be honest; it was how I tended to interact with most men. But Mick was married with a baby, my boss and about ten years older than me. I didn't expect anything to come of a little harmless flirtation.

The way he looked at me with those piercing blue eyes—with a confidence and desperate hunger that boys my age did not possess— made me feel like a cold drink on a hot summer day. Or a perfectly prepared steak, with him in the starring role of starving man.

I still felt he was out of my league, but the more we talked, the more it became a challenge—a dangerous, thrilling challenge.

"I have the most beautiful garden in the back of the house I live in. There's a pond with big goldfish and little white lights on all the bushes. It's calm and secluded. It's only about a ten-minute walk away," I dangled like a carrot.

"I'd like to see it," Mick said plainly. An exchange with so much implication. We both knew exactly what we were really talking about.

Once in my backyard, it was a fairytale. A smutty fairytale. We were surrounded by little white lights, lush shrubbery and flowers while the water trickled in the pond's fountain, and it was perfect. Mick took my face in his hands and kissed me. It hit me like a ton of bricks and, given that I was quite intoxicated, I must have faltered.

He picked me up, wrapped my legs around his waist and sat down on the little blue bench tucked into the bushes. We kissed and groped. It felt amazing but no doubt looked less than glamorous—two drunk fools pawing at each other in the dark. All of a sudden, we heard a noise nearby and looked up to see a guy I'd been flirting with earlier; another guy from work.

"Oh. Sorry," he stammered. "I, uh, thought I'd check that you got home okay." Poor kid. I'm sure he was hoping to get laid and never imagined he'd find me making out with our married boss.

"I'm fine, Darryl. Thanks for checking. I can trust you to not tell anyone what you've seen? You can imagine…" I trailed off, letting him fill in the blanks. He nodded dumbly but continued to stand there staring at us.

"Okay. Goodnight, Darryl. See you at work on Monday," I said sweetly but firmly as I gestured toward the driveway. He wandered off.

"Do you think he recognized me?" Mick whispered. He hadn't said a word before.

"Yeah. It's dark, but it's not that dark," I replied. "So, at this point, things haven't gone that far. Let me call you a cab. If this gets out, at least it will only be drunken smooching and not more." A wave of rationale and guilt crested over me.

Mick stood firm: "I know what I'm doing, and I don't care. I want this. I *need* this." But I wasn't so interested anymore; I didn't want to be the other woman. "No," I held equally firm. "I'm calling you a cab now. When we're sober, we can talk about it."

On Monday I put extra care into my appearance. Whatever happened I wanted to look good for it. I was torn between wanting to be desired by a man I felt was out of my league and not wanting to be a mistress, like my mother had been. Mick called me into his office straight off, which got several curious glances from other staff members. Mick never had meetings with the telemarketers. Only managers.

"I've given a lot of thought to what happened, and I'm glad we didn't go any further. You were right. I'm a married man. I have a baby. I'd like to pretend the whole thing never happened," he shrugged as he furtively drank in my body with thinly veiled lust that could've cracked like crème brûlée at any moment.

"No problem," I replied softly, but I had a sense this wasn't over.

I took the next day off. The sun was shining, and I wanted to lay out in my backyard and sunbathe. Things were stressful at work, given that the company was shutting down and my interactions with Mick had turned weird. I had no intention of dealing with it.

Late morning, the phone rang. It was Mick asking why I didn't come to work. I said I didn't feel like it. I was going to sunbathe in my backyard instead. I heard him groan a little. I asked how he got my home phone number, and he replied that he'd gotten it from personal records because he was worried about me.

"I'm fine," I replied lightly. "Just taking the day off."

"I need to see you. Can I come by on my lunch break?" he asked.

"Sure," I said reluctantly as my heart started to gallop and I again felt torn between the thrill of being wanted and guilt over being with a married man.

I put on the only bikini I had. It was navy with white polka dots and little ruffles. I oiled myself and laid out in the sunshine, knowing full well how I was presented. Even the remotest possibility in his mind that he wouldn't fuck me would be annihilated the instant he saw me.

Sure enough, when Mick strolled into my backyard in his business suit and saw me laid out like a buffet, he wasted little time.

"I need this. I want you. I can't stop thinking about you," he growled the cliché lines that inevitably fall out of the mouth in these situations.

We went up to my bedroom and, with the sun streaming across my buttercup yellow walls, had sex for the first time. To say we made love would be over-selling the romance of it. Fucking: that's what my neighbours would call it. He tied my wrists together with a shoelace and peeled the bikini off my sun-warmed body. He took me the way you would expect a man on death row to, a man who was losing his business and was cheating on a wife who hadn't fucked him since the baby was born. He took me hard and fast and then took me again almost immediately. For that time, nothing else existed. I was consumed.

It was when we came downstairs and my roommates commented

that they thought the ceiling would come down that I realized how loud we must have been. In the moment, I hadn't even registered that I was moaning.

I didn't know where we stood, and Mick didn't have time to discuss it. He'd been gone from the office for far too long, but he was reluctant to go back.

The next day at work, I tried to pretend everything was normal even though I could still feel him between my legs. Mick called me into his office and gave me the speech about that not happening again; how it was a one-off, and he felt bad about it.

"The right thing to do is to end it here. I'm sure you'll agree?" he chuckled, hoping that I would try to talk him out of it. I shrugged, knowing already that he was weak, that he would be back.

A week or so later, he called me at home in the evening. He told me that his wife had taken their baby to visit her parents in British Columbia for a month.

"I know this is crazy and wrong. I wouldn't blame you if you told me to fuck off. But... I'd love for you to spend the night with me. I can't stop thinking about you." A desperate man with a failing business, a wife who didn't want to fuck him and an ego in need of stroking and soothing by a younger woman; losing himself in uninhibited sex was the perfect balm for his tattered life. He'd had a taste and needed more.

We started our month-long immersion. I spent every single night with Mick. We fucked, we talked, we fell in love. Fucking morphed into lovemaking, and we couldn't get enough of each other. He had grown up a little too fast, been overly ambitious with his career, married and settled down before he was genuinely prepared for the cold realities of that life. I was his fountain of youth. He wanted to know my thoughts and feelings, finding my lighthearted youthful optimism refreshing. At twenty, with the special fragrance of a new adult, I'd yet to take on the weathered leathery smell of jagged bitterness.

We were playful and experimental. Mick got a pair of self-release handcuffs and made a big show of being all dominant. He left me bound to the bed in the dark as he wordlessly went to get ice. I could hear the freezer door open, the clink of the ice cubes in a bowl. I released myself and hid behind the door. When he came back in, I let him have a split-second to see the empty bed before I jumped out and grabbed him. He shrieked like a girl, sending ice cubes flying in all directions. We laughed until we fell on the floor, tears streaming down our faces, then made love right there, breaking out into laughter over and over.

He talked about his wife a lot. "She seemed perfect in the beginning. Beautiful, loving, fun, supportive and a good person. But," he continued, "then she became so religious, and it was like she thought sex was dirty. She's disgusted by it, especially since the baby was born. I love the baby so much, but Sara and I bicker all the time."

There were pictures of her in the house. She was beautiful. Sometimes when I was alone in the house I would look through her things, her clothes and jewelry. I'd try to figure out what kind of person she was, what their relationship was like in quiet moments.

Mick and I thought we were clever and discreet. We would avoid looking at each other at work. He would pick me up from random locations and I'd slide down in my seat when we were in areas where people he knew might see me in his car. He would park close to his door and I would crouch and duck in so that the neighbours wouldn't see me, and I wouldn't walk in front of the windows in his house. I hated the sneaking around, but trying not to get caught also felt like a game.

As the month came to an end and Mick's wife and baby were about to return, reality came flooding back to drown our fantasy life. As we tidied the house, making sure no evidence of my presence remained, he offered me his daughter's DVD of *Cinderella*. I had mentioned that it was my favourite. It was then that I broke down, sobbing, "I don't want it. There are no 'happily ever afters' in real life." Disney: the great lying mouth, setting entire generations up for crushing disappointment.

We embraced and cried. We had fallen in love, yet it was impossible for things to continue. I told him in no uncertain terms that I would not be his mistress. I had seen my mother go through that for two years and swore I'd never do that. The idea made me sick—even sicker than the idea of losing him. I didn't think he should leave his wife and kid for me either. I didn't want to be *that* woman. Nothing could be done about it; it was over, and I was crushed.

I went home so that Mick could spend the night alone in his house. He needed to get his head together since his wife and baby were coming home the next day. I stayed home and cried all day. That night he called me.

"Sara knows everything. I've asked for a divorce and left. I'm staying in a motel tonight. I'm pretty messed up. I only got to see my daughter for a couple hours while Sara and I fought the whole time." He sounded exhausted.

"What do you mean she knows *everything?*" I asked in disbelief. "Everything" was an awful lot. It didn't make sense... and divorce? Surely not for me—but *hopefully* for me. I was conflicted between my heart and my head. My mind raced. Would I be expected to be a stepmother to the baby? An endless, blazing road of unanswerable questions.

He chuckled in disbelief as he whispered, "Yeah, pretty much everything. Turns out Rhonda from work had been suspicious earlier in the month and had been following us in the car. She had known for weeks what was going on. She was the one who picked Sara up from the airport today and told her all the details." He paused, then followed up with an incredulous laugh, "As soon as Sara got home, one of the neighbours came over and told her what they had seen: her husband bringing in another woman the entire time she was gone."

I couldn't believe he was laughing about it, but I soon understood he was actually laughing at how stupid he had been to think that he could get away with it, laughing at how completely busted he was. I was horrified. I felt like a terrible person and couldn't even begin imagining how humiliating that must have been for his wife. I couldn't believe Rhonda had known for weeks, and I didn't realize it. She was the head of HR, and though I didn't interact with her often, I did see her around the office.

I said, "This is terrible! How can you be laughing?"

"It's all so dramatic. This isn't my life. This isn't me. I thought we were so careful. I was so stupid. But the truth is that I don't want to be with her anymore. I realized it the moment I saw her." He went on to explain, "I want to be with you. I was the one who asked for a divorce and left. She wanted me to stay and work things out."

I let that sink in for a moment, feeling elated by his need and horrified by the resulting collateral carnage.

"What happens now?" I asked.

"Well, I'd invite you to stay here or I'd come to your place, but Sara keeps calling to talk about things. She's freaking out. I need to try to support her through this and take her calls. So for tonight, I'll stay on my own. I'll try to make it into the office tomorrow. Come in or don't, whichever you want. Rhonda has quit, so you won't see her, but I don't know who else in the office knows. It's all getting shut down soon anyway, so I guess it doesn't matter, but still…" Mick trailed off, and I wasn't sure what he was feeling.

I barely slept that night. I didn't want Mick to leave his wife for me, but he was deeply unhappy. They had a baby, and I knew he loved his daughter more than anything. It was complicated and stressful. I didn't go in to work the next day. Or the next. I tried to give Mick space. He called several times a day with updates.

He reported, "Sara is consistent, and she wants to work things out. She said the Lord would help her forgive me since we made vows in the eyes of God. She even said she understood why I would stray, because she hadn't been a good wife to me that way. She wants to fix that. She thinks this is purely a sex-type thing between you and me. I don't have the heart to tell her that we've fallen in love."

I listened in disbelief. There was no God in my world; his wife sounded like a bit of a loon with all the God talk. God, God, God. I asked, "Do *you* believe in God? Do you feel the way she does about forgiveness and your vows? Are you into all that religious stuff?"

"I'm not sure," Mick replied with a chuckle. "Not as much as she does, but she might have enough faith for the both of us."

I didn't know what to say, so I listened mostly, feeling torn. I had been through my parents' divorce and had witnessed Jim's divorce peripherally—but I was twenty fucking years old! What did I know about religious thirty-year-old couples with babies divorcing, or surviving an affair like this? My heart was breaking and bursting simultaneously. With everything Mick said that indicated he might go back to his wife, my heart broke, and with everything he said that sounded like he might leave her for me, my heart swelled with hope. I felt so in love with him—intensely and overwhelmingly.

My adrenaline was constantly pumping. I didn't know when the phone might ring or when he might come to my door. I could barely eat or sleep. I eventually came back to work after a few days to find dark circles under his eyes; he wasn't sleeping either. We avoided each other as best as we could while thinking about each other constantly. I was on autopilot:

Hello Ms. Sanders, I'm calling on behalf of Sears Professional Carpet cleaning. We'll be in your area this month, and I'm wondering how your carpets are looking? Do you think they could be spruced up a little? (I wonder how Mick is doing? I miss him. I ache for him.) *I'll let you know the price right off the bat since that's almost the best part. It's only forty-nine dollars for two rooms and a hall.* (What if he goes back to his wife? Oh I feel sick. Maybe he should? I'm not ready to be a stepmother.) *It's steam cleaning, Ms. Sanders. Created for those with allergies to help improve the air quality in their home.* (How could we not see each other anymore? We have something so special.)

That night Mick picked me up and brought me to his motel room. In between lovemaking, he took calls from his wife. I was trapped, half-naked, still aroused, hearing her voice through the receiver. She would get him to pray with her. She would try to reason with him. She would put their baby on the phone, and I could hear her coo as her daddy chatted with her. Then he and his wife would laugh about how adorable their daughter was. "I am an impossibly enormous piece of shit," I thought.

Mick went back and forth for about a week, undecided and conflicted, before he got an apartment and moved out of the motel room. He kept telling me he wanted to be with me, and I wanted to believe him. In another week he formally filed for divorce, and they put the house on the market.

I tried to be rational. I would repeat what I was thinking: "Mick, I'm only twenty and not ready to settle down. Not only can I not see me being a step-mother; I can't imagine Sara ever wanting me near your daughter. I am the young bimbo who broke up your marriage. No way this ends happily for us. This cannot work."

And yet, neither of us could resist. Who can tell the difference between love or lust when they're in the thick heat of it? Surely, not a twenty-year-old. Indeed, love and lust are complete madness, as Shakespeare wrote, and when you're drowning in it, it's pointless trying to define which it is. Though, if you asked me then, I would have said we were in love—and my answer hasn't changed in twenty years.

I think Mick thought he'd have more time to figure things out, but the house sold immediately and Sara made an unpredictable snap decision to take their daughter back to British Columbia and live with her parents until Mick came to his senses—or as a way to force him to. She told him that he would not see his daughter until he dumped the bimbo and came back to her. It was a devastating blow and, despite all efforts, he couldn't stop her from leaving. In less than a month from the day she returned, Mick's wife was back on a plane, taking their daughter away again.

Mick was crazy about his daughter. He spent every possible moment with her before she left and video chatted with her every opportunity when she was gone. Sara encouraged all of that. She wanted to keep the bond strong, knowing this was the most likely way to get her husband back.

In the months following their departure, the call centre closed down. Mick took a well-paying job managing a different company. It was a lateral move in his career, but, to be fair, he had overreached starting that big call centre. Plus, he was under a lot of personal stress. He needed a job he could do without adding any more stress to the pile.

Mick used his connections to get me a decent inside sales job with AT&T. I set up appointments for outside sales reps to go to businesses and switch their long-distance calling service to AT&T. The staff were unceasingly conservative and dull; there were no after-work drinks here. And I was calling faceless corporations and had to be professional. I preferred calling regular folks at home in small towns.

Mick and I focused all of our time and effort into two tasks: having sex and talking about what he should do. He went back and forth, stuck in a thought loop: "I want to be with my daughter. I'm good for her, and she needs me. I don't want to be with Sara anymore. I did love her once, though, and she refuses to give up on me. Her faith and loyalty is remarkable."

The subtext was also always the same. He was trying to decide between me and them. I would say, over and over, "Your daughter is and should be the most important thing, but a marriage kept together for the kids can be horribly damaging. I know from experience. My mother telling me she only stayed with my father for me was a terrible weight to bear. I can't promise you lifelong loyalty. I'm only twenty. I am in love with you now, but I'm too young to make a commitment like Sara is offering. I'm not ready to settle down. Don't make the decision between Sara and me. Choose to be with Sara or not regardless of your feelings for me."

Around and around we would go. If Mick and I went through a rough spot, the scales would tip in the other direction: he'd spend more time on the phone listening to Sara try to convince him to work on their marriage. If things were going well with us and we were having fun, he would be more firm with her, telling her he was never coming back to her. I would sit outside the door, listening to him talk to her on the phone, trying to gauge which way he was leaning. It was incredibly stressful, for everyone.

Mick's whole family and Sara's thought he'd lost his mind. He was having an affair with a young floozy from the office, had left his wife and kid for her, and continued to stay with her. Mick and I broke up dozens of times. He'd keep "coming to his senses" and say he had to end it. We'd cry and cling to each other, spend a day or two apart and then get back together again.

We escaped to a beachside cottage near a quaint fishing village. One afternoon, out walking on the beach, heavy fog blew in, and we found ourselves inside a cloud. We couldn't see more than a few feet away; everything was still and peaceful. Socks and shoes off, we stood on the firm, wet sand. The tide lapped and hissed. Nothing existed in the entire world except us. We kissed, laughed and kissed again even more passionately. He swung me around. His eyes were glistening—he was so happy. I hadn't seen an easy smile on his face in so long. Our hands slid beneath each other's clothes and undid zippers. Half-naked on a public beach with cottages right there, yet totally invisible. He hoisted me up and slid me onto his cock. I wrapped my arms and legs around him as we pumped away, the mist making us dewy and the sex making us flush. Nothing else existed, except the thrill of possibly getting caught. Mick thrust hard with a big smile on his face and came inside of me. We kissed passionately, and I slid down to stand, the insides of my thighs slippery. We looked at each other, surrounded by mist, with bittersweet salt tears. "I wish we could stay like this, you and me," I whispered into his shoulder.

"Me too," he replied.

After one of our more dramatic breakups, Mick surprised me with a weekend trip to Boston. Our first night, we went out on the town. It was liberating—walking down the street together, holding hands and kissing, not worrying that we would see anyone who knew us. The freedom and booze made us brave, and we kissed and groped openly. When we got back to our room, we were so stirred up that we threw all the cushions on the floor of the suite and constructed a grand "sex fort." Mick used his necktie to bind my wrists to the leg of the sofa. He took me powerfully, but the alcohol must have made it difficult for him to cum because we fucked for what felt like hours. It was loud, and the front desk called to say other guests were complaining. We giggled like kids who had gotten into trouble.

The next day, I came down with a bladder infection and was painfully glued to the toilet with a constant urge to pee, and when I did it was razor blades. I sent Mick out for cranberry juice, which threw a monkey wrench into our sightseeing plans for the day. He complained that it was the same with Sara; she was always getting ill. He had liked that I appeared to be in perfect health. That hurt, as did his constant comparisons between me and her, knowing that he was inputting dozens of pieces of data into his decision-making machine. We made the best of the day, though, and that night we went to the House of Blues and listened to a great band, The Bubble Fish. We were as in love as ever and wished we could escape permanently—go to a new city and start over, together.

CHAPTER 14

Get Out

We talked about what I would do if Mick and I broke up for good. I was ready to spread my wings and see the world. I felt I had done well in Halifax. I was one of the only people my age who had any savings; most in the area were collecting pogey—unemployment insurance. Mick had lived in Vancouver for a few years before and thought I would be happy there. Jim's son and girlfriend lived near Vancouver, so I could stay with them until I got settled. Therefore, when Mick's scale had finally tipped toward returning to his wife—we were finally breaking up—I gave notice on my apartment and bought a ticket to Vancouver. I had a couple of weeks to get things in order. I was broken-hearted, but I was also tired of the roller-coaster ride. It had been going on for months and was like living in a romantic drama movie that kept having alternating happy and sad endings.

Predictably, immediately before I left for Vancouver, Mick had yet another change of heart. I was taken aback. I had given up my place, sold or given away my things, quit my job and said goodbye to my family and friends—so what was I supposed to do now? But Mick said that if I moved to Vancouver, he would come there and do everything in his power to bring me back. He was 100% sure he wanted to be with me and couldn't live without me. It was the certainty that I'd been waiting for. It felt different than the times before. This time he was truly decided. Somehow we'd make it work. We'd figure it all out, like in the movies.

I still decided to go to Vancouver for the weekend, though. A round-trip ticket was cheaper than a one-way at that time, so I booked the return for a few days later. I flew there, and my step-brother and his girlfriend picked me up. We spent a few days doing the touristy sites of Vancouver. Even though it rained the whole time and I never glimpsed the supposedly majestic mountains, I knew that I liked it there.

Everything appeared fine when I returned. Mick picked me up from the airport in Halifax and was still as in love as he had been before I left; no time had passed in the eyes of his heart. I moved into a little hotel room that rented by the month until we figured out what to do next. Sara and the baby were making occasional trips back from BC so that Mick could see his daughter, and since they were staying at his place, it hadn't made sense for me to move in with him at this point.

A couple weeks after I returned from Vancouver and Mick was away on business for a couple days, the phone rang in my hotel room. A female voice came through the other end: "This is Sara, Mick's wife. Please don't hang up." She wasn't yelling. She didn't sound angry, but there was a tense, urgent tone that kept me from slamming down the receiver in panic. I could tell she was shaking but willing herself to sound calm. She went on, "I felt like I needed to reach out to you to let you know that when you were in Vancouver I flew back here to Halifax, and Mick and I reconciled. We made love all weekend, and he intended on calling you to break it off. He changed his mind at the last minute, but you should know that there is still a lot of love between us and the best thing for our daughter is for us to get back together. I'm asking you to do the right thing and let him go." I could picture her mouth on the other end, close to the receiver, saying these words, trying to sound reasonable.

It felt like Tommy Lee from Motley Crue was doing a drum solo of "Kickstart My Heart" in my chest. With muscles straining in my neck and fingers gripping the receiver like it was the only thing holding me up, I said nothing. I didn't want to believe her. My mind replayed Mick's face telling me he wasn't attracted to his wife. Why would he have sex with her? Why would he not have told me she flew back for the weekend when I was gone?

She went on, pleading, "Please let him go. If you end things with him, I know he'll come back to us. You're only nineteen, just a kid…"

"I'm twenty," I interrupted.

She kept going as if she hadn't heard: "Mick's daughter needs her father. We made vows in the eyes of the Lord and we must honour that…"

At that point I hung up. I thought my heart was going to rip out of my chest. Sweating, flushed, I felt as if I'd sprinted a mile but hadn't moved an inch. The room tilted, and vertigo turned the world to jelly. My hand on the silent receiver, staring at the blank wall of my hotel room, I did the only thing I could think to do: I called my mother. She was still my best friend even though we'd grown apart. I told her about the phone call and never in a million years would have expected her response: "I know. It's true. Mick came to us while you were away and wanted us to call you in Vancouver to suggest that you stay. He said he would mail any of your things out. Then the next day he changed his mind; he called us and told us to please not mention anything to you. We didn't know what to do, but decided to not tell you and let things play out."

The room was a keeling ship. Betrayal. The inconceivable image of Mick sitting with my parents, telling them he was ending things with me and going back to his wife, asking them to break the news to me. I felt humiliated and small, stupid, disrespected. Too much. All too much. With my adrenaline already reaching the zenith from the first call, I sunk to the floor. The first sob washed over me, and I shook. I could barely keep my grip on the phone-receiver lifeline as the distant voice of my mother warbled, "We're going to come get you."

Have you joined me on the floor, reader? Have you ever had an occasion to crumple to the floor, a marionette whose strings have been cut? It's done in movies, isn't it? A character gets some terrible news on the phone and slides to the floor like an imploded building. It's an interesting thing how these sticks we call legs carry us along so well most of the time, but an emotional shock will take them right from under us, turning them to jelly. Amazing how connected our physicality is to our emotions.

I cradled the kind, generous toilet as it received my lunch, cried and ignored the ringing phone. Mom and Jim packed up my things and checked me out of the hotel. On the way out, the hotel staff told me I had several messages from Mick. The last one was urgent. A large bouquet of flowers from him was lying on the counter. I sat in the back seat, loosely clutching the obscene, lying flowers. Childish, foolish, humiliated; my trust had been shattered. Jim said, "You see those flowers? Men send flowers like that when they've screwed up. They mean that they're sorry. Don't be a sucker. Flowers don't make up for mistakes."

When we got back to my parents' place, I put them in a vase anyway. They were stunning in their meaningless glory. Long-stem white roses; a dozen of them. I'd never seen flowers so beautiful in person, and no one had ever had flowers delivered to me. They must have cost a fortune. I couldn't bring myself to throw them away.

I went to bed and stayed there. For two days I was sick, crying, barely eating, sleeping a lot and refusing to take Mick's calls. Mom nursed me, and it was nice to be cared for. I slipped into a comfortable place where my mother was really my mother, like I was still a little girl, and taking care of me was the most important thing in the world to her. She felt guilty for not telling me about Mick's visit, and she took care of me so sweetly that I felt I could live on that little window of love for the rest of my life.

After a couple days of Mick calling relentlessly, I finally took his call. He begged to see me, to talk about what had happened. I reluctantly agreed to meet up with him briefly. I expected Mom and Jim to try to dissuade me, but Jim said, "I would like you to help your mother pack for her trip tomorrow when you get home. She's never flown before, and she's nervous."

It sounded silly to me. Mom and Jim were going to Montreal for a few days on a business trip. My mother was a grown woman who surely knew how to pack for a short trip in the same country with the same climate in which she lived.

Mick pulled into my parents' driveway and waited in the car. I looked out and saw his blue eyes anxiously looking for me. "Coward," I thought. "Can't even come to the door and face my parents."

I opened the car door and slid into the seat. I turned to Mick and saw that he was already starting to cry. Neither of us said anything as he backed out of the driveway. I'm sure he wanted to get the hell out of there as soon as possible.

Once on the road, he finally spoke: "I was so worried about you when I couldn't reach you."

"Worried that I'd found out about you fucking Sara and trying to get my parents to tell me to stay in Vancouver, you mean?" I spat back.

"I figured you had found out, and I wanted to explain. Yes, Sara and I had sex that weekend, and it was the best sex we've had in a long time. It gave me hope that maybe we could work things out, and that would be the best thing for the baby. It's what you and everyone else have been telling me the whole time. I figured that since you were already in Vancouver, you should have the option to stay there and start a new life," he explained.

"Oh, so you were being considerate? Ha!" I snapped.

"I had a short window to make a decision. I went to your mom and Jim to get their opinion, and somehow the whole thing got twisted into me asking them to break the news to you. It wasn't exactly like that. We agreed that the news might be better coming from them. A phone call like that, a life-changing thing…" he tried to convince me, pleading.

"I wish I *had* stayed in Vancouver. I feel like a fool," I said, looking out the car window at his building as we entered the parking lot. We hadn't discussed where we were going, and I hadn't been paying attention.

Mick parked the car, turned his body toward me and said, "I know. I screwed up. I've screwed up so much and hurt you and Sara over and over. She thought we were getting back together, and then the next day I woke up and realized that I love you in a way that I never loved her. I deserve to feel that way about someone. I can't live without you."

"Well, you're going to have to learn to because I'm not coming back for more. I've had enough, and I've been humiliated. You say that you deserve to feel that way about someone? Well, I deserve to be loved by someone who isn't conflicted about his love for me," I spat with cutting finality.

There was heavy silence as his eyes welled up with tears, and he realized that he had probably lost me for good. I stared back, trying to be strong, but my heart was breaking. I wanted to touch him, to be held by him, to disappear into the mist again. Our love was so strong, but everything beyond that... well, it just couldn't work out.

"Since we're here, I'll come up and get the few things I left," I said.

Once inside his apartment, the mood was lightened. Mick cracked a joke about something, and we both laughed, grateful for a break from the gloom. I gathered up my stray items, and Mick quipped, glancing at the bed, "How about one for the road? Maybe I'll be able to convince you to stay?" We both laughed, but it was a foregone conclusion. No matter what was happening, we could never, ever keep our hands off each other. We had sex for hours, and by the time I realized it was late, it was too late to call home. I knew Mom and Jim would be going to bed early, and I didn't want to wake them, so I stayed at Mick's.

In the morning we were civil. We both needed to get to work, so we focused on that. I asked Mick to drive me back to my parents' first so that I could change my clothes and then drive me to work. On the ride there he checked again, "So we're really done? This is it?"

"Yes, Mick," I said firmly. "I don't know how we're going to do it, but we have to. I can't take this anymore. I guess I'll stay with Mom and Jim while I get things in order, and then I'll move to Vancouver."

"Okay. Well, I'd let you stay at my place, but Sara is bringing the baby tonight and staying for the week," Mick explained. "She knows that we're not getting back together, but she wants me to spend time with the baby."

"Ha. I can understand why you didn't tell me that last night," I shot back, adding, "I'm so done with this drama."

"I am in love with you. I will always love you," Mick said.

"Love isn't enough, Mick," I replied matter-of-factly.

We pulled into my parents' driveway, and I let myself in with the key they had given me. I started to go to my room for a change of clothes but heard Mom and Jim in the dining room and went to say hello. Jim told me to sit down and started lecturing with a vigour that caught me off guard. "You have deeply disappointed your mother and me. You were supposed to help her pack last night. It was the least you could do after everything she has done for you. All that she has sacrificed for you!"

I looked directly at my mother in disbelief. Was it true that it had been that important to her that I help her pack? Really? She was just staring at her plate of half-eaten toast. She wouldn't even look at me.

I tried to explain, "I'm sorry. I didn't realize it was a big deal. I had meant to come back, but one thing led to another, and it got late. I didn't want to call and wake you up because I thought you'd be going to bed early..."

Jim bellowed, slamming his hand down on the table, "If you are going to live under OUR roof, you are going to abide by OUR rules!"

The white roses Mick had sent me were in a vase on the table. They were starting to droop, and the vibration from Jim slamming his hand on the table made them tremble as if in fear.

"Your rules? What do you mean? What are you talking about?" I stammered, genuinely confused.

Jim sniffed, puffed up his chest and said, "Go pack what you can carry, leave your key and get out. We're not having you in this house while we're in Montreal. You can't live here. Go."

I looked at Mom again, who was still looking at her plate but crying now. Jim had made a fist with one finger jutting out and was pointing at the table in front of him, indicating that I should put my key there right now.

I felt like I was choking. Mick was sitting in the driveway waiting for me, and I had work that day and no place to go afterwards. Sara was staying at Mick's place that night. I had alienated any other friends I'd had with this dramatic, all-consuming roller-coaster ride of a relationship. I couldn't believe Jim was kicking me out—and that Mom wasn't trying to stop him.

Jim pointed firmly at the spot on the table again. His face was red—he looked like he was going to explode any second.

I looked down at the keys in my hand, and that's when I realized I was crying too. Tears dripped onto the keys. Everything started to go in slow motion, and I was in a tunnel; everything in front of me was clear, the periphery a blur. I saw my hand lift the keys up and set them on the table. I saw myself walk down the hall to my room and numbly put some things in a bag. I could hear my mother sobbing in the dining room and Jim muttering angry comments to her. I looked at the bed where I had spent the last couple of days being cared for by my mother. The mother that was now allowing her boyfriend to kick me out with no place to go. The people who had rescued me a few days before and nursed me were now turning their backs on me. They had kept Mick's secret; now this—more betrayal. A sour taste bloomed in my mouth as my jaw clenched and heart closed. There wasn't a soul in this world I could trust.

I went to the car, sobbing with such intensity that I could barely explain what had happened. Mick was late for work, and I refused to accept his comfort. I told him to drop me off at the bus stop; I'd take care of myself. Myself: the only person I could rely on.

At the bus stop I grabbed a newspaper, and on the ride downtown I looked up boarding houses in the classifieds. From a payphone I called in sick for work and then tried various boarding houses until I found one that I could move into that day: a tiny room with a single bed and a hot plate, and a shared bathroom down the hall. At least it was clean. I wondered, what kind of person lives in a place like this? My circumstances were unusual; I needed a place immediately but temporarily, for an indeterminate period of time.

For a week, I licked my wounds. No, that's not true, as it implies kindness. My heart had closed, and I spent the week reinforcing the door with cold iron. I was bitterly angry with my mother for allowing Jim to kick me out. Disgusting, weak Mom. I had opened up and allowed myself to feel nurtured by her, allowed myself to be vulnerable; I should have known she'd abandon me again. Sucker. She had been abandoning me for years, so why did I trust that she would be there for me when I needed her more than ever? How could I be so foolish? And so I spent the week thoroughly beating myself up. I put the cold, hard armour on, vowing to never let anyone get close enough to hurt me again. Though Mom had attempted to prepare me for life's challenges—"You need to be tough; life is hard"—ironically, it was she who caused the most harm.

However, a week after I moved into the boarding house she came for a visit. She looked at my tiny, shabby, lonely room with palpable sadness.

"It was all I could find on short notice. I had nowhere to go that day," I informed her. I felt like she was being judgmental.

"We thought you would go to Mick's place. We presumed you got back together again—" she defended.

"You didn't bother asking," I cut in, ice cold.

Mom reached for her cigarettes shakily. "Can I smoke in here?"

"No."

She stuffed them back in her purse. Her fingers kept fiddling with the pack, her eyes glancing at the door. She was dying for one, I could tell. I watched her silently. "How long do you think you'll stay here?" she asked, almost apologetically.

"Not sure. I don't have much left to keep me here, so I'll probably move to Vancouver soon." As if leaving the only place I'd known and moving 4,000 kilometers across the country was the same as deciding what to have for supper.

I watched her moving slowly around my room, taking it all in. The hot plate. The single bed. She avoided looking me in the eye and suddenly straightened, her nose twitching in the way it does whenever she said something with conviction or had to say something difficult. "I'm sorry I didn't stop him. I didn't know what to do. I was sick the whole time in Montreal. Terrible throwing up and diarrhea. I've been so upset." She presented an image of her painting the inside of a toilet with her grief and guilt like it was something precious she'd made especially for me.

"I had no place to go," I interjected. "I let you take me in. You checked me out of that hotel. Then you kicked me out with no place to go. Why? *Because I didn't help you fucking pack?!* Or because you thought Mick and I got back together? I know it's been dramatic, but for fuck's sake if ANYONE should have understood, it was you and

Jim! You were his goddamn mistress for two fucking years!" I said, punctuating the profanity. I was angry, and I wanted her to suffer.

"I know, I know," she pleaded. "But it was Jim. I didn't know he was going to kick you out. I don't think he planned it. He lost his temper. If you had said you didn't have any place to go—well, as I said, we assumed you would go to Mick's. If you had told us…"

"If I begged? You know me better than that; you raised me better than that," I hissed. My blood was boiling as she shrank further, ashamed.

"I can't imagine you moving across the country. You'll be so far away," she whimpered.

"That's exactly the point, Mom. Far away from Jim, who I will never, *ever* forgive. And for as long as you're with him, the farther I am from you, the better. Farther from Mick, so he can try to put his family back together. He sure as hell can't do it with me living in the same city." I starting to calm down as the direction of the conversation moved to the future. A future I felt genuinely optimistic about.

Mom made a move toward her cigarettes once more, and I said, "You can smoke outside, Mom. You can go. I'll see you before I leave."

The truth was that I felt sorry for her; no doubt she was telling the truth about being ill in Montreal, sick with guilt and worry. No one could have come away from that situation feeling good about themselves. She was a coward. She had abandoned her daughter once again, and even if she didn't have the emotional intelligence to verbalize it, in her gut she knew. She couldn't verbalize, so she threw up and had diarrhea instead. As angry as I was, I couldn't send her off in that state. I hugged her, a baby bird in my embrace. Through tight jaws I passed an "I love you." I heard her sniff, and her voice caught as she told me she loved me so much.

I booked my flight to Vancouver and prepared to go. The next couple of weeks, Mick and I still saw each other frequently. As I said, as long as it was physically possible, we couldn't keep our hands off each other. As the reality of my departure set in, Mick and Sara drew closer. They started to discuss the logistics of coming back together—where they would live and so on. He was relieved to have things decided. I didn't decide for him; I made it a little easier for him to make the decision he needed to make. As Sara said, I needed to let him go. It wasn't easy for either of us though, and we slept together until the bitter end. Sara and their daughter passed me in the air; my flight to Vancouver was on the same day as their flight back to Halifax. Mick went to the airport twice that day, once to drop me off and again to pick them up.

On the way to the airport, he said, "One of the hardest things you can ever do is drive someone you love to the airport knowing you'll never see them again."

We wept and clung to each other—my entire body screaming for me to stay. I loved Mick with all my heart. I didn't look back as I walked away, tears streaming down my face. I cried on and off during the whole flight to Vancouver, but what sweet relief it was to be off that roller coaster. Or was I? Would putting that much distance between us be enough to end this craziness? What if they broke up again in a few weeks, months or years? Would we get back together? Finally deciding I couldn't let myself think that way, I looked out the plane window and started planning the next chapter of my life as the majestic Rocky Mountains came into view.

CHAPTER 15

New Life in Vancouver

Almost twenty-one and starting a new life in Vancouver, I had become harder, colder and more determined and ambitious. No chance of failure.

I immediately found work in another call centre. That was the easiest thing to get quickly, but because the economy was much better in Vancouver, call centre work wasn't considered a good job. I gave it my all, though, and called people at home to sell them long-distance phone packages.

That went well for about a month, until one magical day. I was approaching the door of the office building carrying two cups of coffee, one in each hand. A friendly-looking man held the door for me and stood nearby waiting for the elevator as I chatted with a coworker about having just moved from Halifax. In the elevator, he gave me his card and said, "I'm from back East too and would love to help out a fellow Maritimer."

Eric was a cute, clean-shaven, pale-skinned man of about thirty clad in business attire, with neatly cropped brown hair, an easy smile and a twinkle in his eyes. I looked for a wedding ring and didn't see one, so I called him the next day and we went for lunch. He immediately started talking about his wife and kids. I felt sick. The last thing I wanted was to get involved with another married man. He went on to ask for my resume, saying he could help me find better employment. I was polite but tossed his card and meant to forget him.

Eric persisted though, calling my work and leaving messages, and I continued to ignore him. Eventually he called just as I was passing the reception, and I had to take the call. Eric explained that he had the best intentions, that I was working a dead-end job that I was too good for and that he had set up an interview the next day for me at a solid company. He was so assertive that I reluctantly decided to go.

I arrived at the posh new offices of JULCOM Technology Services. My meeting was with the HR manager, who explained their previous secretary had moved up to assist the president and that they were in need of a new receptionist for the busy, growing office. I had none of the required skills; I barely knew how to use a computer, let alone how to work a complicated switchboard. I didn't know how to use the photocopy machine, how to keep an inventory of a supply room, or how to juggle incoming and outgoing packages. On top of all that, I didn't have the right business wardrobe for a front office job.

Despite all that, the manager explained that Eric highly recommended me and that they were willing to pay for all the required training. I had no reason to be cocky—I was probably the worst possible candidate for the job—but explained that I would need a clothing budget on top of the salary they offered me. Both Eric and the HR manager laughed about that for years.

I started that week, and it was an unmitigated disaster. I did not possess the sticky sweetness and plastic smile that is universally required of reception customer service personnel. Nor did I have the patience to juggle a hundred things at once: the phone ringing constantly, worker bee couriers coming in and out, clients arriving, coordinating meetings, learning to use the computer, etc. All this swirled within the furious onslaught of my fellow female employees' hatred, centering on me due to the inescapable fact that I was completely unqualified and had probably been hired exclusively for my beauty and youth.

Eric, luckily, was my ray of sunshine—always with a smile and an encouraging word and never flirty or inappropriate; he was a genuine angel there who helped me through it. The carrot pulling me through the mediocre hell of office life was the fact that the company paid 75% of any training I wanted to take. It didn't matter if it was related to the job. So I soon enrolled in night courses in sales, marketing and public relations. Eric had always been clear that he didn't see me as a receptionist; this was simply a great opportunity to better myself, to climb higher.

I worked and went to night school for a couple of years, and I eventually got the hang of the job. I learned a great deal about the corporate world, office politics, business and marketing.

The aggressive saleswoman inside me was alive and well, and she was tired of being a receptionist. I befriended the vice president of the company and convinced him I should be promoted to a particular type of sales position, one similar to a telemarketing role—something the company didn't have at the time. The business wasn't doing especially well, partly because of a shift in the market and partly because the sales manager was incompetent, but even the sales manager could tell my idea didn't make sense. Despite that, the VP ordered him to promote me, and he did so, begrudgingly.

In the next few months, the sales manager was fired, and Eric took his place. One of the first things he did was lay off about 25% of the employees—including me. He looked sad as he slid the severance package documents across the desk and said, "I did the best I could." I would get a month's salary. I beamed, thanked him and went straight to the travel agent to book a flight to Thailand.

At this time I was dating a sweet lad by the name of Calvin. He was handsome and focused on climbing the corporate ladder. He came from a lovely family, played hockey in an amateur league, golfed, was a good cook and treated me like solid gold. On paper, he was perfect husband material.

He had stolen me away from "Premature Ejaculator Stewart." Stewart was a nice enough guy but regularly came in his shorts when we were making out. He learned some self control, but sex was always tentative because I never knew how long it would last; I just couldn't relax into it.

Sex with Calvin was great at first but got boring quickly. He always wanted to make sweet love, sensually, slowly. His orgasm face was alarmingly womanly, curling his mouth into an "O," gasping in breathy high-pitched moans. I typically stared at his face in shock during his climax.

Deciding I should spice things up a bit, I went to the youth section of a department store and got all the pieces for a naughty schoolgirl uniform: a short, pleated plaid skirt; a crisp white shirt; white knee-high socks; and black patent leather Mary Janes. I wiggled into my tight new clothes, put my hair up into messy pigtails, stuck a lollipop in my mouth and turned "Only Happy When It Rains" by Garbage way up. When Calvin came home from work and opened the door, it must have been quite the sight. My engine was certainly running as I skipped up to him and pressed myself against him. He stiffened, but I persisted and dragged him to the sofa by his tie, pushed him down and sat on his knee. I sucked on the lollipop while looking into his eyes, measuring his reaction. He looked uncomfortable; he wasn't into it.

But Calvin was committed to me, and we had a good relationship. Steady, secure, safe, easy, dull. So when I had the opportunity to go to Thailand for a month on my severance package from JULCOM, he encouraged me to go on my own. He was that kind of guy.

So off I went, armed with a sense of adventure and an engorged backpack bursting with useless junk. Thailand in 2001 was genuinely wild, and I was dangerously inexperienced and totally unprepared. I managed to get food poisoning on the flight there and arrived at 1 am pale and sweaty, having thrown up for the bulk of the 17-hour flight. A minibus shat me out into the notoriously debaucherous slum of Khao San Road in Bangkok. Stray dogs, rats and cockroaches the size of hamsters weaved around vendors selling mystery meat on sticks. Ladyboys flirted with drunk tourists, plying their wares. Rotting wooden planks creaked over streams of filth. The mingling smells of piss, vomit and charred meat were overpowering. In a stupor, I followed a couple I met on the plane who had taken pity on me. They found a hotel and said I could share their room. In the morning they were gone.

I descended from my haven to the bustling tourist area. The heat was suffocating, but the bright sunlight put a friendly face on the shitshow. There were loads of racks selling clothing and many shops selling bus tickets to other parts of Thailand. I decided to go to one of the picturesque islands; why not?

I waited in a coffee shop until it was time for my bus to leave. Dark wooden chairs and tables, large fans on the ceiling pushing the steaming heat around, incomprehensible Thai music playing loudly. As I ordered water, I noticed a stick of a man looking at me curiously. He was dressed in practical but fashionable khaki clothing and sturdy, well-worn hiking boots. His Germanic face was well tanned, and his white teeth gleamed as he smiled at me. I smiled back. He was nice enough. He politely asked if he could join me and then spoke to the waitress in Thai. I was impressed.

"You speak Thai?" I asked.

"Yes, fluently," he replied with a grin and went on. "I've lived here many years. I'm a gem trader."

I thought that sounded rather fancy.

"Do you like gems?" he inquired.

"I don't know anything about them," I said, realizing that I didn't really know much about anything.

"Let me guess," he said smiling warmly. "This is your first time to Thailand, and you've just arrived. Am I right?"

"Yes," I said with a laugh. I'm sure it was obvious.

"And you're waiting for a bus, I presume? Where are you heading?" he asked.

I wasn't sure I should tell a stranger, but I couldn't come up with a passable lie, so I told him the truth: "Koh Chang."

He looked disappointed, like he was deciding if he should say something controversial, when his coffee arrived. He and the waitress exchanged a few sentences. He was showing off his Thai, but she wasn't terribly impressed. I became wary of him.

"Koh Chang is fine," he said smoothly, "but it's a tourist trap. I assume you're travelling on your own because you want an adventure? Have you heard of the River Kwai? As in the movie *The Bridge Over the River Kwai*?"

I confirmed I'd heard of it but hadn't seen the movie, so he went on. "It's a beautiful place in the jungle. Not touristy. That's where I'm heading; that's where I stay and source the gems I trade. You're welcome to come with me and see something truly special."

I looked hard at this man I'd only known a few minutes. He had a warm, open look about him, but he was also slick—a little too slick. I was a naive, vulnerable looking girl in her early twenties, an easy target. So far he hadn't flirted with me, so why would he want me to come with him somewhere? I imagined I would be a burden. I had heard of human trafficking, and all of a sudden I felt certain that's what this was all about.

I got a chill, despite the heat. I shifted in my seat and went to reach for my water but stopped. How carefully had I been watching? Could he have slipped something in my drink? I brought the glass to my lips but didn't drink from it. Then I explained, "Thank you, but I'm meeting friends on Koh Chang, and they'll be worried if I don't turn up there tonight."

"Oh, it's Thailand! Plans change. I'm sure they'll understand. You could come with me for a few days and then go meet your friends after," he pressed.

His persistence reinforced my fears. I pushed back, "Why would you want me to come with you? You've just met me."

I thought I noticed a flinch in his smile. A crack on an icy pond when you first put your weight on it. A warning crack.

He answered lamely that he was only offering the opportunity for me to have an adventure, to see a part of Thailand that most tourists don't get to see. He continued trying to persuade me with increasing pressure, assuring me I could trust him, but I was already sure I didn't want to go anywhere with this man. I tried to be polite and disarming until my bus came. He insisted on carrying my backpack for me to the door of the bus, and as I took it from him he had a look in his eyes that I perceived as an animal who had just lost his prey. As the bus drove away, I looked at him standing there watching me go, unsmiling.

Was I nearly abducted by a human trafficker posing as a gem trader? Or something else? I'll never know for sure.

On Koh Chang I got the cheapest available bungalow I could find and spent a horrible night next to a smelly kitchen in a mosquito-filled room with a flooded bathroom. In the morning the sun shone on stunning white sand and turquoise water. I put on my bathing suit and went for a swim. I thought things might be okay after all, but upon returning to my bungalow I was scared to death by a gecko on my door. How was I supposed to know they're harmless?

I decided to explore the area and look for a better place to stay. As I walked, the bungalows were either shabby or more expensive than I could afford, though I admit I didn't fully understand the exchange rate. When I ran out of beach, hopelessness set in. I had barely eaten in a couple of days, still had severe nausea and was exhausted, confused and sad.

As I stood there alone, crying and feeling sorry for myself, I heard a woman's voice say, "What's wrong, Angel?"

That was Lina. A fifty-year-old Swiss artist who would be my saviour. She nursed me back to health, found me a better place to stay and planned the rest of my trip for me, including helping pre-book all my travel and accommodation for Chiang Mai and Koh Phangan. She even called ahead for her friends to meet me and look out for me. I have no idea what would have happened to me without her help, but the remainder of the trip was blissfully uneventful.

I returned home to Calvin, and life went on. I briefly took a sales assistant job at a boring company in the business of employee assistance programs and then changed to a more interesting job in customer service and marketing for a chat line company. Straight and gay chat lines. It was a fun place to work.

Then one day, out of the blue, I got a call from Mick. He took a real risk calling and had phoned my mother asking for my number. She explained that I was living with someone, but Mick was persistent and promised he wouldn't cause trouble.

"It's Mick—please don't hang up," he started, the hope straining his voice. Then, revelling in the shock he knew I must be feeling, he added an easy "How are you?"

"Why are you calling?" I cut right to the chase.

A nervous laugh trickled through the receiver, and realizing I didn't want to torture him, I apologized. "Sorry, I'm just taken aback. I'm living with someone, and we're going to be married. We just got a kitten. He's purring away on my chest. Say hello to little Noah."

"Noah?!" Mick sounded alarmed. He stuttered, "Why did you name him that?"

I replied that my boyfriend had named him.

Mick paused and laughed nervously again, sounding shaken. "That's what we named our son. He's a year old now. A baby to fix the marriage... you know how it goes."

"Wow. I didn't know. Seriously. A band-aid baby, eh? How's that working out for you?" I said, not even trying to hide the sarcasm in my voice.

He didn't answer but said he wouldn't keep me; he only wanted to let me know he was coming to Vancouver for business in a few days. "Would you join me for dinner? Just dinner." He asked with an edge of desperation.

How could I resist?

It had been a few years since I'd seen him, but the moment I saw him I knew that my feelings hadn't changed. I was as in love with him as I always had been; it was as if no time had passed at all.

We caught up. Despite a lot of couples therapy, their relationship hadn't improved. I told him Sara used to call me every couple of weeks—drunk, angry, sad, etc.—to tell me how they were doing. She bitterly spat that she should have let him be with me since he loved me in a way that he would never love her. It was a horrible life for them to live, but they had made their own choices.

I went home that night and broke it off with Calvin. I explained that I didn't love him the way he deserved. I could marry him, give him a child or two, go through the motions, and we would be content, but he deserved someone who loved him passionately, fiercely, fully. We shouldn't be with people just because they look good on paper. Our hearts should be in love with their souls.

I knew Mick and I wouldn't be together, but I vowed to never stay with anyone I wasn't crazy about.

CHAPTER 16

The Power Exchange

I had a fling with Thad, a man who was terribly homely—the most physically unattractive guy I ever had sex with—but he had an edge. I first glimpsed his edge while he was biting my earlobe. Hard. The rush of pain was refreshingly thrilling after a couple of years of soft lovemaking with sweet Calvin. I only wanted a quick rebound thing, but then tragedy struck. Thad's brother died by suicide, and a week later his grandmother died too. I found myself in a room with his whole family in mourning. His eight inquisitive aunts were all trying to figure out why this beautiful, poised young woman was with their strange, unattractive, awkward, alcoholic nephew. Thad had never had a girlfriend, any girlfriend, and he was thirty.

I stuck around for a couple more months while Thad spent most of his time drunk in bed in the dark, unbathed. I figured that was mourning, and I felt I was doing the right thing by not breaking up with him, but it ended badly anyway. I tried to break it off delicately but still got a drink thrown in my face and later a series of threatening phone calls, which led to me getting a restraining order.

About ten years later he reached out, asking if we could meet so he could apologize for what happened. I accepted, and it went well until he told me about a girl he had dated for a while, a Marilyn Monroe impersonator. When I asked if he meant "Malina Marvelous," he looked like he'd been caught with his hand in the cookie jar. I explained that I had dated her and that we were still friends. He back-pedalled and said that it had been brief and casual. I called her later, and she wasn't sure who Thad was but thought he might have been a regular customer at a strip club where she had worked. Poor Thad.

It was around that time that I took a trip that would change my life. I went to San Francisco with Francois, my platonic male friend. We did all the usual touristy things: Fisherman's Wharf, the tour of Alcatraz, the Castro. I was looking for something more exciting, so I struck up a conversation with the hotel concierge. I asked him if there was a place he could recommend—nothing was out of bounds. I explained that I expected a big American city to have something that would blow my mind.

"Don't even tell me what it is," I told him. "Just give me the address for the cab. I don't want to know where I'm headed." He smiled nervously, wondering whether I was looking for a club or a good club sandwich. I was a petite, conservative, naive-looking Canadian in her twenties. I reassured him, "It's okay. I'm looking for a memorable experience." So he wrote down the address and handed it to me with a smile and an "Enjoy."

I fetched Francois in the room, explained that I had a surprise for him and off we went. When I handed the cab driver the address, he looked back at me and said, "Are you sure?" I nodded yes confidently, grinning to my nervous friend. Ten minutes later we were dropped off in front of a shady-looking place with a burly bouncer at the door. As we stepped inside, a big sign with a list of rules greeted us. Among these were "Condoms are required for penetration" and "No touching without permission." Welcoming, yet firm.

We had arrived at The Power Exchange, but I still wasn't sure what it even was. We paid, put our things in a locker and entered the first room. It was decorated as a medieval tavern. An enormous fireplace complete with roaring fire took up most of the far wall, a solid rustic table with benches filled most of the space, and torches and candles adorned the walls. It was dark except for the firelight, which lit up a stunning naked woman. She was bound to a heavy wooden cross, getting whipped by a large barbarian of a man wearing fur pelts. Off to the side, a small, ordinary-looking fella sat watching. She was howling in pain—or was it ecstasy? After a moment the regular-looking man approached her from the front and started fucking her pussy with his fingers while she was getting whipped. Her moans rose higher as she climaxed, quivering against her restraints. They unhooked her, and they went off to cuddle in front of the fire on a bearskin rug.

I turned to Francois. He was speechless, as was I. A couple of other voyeurs were shuffling off down the hallway, so we followed. We passed a room with a stripper pole. A half-dressed woman slithered around the pole, obviously not a professional dancer but enjoying the attention of a few men watching her anyway. One of the men watching was stroking his cock, and she encouraged him. We kept moving past a few cages that held men dressed as dogs. They whimpered at us as we stared at them.

Down some steps and a narrow hallway, we noticed peepholes in the wall. Looking through one, I saw a young woman dressed in a schoolgirl costume lying on a medical table and masturbating with a vibrator while a man sat watching her. In another room, I saw a woman with a strap-on cock pounding a heavy man dressed entirely in leather from behind.

We then came into a room with a wall of TVs all playing different porn scenes. An attractive couple laid on a bed watching the porn, fondling each other while a pair of guys watched them, stroking their cocks under tiny towels wrapped around their waists. In a darkened corner, a woman stood against the wall getting fucked from behind by a goblinesque man. She didn't look at him, not even a glance. He blew his load, and another random guy stepped in to take his place. She didn't look at him either. She kept her eyes clamped shut as men took turns with her, revelling in the thrill of not knowing.

We came across a man secured to a pole with plastic wrap. His eyes were wide, taking in the crowd of voyeurs. A busty goth woman clad in a shiny black dress was busy abusing his genitals. Drips of hot red wax fell on his cock and balls, only to be smacked off with a riding crop as soon as it dried. He whimpered softly, his face creased in pain, eyes darting from her, to his mutilated genitals, to those watching, and back again. The crowd swelled. Men and women gathered to see what she would do next. Out came the needles, and she started on him like he was a pin cushion. His cock and balls soon resembled a porcupine. Despite everything, he was rock-hard, his cock straining and drooling pre-cum. She kept dipping her finger in it and bringing it up to his lips to clean up.

This whole time Francois and I said nothing to each other. We drifted from one mind-blowing scene to another, exchanging glances but also trying to avoid each other's eyes.

We came upon a large crowd gathered around a big caged-off area. Inside was an attractive, slender, thirty-something brunette bound to a board that was raised up a few inches off the floor and tilted slightly. She was restrained with her back against the board and facing the crowd, and an alarming number of clothes pegs quivered on her breasts and genitals. The man who was attaching the clothes pegs looked intensely serious.

"Tell them what you did to earn your punishment!" he barked at her, an inch from her face.

Meekly, in almost a whisper, she confessed, "I burnt his toast."

The crowd broke out into unexpected laughter, and so did they. He no longer looked so severe, and the tone of the scene became less intimidating. It was at that moment that he looked into the crowd and saw me. He smiled slyly and gestured for me to enter the caged-off area.

Not looking at my friend, I dipped under the chain and approached them. The man quickly and efficiently delivered a bunch of information to me while she nodded and smiled. He explained that she was his submissive and they had played together for a long time. She was a consenting adult and enjoyed what they did, even if it hurt. He explained safe words, that she would say "amber" to slow down or "red" to stop the action. He then handed me a vibrator and asked me to touch it to the tips of the clothes pegs on her breasts and pussy. I was welcome to shove it right into her pussy if I wanted to. I did exactly that, checking her face for a response. She was biting her lips and moaning in pain or pleasure; I wasn't sure.

He then put a rubber glove on my hand and asked if I had ever fisted anyone before. I shook my head no, and he laughed. He said that I had small hands and that he fists her, so she'd be able to take my whole hand no problem. He lubed me up, and I slowly, gently started to work my hand into her pussy. It felt too tight for me to get my whole hand in, but he encouraged me, coached me through it, smiling the whole time. Here I was, in front of a large group of people, in some weird sex club, fist-fucking a woman I didn't even know. It occured to me that she looked like she was my hand puppet.

"Now," the Dom said, "it's boot shine time." He took the clothes pegs off while she howled in pain and then released her from her restraints. There were a couple of chairs nearby, and he gestured for us to sit down. Not her though—she kneeled on the floor beside us. He theatrically announced to the crowd that his slave was going to give a special boot shine. She then straddled his leg, pressed her pussy against the toe of his army boot and started grinding and writhing. I made eye contact with Francois; he looked stunned.

She then moved on to my boots, which were black leather with a softly pointed toe. She didn't just shine my boots; she fucked them—getting most of the boot into her juicy, freshly fisted cunt.

The Dom asked, "Want to know what it feels like to be flogged?" I had no idea what he meant but said, "Sure." He was gentle but firm in his instructions. He repeated the safe words and how to use them. He told me to stand up on the ledge of the torture board and drop my pants, but that he wouldn't tie me up the first time. His slave held my hand and talked sweetly to me, telling me what to expect and that I could stop it at any time.

Just over her head was a large crowd of mostly guys, many of whom were wanking, and among them, my poor friend, wide-eyed and shocked. Right beside me was a buxom, boisterous women getting fucked in a sex swing; to my left, on the floor kneeling on a blanket, was a man naked (except for a gimp mask) masturbating.

Behind me to the left was a woman on her hands and knees getting fucked from behind while another man was fucking her mouth and a third man filmed it. Lastly, as I turned my head further, feeling my pants around my ankles, my ass bare except for a purple g-string, I could see the Dom clad all in black leather, looking intimidating holding a monstrous instrument of torture: a big leather-covered handle with many long soft-leather strips. It was huge, and when it came down on the flesh of my ass and back it felt like what getting tackled by a football player must feel like.

Thud.

Thud.

He started slowly, but as he built up speed and pressure, it knocked the wind out of me. I began to sweat. It was an unusual sensation: not exactly *painful*, but not exactly *not pleasurable* either. I noticed at least a couple of men reach climax, ejaculating into their condoms as they watched. I loved it. As though it was a drug, I was immediately addicted to this new rush—the thrill of being watched.

We exchanged information afterward, and our paths would cross again. That night though, Francois and I lay in bed for hours staring at the ceiling, thinking about all that we had experienced, replaying scenes in our heads, trying to process the sensory overload. I was forever changed.

CHAPTER 17

Boys, Boys, Boys

I moved jobs again and started selling DNS and DHCP software for a high-tech company. I didn't understand the technology and I wasn't terribly good at my job, but I started an affair with the cute secretary, Aiden, which kept things interesting at work. Aiden had a mixed ethnicity: Trinidadian, African, Spanish. He was beautiful. I could look into his big, brown eyes all day long. He showed me a trick to make more money at my job by contacting existing customers and renewing their service license. It wasn't what I was hired to do, but it was a moneymaker for the company, so they didn't mind.

Those days I changed jobs and men about as often as you change the oil in your vehicle. My next paramour, Dick, was an emotionally detached and fiercely selfish go-getter. He was on his way up the corporate ladder, and I found his ambition attractive. He never missed an opportunity to advise me that I should wear more makeup, do my hair better, dress sexier or work harder. He loved to keep me feeling that I wasn't good enough for him.

Dick introduced me to the infamous party drug, ecstasy, and I loved it, but he still somehow found a way to screw up something called "ecstasy." The second time we did it together we were in a club. I noticed him checking out other women and paying no attention to me at all. High, in a huge crowd, I felt completely alone. I told him I understood he didn't want to be with me and that we should break up. He agreed but then later that night seduced me back, simply because his friend was showing interest in me.

I brought Dick to San Francisco with me the next time I went. I met up with the Dom who flogged me at The Power Exchange, and we went to a huge fetish party. We even got to help backstage, body-painting people for a shibari rope-tying performance by the famous Midori, who wrote *The Seductive Art of Japanese Bondage*. It was exciting to meet her and to see all the amazing stage shows that night.

I had an opportunity to submit to a well-known and well-respected Dom while Dick watched. I was spanked, experienced electric play, tied up and flogged. I didn't like the pain, but I loved the exhibitionism. I loved all the people watching. I felt high. It registered that Dick looked unhappy, so I checked in with him. He said he was fine, and the play continued. I closed my eyes and felt the pain. As my adrenaline kicked in, I tried to breathe through it, opened my eyes and made eye contact with people in the crowd. What a rush it was seeing the arousal in their eyes! Couples fondling each other watching me, whispering about what they liked, men wishing they could touch me. I felt safe and alive at the same time—until I made eye contact with Dick again. Disgust. I walked back over to him again, and this time he started to rant about how much he hated the whole thing. "It's too fucking weird. I'm not going to stay here and watch this. Watch YOU do this." He put the stamp on his complaints by saying he was leaving with or without me.

I felt crushed, like I'd been dropped off a cliff. I tried to hold back the tears, but it was pointless; they welled up and spilled down my cheeks. I could barely see through the tears as I tried to keep up with him while he worked his way through the crowd, heading to where our things were behind the stage. We ran into people that we met earlier, and I was embarrassed to be seen crying. We made a fast exit and spent a silent, sleepless night in bed together. I cried. He said nothing.

The next day as we were about to fly home Dick got into a petty argument with a male flight attendant before the plane took off. We were escorted off the plane by security and had to catch the next flight.

Not long after, Dick forgot my birthday, and that was the last straw for me. I broke up with him over email because he didn't even deserve an in-person discussion. The whole thing didn't last more than a few months, but it shouldn't have lasted even a day.

Despite that, I was feeling awful after the breakup. My self-esteem had been pummelled. A blossoming part of my sexuality had been judged as disgusting. A good friend asked me to come to Wreck Beach, located near the University of British Columbia in Vancouver, because he thought it would elevate my mood. I'd never been there before, but the beach sounded exactly like what I needed.

When we arrived, I realized it was a nude beach. I was happy to strip off; I wasn't shy. I was hanging out at the water's edge when I saw the cutest beach boy—tanned, white-blonde hair, piercing blue eyes. He was approaching our blanket, so I came back. He was selling beer to my friend, and he smiled at me. I smiled back, pretending to be bashful.

I came back to the beach a few days later with a different friend. This time I crossed paths with the beautiful beach boy at the water's edge, and it afforded an opportunity for him to inquire if I was single. I said yes. He asked for my number, and I gave it to him. He then reached out and took my hand as he walked away, and it was magical. That was Tyler; he was one of those people who would drastically change my life.

CHAPTER 18

Inspiration

Our affair started out full of sweetness and passion. Tyler liked innocent girls, so I kept my mouth shut and went with it. I appeared to be a nice, sweet, naive girl. The sex was phenomenal, and the rest of the time I simply observed him. He was the happiest person I had ever met. He spent his summers selling beer and cannabis on a nude beach to pleasant hippies. He partied at night and had as many lovers as he could juggle, as well as a fun group of friends who worshiped him. He sang and played guitar. In the winters he travelled to exotic destinations like India and Africa. I truly had never met someone so happy. He was doing his own thing, living off the grid, whereas I had been surrounding myself with people who were climbing the corporate ladder or conforming to society's mould for general acceptance. The idea that I could do what I wanted, create a life customized specifically for me, and be happier was an extraordinary revelation.

Tyler showed me inspirational pictures of him in India and encouraged me to travel. He encouraged me to sell tequila shooters at the beach in my free time and take a break from my soulless job selling used office cubicles to other companies.

He also made me feel beautiful. When we had sex, he gushed

over how sexy I was, and I savoured every bit of it. After Dick, I was thirsty for the compliments. I dragged it out for as long as possible, keeping my bigger personality quiet, knowing that who I really was would turn him off. I was too kinky, too coarse, too hard, too strong. I was not the soft, sweet and innocent girl he thought I was. If I were, I might have thought I was the only one he was dating, or I might have thought that we were dating in the first place. Tyler was a player; he always had a few girls on the go. But he didn't want to hurt anyone. He just loved getting swept up in a moment of passion and was able to do that with a lot of women. He was disarming and fun. He was like Peter Pan with a youthful playfulness. As long as he made me feel special, I didn't care who else he was sleeping with.

I started working at the beach evenings and weekends. I walked up and down the beach naked selling tequila shooters, and I loved it. Everyone was so nice to me, so welcoming, so friendly. I had never felt such a sense of community.

As Tyler and I drifted apart, I started a fling with a coworker named Vince. I guess I never learned the whole "don't shit where you eat" concept. I was spending my days in a shabby office cubicle, cold-calling companies to ask if they were expanding or renovating and whether they needed any office furniture, and sending them follow-up emails. Mostly, I was just harassing people. Vince and I flirted at work and partied on the weekends. He loved to drink, and it took me a while to figure out he was an alcoholic.

Tyler and I still saw each other at the beach all the time, and the attraction wasn't gone. We flirted all the time, and I knew exactly what was going to happen. I didn't want to cheat on Vince, so I broke up with him, and Tyler and I spent a weekend together, making love on the beach by the campfire, him singing to me, me lapping it up, knowing it was temporary.

As summer started to turn into fall, I was feeling restless. So, inspired by Tyler's winter travels, I decided to go to India. I didn't have much money saved, but my plan was to charge it on my credit card and figure it out later. Instead, I met someone at Wreck Beach who had a better idea.

Elaina was beautiful. Tall, with auburn hair that brushed her perfect breasts, and eyes that were big and soft in a way that made her look constantly aroused. I wouldn't have described her as especially intelligent, but her mix of soft-spoken hesitation and giggling shyness was endearing. I developed an instant crush on her and would have followed her anywhere. We would get drunk and make out, but that's as far as we went physically. Elaina had worked in Tokyo as a hostess and planned to go back.

"Come with me and make money for your trip," she invited. "I know it sounds crazy, but it's safe, and I'll be there too."

I made the arrangements, gave notice that I was moving out of my apartment, quit my job and told Vince I was leaving for an undetermined amount of time. We had sort of gotten back together and, although it wasn't serious for me, I should have seen that it was serious for him.

Two days before I left, Vince's father died suddenly of a heart attack. They hadn't spoken in a decade—since Vince's father had called the police and reported his son for driving under the influence. Vince was stubborn and wouldn't forgive him for it, but the moment he learned of his father's death, he suddenly realized how foolish he had been. He was devastated.

I was torn between being there for a friend during a horrible time and moving forward with my life, knowing there was no future for us together anyway.

The last day before I left while I was packing up the last of my things, just as I was about to unplug my phone and put it in a box, it rang. It was Mick. I had to sit down. I did everything I could think of so that he wouldn't be able to find me. I had an unlisted phone number. I had never told him where I worked. I had tried to avoid this very thing, and yet I was so happy to hear his voice.

He explained that he had accepted a job offer in British Columbia, and in his first week he was looking for office furniture. His secretary sent him my email; turns out I'd cold-called his company to sell them office furniture. "I couldn't believe it," he said. "It was *your* name." He had been trying to find me, but my mother wouldn't give him my contact information this time. So he called and was told I had left the company. He smooth-talked the receptionist into giving him my personal number. "I don't know that I would have bothered, but it was too crazy," Mick continued. "The way it all fell into place, I felt like I had to try." He was in my city, and he was there to stay, with his wife and daughter and son.

"I want to see you," he added, filling the silence hanging over us. I hadn't said a word.

I finally mustered, "I don't think that's possible."

I explained that I was sitting in an empty apartment, that I was boarding a plane the next day for who knows how long and that my "kind-of" boyfriend's father had recently died. It was crummy timing; it wouldn't work. We said our farewells, and I unplugged the phone from the wall, feeling overwhelmed as my past, present and future collided.

CHAPTER 19

Tokyo

Elaina and I arrived in Tokyo at night and went straight to the club to sign our contracts. I met my boss, Woody, a tiny Pakistani man with a grating, disrespectful attitude, and I immediately wanted to punch him in the face. He was annoyed that Elaina had lied about my age. I was twenty-six, a year older than the cut-off age of twenty-five. "You're lucky you look younger," he said with a sneer, "or you'd already be back on a plane to Canada." He instructed me to tell customers that I was twenty-three.

Next, we were taken to the apartment provided for the girls working in the club. A cockroach scuttled under the bed as we opened the door and turned on the flickering fluorescent lights. I guess the cockroach was the welcoming committee. Tokyo is known to be infested with cockroaches, and I would learn to live with many of them just as I learned to live with the futuristic silent trains, spotless streets (despite there being no trash cans) and having to unwrap cookies individually. I noticed that the walls did not reach the ceiling, so we had visual privacy but no soundproofing for the three bedrooms in the small, basic apartment that we would soon be sharing with a couple more girls coming from Vancouver.

The next night we walked to work at Club Lucky in the bustling

Roppongi district. The neon signs, ultra-modern little cars and sheer volume of humanity was overwhelming despite its incredible organization.

The club was a surprisingly small room, dim and smelling of stale cigarettes, with booths for karaoke. Woody showed us around while running down his list of rules and expectations. We were to be weighed that night, Woody told us, and we would be weighed every Monday. If we gained more than ten pounds during our three-month contract, we'd get fined 10,000 yen each week that we were overweight.

Then Woody moved on to explain the pay scheme: we would receive a base pay, but bonuses were based on popularity. Everything—customers requesting we sit with them, wanting to take us out for dinner, etc.—had a bonus. Curfew was 6 a.m., and they would call us to check that we're home; if we were not, we'd be fined. We were prohibited from having sex or any sexual relations with the customers. This club was for companionship only, and they did not want to be associated with or confused with clubs that had prostitutes. We were there to make conversation, sing karaoke, pour drinks, light cigarettes and provide entertainment for stressed-out Japanese businessmen. We were encouraged to drink with our customers, but if we got "drunk-over" and passed out, we would be fined.

We all sat in our alluring but not-too-slutty dresses in the bullpen where customers could see us and pick what they liked. One gal from Australia, one from New Zealand, one from France and one from America. The rest of us girls, about a dozen more, were mostly Czech or from Vancouver. It was an ambitious recruiter in Vancouver who had ensured the steady supply of Canadian girls. And beautiful Czech girls trying to find ways to make money? Well, they're almost a cliche commodity, aren't they? Years later it was suggested to me these Czech girls were possibly being trafficked, but the thought hadn't occurred to me at the time, so I have no idea. Whatever it was, they all stuck together and hardly spoke to the rest of us.

I was abundantly nervous and unsure of how I was supposed to behave. From the first night, Elaina changed too. She became quietly cutthroat, doing whatever she needed to do to make money. She didn't even try to make friends with the other girls. I felt decidedly alone and out of my depth.

Woody sat me with Japanese businessmen, and I clumsily tried to do my job, but I was such a horrible karaoke singer that most customers politely traded me in for another girl after my first song. I found catering to their needs dehumanizing, even though it was only pouring drinks, lighting cigarettes and pretending to enjoy the awkward conversation. Being a hostess in Japan is like being a modern Geisha: my job was to pamper, serve and entertain. Woody would impatiently snap at us, "Girls, hurry up! Sit down and shut up. The customers will be here soon, and they don't want to hear you yapping to each other. At least try not to look stupid."

It brought my issues with authority to the surface, and I felt the need to rebel. I started taking pride in being bad at my job, considering it to be a failing of character to be good at such a degrading role.

More Vancouver girls showed up the next week. They were party girls who ran with a rough crowd in Vancouver, did lots of drugs and dabbled in petty crime. I felt abandoned by Elaina, who by the third week was already sleeping with the elderly Japanese owner of the club. He was a hedgehog of a man: short, chubby and with a scrunched-up face. So I bonded with the bad girls from Vancouver, who appreciated my rebellious attitude and constant mocking of Woody and the customers. I kept them laughing and got in trouble often. My way meant less money though, so they all at least tried to be good at the job. They did so almost apologetically, but you couldn't argue that their approach was more lucrative than mine. Most of them ended up with regular customers while I sat alone on the bench, batting away insults from Woody, who frequently reminded me that I was the worst hostess they had ever had.

The Vancouver girls talked a lot about drugs. They explained that some people take drugs by dropping them in their eye or sticking them up their asshole. I was shocked. They described girls putting straws in their asshole while someone blew cocaine up their butts instead of snorting it, or "parachuting" ecstasy by wrapping it in a bit of toilet paper and swallowing it. They talked about how drugs can be absorbed different ways for different reasons and that the butt is great for drugs that might burn your nose—plus it absorbs quickly through the lining of your anus. I was equally fascinated and mortified. At that point, the full extent of my drug experimentation was taking ecstasy twice, but these conversations would end up saving my life only a few months later.

I tried cocaine for the first time in Tokyo. One of the Vancouver girls had a flap mailed to her in a magazine from her drug-dealer friend in Canada. I asked to try it, and she was reluctant: "I don't want to be the one to introduce you to coke." Finally, she gave in and let me have a tiny bump. I loved it.

Elaina and I were still barely speaking, and she was often out with the owner of the club. He'd take her to fancy restaurants and buy her expensive jewelry and clothes. She was allowed to come and go as she pleased; curfew and rules didn't apply to her. All the girls hated her and were disgusted by the thought of her sleeping with that gross little hedgehog. She often seemed unwell, picking at her food, not eating it.

Then, in our third month, one of the owner's other girlfriends came back into town, and he tossed Elaina aside unceremoniously. It was humiliating for her. She was just a regular girl now, having to work like everyone else while all the other girls hated her. I accidentally caught her throwing up late one night. She was drunk and crying. She confessed that she was bulimic and had been throwing up for years. She said that it was hell going out for all the fancy dinners with him and trying to get to the bathroom to throw up after; that she couldn't always do it and kept gaining weight, which he never hesitated to point out. She knew that part of the reason he broke it off with her was she was getting too fat for him.

Despite our fractured relationship, I felt sorry for Elaina and tried to be a friend to her for the rest of the trip. I even defended her to the other girls. She was so fragile, and I worried about her. At the end of our three-month contract she went back to Vancouver, and I headed to Thailand to try to find a travel companion to go to India with me.

CHAPTER 20

Ass-oooh-ru

For three months, I had been drinking six nights a week in a tiny, smoke-filled room with stressed Japanese men who were miserable workaholics, young women using their looks to make money, and a boss who despised everyone, himself included. I spent most days sleeping off hangovers instead of taking advantage of my incredible opportunity to explore Japan. I had gained a full ten pounds, so I took a load of ex-lax the day of my last weigh-in and barely made it under the mark to avoid the fine.

I hadn't had sex in three months, although I could have once with a kinky customer who was always talking about wanting to touch our bum holes. This was particularly naughty because customers were expected to behave only respectfully toward the girls—no groping, fondling, etc. But this guy was always trying to slip his hand under our bums and then giggling like a child. I at least found him interesting since most other customers were so boring. I indulged his groping and encouraged him to tell me more about what he was into. As it turned out, he was rather twisted. I convinced him to bring me a kinky, pornographic Japanese magazine. He brought me a good one, filled with photos of Japanese women in schoolgirl outfits tied up in muddy ditches and at abandoned houses. Another depicted Japanese women being tied up and covered in hot wax or used as ashtrays.

I asked him if there were any fetish clubs he could take me to. He said yes, and we had a "date," which was permitted by the club within certain parameters. I expected a fetish party, but we entered a discreet door and found ourselves in a room with gaudy red-and-gold decor that resembled a hotel lobby. The poker-faced, well-past-her-prime Japanese women behind the desk handed us a book with photos of various rooms. Each room was decorated like a dungeon or torture chamber. Bondage equipment, spanking benches, St. Andrew's crosses, whips, paddles, floggers, a classroom, a kinky medical room. It dawned on me that we had had a misunderstanding. I wasn't even sure which one of us was supposed to be the bottom or top, submissive or Dominant, but there was no way I was entering one of those rooms with that man. I felt an uneasiness in my stomach and wondered how I was going to wiggle out of this one.

I had been so sure that the rules about there being no sex between the customers and hostesses would be respected that it didn't even occur to me he would try to get me alone in a BDSM by-the-hour love hotel. I apologized for the misunderstanding, and luckily he was gracious about getting us out of there immediately. In broken English, he suggested we use our time to go to a karaoke place instead. That sounded safe, until he booked a cozy private room and immediately pressed himself against me eagerly, sliding his hand down and under my buttocks aiming for the target of his obsession: my "ass-oooh-ru," as he called it. He pressed his sloppy, wet lips against my mouth, and I felt his tongue sliding out eagerly. It was easy to fend him off; he was a clumsy fool who was scared of getting banned from the club for crossing the line. All it took was one shove and a firm "no" for him to jump off me like a dog that's been scolded and threatened with rolled newspaper.

As soon as he understood I would not be having sex with him, he brought me back to Lucky's. I later found out that the American girl had had sex with him for a lot of money. She later wrote to me about it, confessing and expressing how Tokyo had fucked with her head, made her feel like it was okay to do it, but then later on she felt disgusted by it. At least one of the Vancouver girls had sex with her regular customer too. He at least was attractive—a Japanese Tom Cruise—but still. She had thought it would be hot and didn't even care about the money he offered her. It felt like she was doing it because she wanted to—until the moment it happened. And I do mean "the moment," as that's about as long as it lasted, she said.

I had been so naive to think that the rules meant anything. Lucky's was not a prostitution club—it wasn't even an introduction club— but where there are women who want to use their looks to make money and rich men who are attracted to good-looking women, sex for money is bound to happen, rules be damned. I suppose the rules were there to protect women who did not want to have sex for money and, as a bonus, to make the men feel special if a woman chose to cross that line.

I was unhealthy at the end of my three months, both mentally and physically, so I arranged to meet my yoga instructor from Vancouver in Thailand. Leaf was an eccentric hippie, the real deal: mid-fifties, with long, grey hair flowing halfway down the strong back of his lean, flexible, body. His tan skin looked like crepe paper from decades of nude sunbathing. His crystal blue eyes twinkled as he laughed like a mad man, which he did often, at everything, especially when he said some profound shit that made most people think he was a complete nutter.

I could learn a lot from Leaf, the Buddhist, non-violent communicator, tantric practitioner, bodyworker, yogi and rebirther— although honestly I never fully understood what that meant—and that is why I had asked him to travel with me in Thailand for a while. I'd cover some of his expenses in exchange for his "spiritual guidance." I feel like a twat saying that now, but I'm not sure how else to explain it. I felt empty after Tokyo, and I was looking for something meaningful.

We had never had sex before Thailand, but we did have a chance encounter years before he became my yoga instructor. I was at a party with people I barely knew. A crowd had gathered around a weird guy cracking people's necks like a chiropractor. I had just moved to Vancouver then; I was about twenty-two. I let him crack my neck even though I was scared he might kill me. He laughed like a maniac, even back then, and was decades older than anyone else at the party. The fact that he didn't fit in at all fascinated me. Someone mentioned that if I thought the neck cracking was cool, I should go to his apartment with him and see what else he could do. I honestly thought it would be more chiropractic stuff, but a moment after entering his apartment he had expertly slid his fingers inside my vagina while laughing in a charmingly disarming way. Though I didn't understand it then, he was probably doing some tantra stuff. It felt fantastic—I was immediately sopping wet—but I was freaked out by how fast it had happened, so I stopped him. He kept laughing; everything was pleasantly hilarious to him.

It was several years later that I ran into him on Wreck Beach while I was selling tequila shooters. He was off his face on mushrooms but vaguely remembered me when I asked him if he was the guy from the party who cracked people's necks. He mentioned he was teaching yoga if I wanted to come to a class, and I ended up doing that all summer before leaving for Tokyo.

So on the second night in Thailand with Leaf, I propositioned him. I hadn't had sex in months, and I was curious about that thing he had done to my pussy years before. I guess I was expecting some tantric, Voodoo, magical hippie sex. Sadly, beyond Leaf pulling out some amber and dabbing it on us, there wasn't anything really unique about the act for me, except for the feel of his skin, which I couldn't get past; there were twenty-five years between us, after all. There are changes that happen to a body—like the loss of collagen in the skin—that feel alien to a person in their twenties. As I moved my hand over his flesh, it felt like tissue paper; loose skin that moved over the muscle in a way that taunt, youthful skin doesn't. The age gap was an unbridgeable divide, a moat filled with persistent discomfort and mild aversion.

We travelled together for a couple more weeks without even mentioning sex. He gave me books to read: *The Work* by Byron Katie, *Nonviolent Communication* by Marshall Rosenberg, some stuff on rebirthing. We discussed where things might go with my life. The path I had been on—climbing the corporate ladder doing sales jobs in various industries—was soul-sucking. We talked about me becoming a yoga instructor, a bodyworker or a rebirther like him, recreating birth scenarios for traumatized people—but honestly I didn't understand most of that stuff.

Leaf had come to Thailand to settle, to make a new life, whereas I was passing through on my way to India. So I went off on my own, seeking the beach and friends my age. I spent only one more week in Thailand before giving up on finding a travel partner and decided to do India solo. The idea was scary, but the Mother Teresa biography I'd read while I was in Tokyo had left an impression, as did Tyler's photos. I *needed* to go.

CHAPTER 21

Don't Eat the Chicken in India

I arrived at Calcutta's simple, grubby airport in the middle of the day. The oppressive heat and stench of rotting shit mixed with curry-flavoured sweat was an immediate punch in the face. Dozens of aggressive taxi drivers yelled at us, the new arrivals, elbowing each other out of position for the next fare. I took a cab to Sudder Street, the backpacker tourist area recommended by my *Lonely Planet* guide, aka "The Bible," as it was referred to among backpackers. Along the way we weaved in and out of traffic amidst honking horns, motorbikes, old cars, cows, goats, dogs, homeless people—*so many homeless people*—and a million other chaotic stimuli. Everywhere I looked there was a tidal wave of poverty, crashing over shacks covered in filthy tarps and children with distended bellies like you see in those infomercials for UNICEF.

I checked into a private back room at The Salvation Army hostel, away from the din of the street chaos. I soon met a slender, American woman named Frannie who was in her mid-forties and had distracting tattooed-on eyebrows, eyeliner and lip liner. She was eager to take me under her wing, so I let her. She showed me around, took me to the places she liked to eat, explained how to survive in my new environment, gave me advice and asked to share my room to save money. I agreed, and we got a room with two single beds. Frannie was an eccentric, but I didn't mind. I noticed that travellers, especially single older ones, tended to be eccentric. They had not settled down like many of their peers in life-long careers and comfortable marriages; they were non-conformists marching to the beat of their own drums. I wondered if that would be me some day.

Frannie asked to use our room for a rendezvous with a homely but nice younger Italian guy, Massimo. He had been flirting with me, so I was surprised when she said they had a date, but I didn't care. I found his bad teeth and lack of hygiene sexually revolting. Frannie didn't mind, I guess. She was at least fifteen years older than him, so maybe his youth was enough of a draw? They both told me I didn't need to leave, that I was welcome to stay—to join in, even. I declined and instead went to a theatre with a nice Indian fellow to see a Bollywood film. When I returned, they were basking in the afterglow by candlelight. Still smooching and fondling, but it was close to midnight, too late for me to be wandering around Calcutta alone at night. I tried to settle into bed and go to sleep, with them in the bed next to me a few feet away. It brought back memories of my mother fucking in the next room, and I finally asked Massimo to leave so that I could get some sleep. He was sweet about it, but Frannie was annoyed. I left the next day.

About a week later, I was in Varanasi on the Ganges River. Even though I had been warned about eating meat in India, I was craving butter chicken and felt brave. I regretted that decision as I projectile vomited while simultaneously shooting watery poop out my ass at such speeds that I'm surprised it didn't chip the enamel. Luckily, my Indian-style bathroom was set up perfectly for this kind of illness: a squat toilet with a water hose right there and a shower, all in one small room with a slanted floor going to a drain. After each round, I was able to hose off the sweat, vomit and shit before collapsing on the bed for a few minutes until the next wave hit. This went on for about twelve hours without any sign of slowing down.

Although I had the medication to fix things, I couldn't keep it down. Every time I swallowed it, it would bounce back up a few minutes later. I looked into the puddle of vomit at the perfectly formed pill and considered giving it another go, but I knew it wouldn't have time to absorb before I vomited again.

I suddenly remembered the conversation I'd had with the Vancouver party girls back in Tokyo about how different people take drugs. I considered crunching up the pill and snorting it like cocaine or sticking it up my ass, knowing it would absorb faster through my anus than my stomach.

So I waited until I finished another wave of power-pooping, hosed off, jammed the pill up my ass-oooh-ru—I laughed thinking of that asshole-obsessed Japanese customer: bet he wouldn't be too jazzed about my pooper now!—leaving my finger in to plug the hole and using my other fingers to squeeze my ass cheeks shut. I passed out on the bed like that, finger up my ass. Hot visual, eh?

I woke up a little while later feeling the urge to puke and shit again, but it wasn't as violent. The medication must have started to work, so I swallowed another pill, and this time it stayed down. I slept, waking up only to squeeze a little more watery poop out of my ass and take more medication.

I only had one opportunity to do the sunrise boat ride along the Ganges and see the burning Ghats. As weak as I was, I dragged myself down to the river, and it was one of the most beautiful and exotic things I had ever seen. Ancient buildings rose up from the river via steps covered in colourful saris laid out to dry in the sun. A dead cow floated by as we passed the burning ghats where they were cremating people. Like a wave passing over me, I suddenly realized that "hooping" that medication might have saved my life. I wept on that little wooden boat rowed by a silent Indian man, enjoying a sunrise I almost didn't see, watching Indians bathing in the holy Ganges, praying, chanting, living.

I continued to be ill for the rest of my trip, even shitting my pants a couple of times in the following days while travelling to

Delhi for a wedding. Indian friends from Vancouver were there for a family wedding, and I was fortunate to attend, even though I was still in rough shape. We stayed in a mansion with servants. I was embarrassed about my shabby backpacking style and spent more than my budget on clothes and shoes to try to fit in, at least at the wedding. It was a grand affair with famous Bollywood directors and other influential people in attendance. The fashion, food, decorations and entertainment were beyond anything you could imagine, and how much the wealth contrasted against the incredible poverty I'd seen in the rest of India was surreal.

The friends who invited me were not exactly "friends." The guy was someone who had pursued me for a long time, a man who I had even kissed on occasion when we were drunk at business networking events. He had been arranged to be married and didn't tell me until days before the wedding. I had met his wife, but she had no idea we had a history.

One night in Delhi, as his wife slept, he crept into my room and lightly placed his hand between my thighs. The blood rushed there as my body reacted, craving intimacy, touch, sex. I started to sweat as alarm bells went off in my cunt. I wanted it, and I loved the thrill of it, how naughty it was, but I came to my senses. I dared not think of the repercussions if I were caught having sex with this Indian man in his family's mansion. This was India, where men get away with anything, and white women are considered whores. I turned him away, told him to leave and to not come back into my room. It wasn't easy, but nothing stopped me from masturbating after he left. I'm sure I made the right choice.

The trip in India was adventure after adventure. I saw the most amazing things, but you'd expect someone to say something like that, wouldn't you? I travelled all over by train, in third-class (the lowest class) ladies-only compartments protected by armed guards. You know you might be in a dangerous place when soldiers with guns are guarding the regular folks.

The Indian ladies on the trains took care of me like a little pet. When it was busy and the train would fill with people, parcels and animals, they'd push me up on the top bunk above the crowd.

They helped me buy food through the window of the train when we stopped at stations. They brushed and braided my blonde hair. They invited me to get off the train and come home with them for dinner, but they barely spoke English, and their tiny villages didn't even show up on my map. I regret not going now, but I was scared of getting stuck somewhere tourists never go.

I spent an entire day alone from sunrise to sunset at the Taj Mahal in Agra. I wanted to see it in every light.

I made friends with a Scottish fellow and an Indian guy in Goa. We hung out for ten days together, swimming in the waves at the beach, eating papaya, listening to the Beatles. It was the only CD they had. Sergeant Pepper's Lonely Hearts Club Band. Lucy in the Sky With Diamonds. Yellow Submarine. Eleanor Rigby. Over and over. I loved it. No sexual tension stirred between us. I later wondered if they were gay and simply good at hiding it. Homosexuality was and still is frowned upon in India.

I went on a camel safari in the Rajasthan desert with a half-dozen strangers who became temporary friends. We travelled to Udaipur after and saw the floating palace.

At one point I was alone in Pushkar, a little village beside a holy lake. It was an entirely vegan place—no meat or eggs—and also no alcohol. That was all right by me; after the butter chicken incident I didn't eat meat or drink alcohol the rest of the trip anyway. I was cautious about what I ate, as my digestion remained seriously delicate. I lost those ten pounds I gained in Tokyo and then some. I looked frail.

In Pushkar, there was a hill with a temple at the top. The Lonely Planet boasted the sunrise view as one of the best and said the hike was easy but took about an hour. I set out early in the morning when it was still dark. It felt risky to be out at that time, but I didn't encounter another person as I made my way to the base of the hill. It was so pitch dark that I jumped at every sound: a dog barking in the distance, a pig grunting somewhere. I started the hike slowly, staying within the limits of what my body could manage. The sky began to lighten about halfway up, and I could make out one cute little monkey hanging out on a tree in the distance. I had never seen one in person before. I was elated.

I continued to hike up, up, up, as the sky got lighter. I looked back and saw the little village beside the lake, and it was majestic. I finally reached the tiny temple at the top and sat down to eat my breakfast of simple biscuits while watching the glorious sunrise. Being the only person on top of a hill that took me over an hour to hike, I felt acutely alone, but peaceful.

Movement in the distance caught my eye, and I realized it was the monkey I'd seen earlier. I tried to take a photo, but it was too far away. I called to it and tossed a piece of a biscuit in its direction. Stupid move, Dumb-Dumb.

Almost instantly I was surrounded by monkeys, and they weren't all cute or little. There were some large, aggressive-looking alpha males, along with smaller males and females with baby monkeys. One of the bigger males came right over and sat right beside me—so close that when I took his picture, it was blurry. He. Was. That. Close.

He grabbed my backpack, and I reflexively grabbed it back. He immediately bared his teeth and took a swipe at me. I pulled my head back, feeling the wind against my face as his claws just missed me.

My adrenaline went into primal overdrive, my heart lurched and tunnel vision partially blinded me while bringing some things into intense focus—sharp teeth. I was outnumbered. This wasn't a fight I could win. I was painfully unprepared for this situation, and the adrenaline pumping through my body could only do so much.

I found myself trying to reason with them, saying, "It's okay buddy; no one wants a fight here. Take the bag if you want it. It's yours"—as if dealing with a drunk in a bar or a mugger. I was half standing on shaky legs and starting to slowly back away from the monkey who first grabbed my bag, but there was nowhere to go. Dozens of monkeys surrounded me at the top of a hill, while the big guy fumbled with the zipper of the bag unsuccessfully.

I watched as the thieving monkey and his buddies wrestled with my backpack, trying to unzip it to get to the biscuits, but they couldn't figure it out. Despite being terrified, I took pictures because that's what stupid tourists do. Eventually, they left the bag and wandered off. I picked it back up and made my way back down the hill on wobbly legs, noticing that the sunrise was indeed stunning—and feeling grateful to have survived yet again to see another sunrise. I later learned that I was foolish not to be carrying a monkey-whacking stick but that I could have used my shirt as a useful weapon too. Apparently, you can swirl and snap it as you do with a towel and monkeys will think it's some magical light sabre or something. The more you know, right?

I ended my trip in India where I started, in Calcutta. I was ready to put in some time at Mother Teresa's home for the dying. I knew that Massimo, the Italian paramour of my old roomie, volunteered there, so I tracked him down. We decided to share a room to save costs, and I insisted that he let me take the floor. I had been sleeping on filthy floors most of my trip to save money, so by this point I honestly didn't care anymore. I had slept on the floor of a crowded overnight train, spooned in between dozens of Indian ladies, and met other travellers, whom I asked whether I could sleep on their floors and split the bill with them, so a few more nights on a floor didn't faze me.

You might be wondering why I was on such a shoestring budget when I had gone to Tokyo to make money for the trip.

Well, I had stupidly sent half the money to my ex-boyfriend Vince before I left. He had agreed to put the money on my credit card, but he didn't do it for some reason. It was tricky to get that money out of Tokyo, and I didn't want to carry thousands of dollars with me in case I got robbed. Then I got robbed anyway by someone I trusted: Vince.

Massimo and I shared a tiny, windowless room. I slept on a sari on the cement floor and used a pile of my clothes for a pillow. During the day we went to Mother Teresa's—Massimo to the male side, I to the female side. I saw things there that will haunt me for the rest of my life. Head wounds so infected that I could see big patches of skull. Skin and muscle rotted away to the bone, maggots eating the dead flesh. Old women so frail that I could lift them out of bed easily and carry them to the bathing area. I would hold their hands, spoon-feed them and help change the sheets on the beds. My role as a temporary volunteer was support and comfort. It was, after all, a home for the dying.

I thought I'd be better equipped to deal with these things from the tiny bit of support I had given my mother while looking after my great-grandmother in her last few years. I had helped administer enemas and dressed bedsores, but that was nothing, really. What I saw and experienced at the home for the dying was infinitely more heartbreaking, graphic and intense. At the end of each day I either felt hollowed out, or I crumpled and sobbed. Luckily, Massimo was wonderfully supportive, having seen it all in the many months he'd been volunteering there.

Massimo was an interesting guy. He worked half the year in Italy, and the other half of the year he volunteered in Calcutta. He also helped other Italian tourists arriving in Calcutta get from the airport to their hotel in exchange for one of his favourite things: Parmigiano-Reggiano. I accompanied him on one of these excursions and saw how happy it made him when they handed him that big wedge of fine Italian cheese. Since we didn't have refrigeration, it needed to be eaten that day. We went to the market to pick up ingredients for a salad, and he fed at least a dozen people in our hostel. It felt so indulgent to eat such fine Italian cheese in India. A real treat for everyone. All these years later, I still think fondly of Massimo every time I see or eat Parmigiano-Reggiano.

CHAPTER 22

The Cost of Breaking a Heart

When I returned to Vancouver, Vince picked me up at the airport. He was a shell of the man I had known six months earlier. I asked where the money that I sent had gone and was told he'd explain later. We caught up—I told him about my travels, and he talked about his struggles. He had gone on a drinking binge after his father died, missed a lot of work and recently met someone new. We went back to his place, and we made love. It had been months since I had been with anyone, and I was hungry for it. The second it was over, though, I knew that it had been a mistake or the last time—or both. Vince shut down, became cold, sad. We parted ways with him promising to explain about the money soon.

A week passed, and Vince avoided me and didn't return my calls. I ran into him and his new girlfriend at the video store minutes after I removed his name from the video rental account we had shared. He'd stiffed me with an overdue charge, and it pissed me off. It resulted in him being humiliated in front of her when she realized he couldn't get a card of his own because he had bad credit.

Like the domino effect in action, the scene devolved into a furious conversation where he revealed he had spent all the money I sent (he didn't even know on what). I guess that's the price when you break someone's heart: $10,000. Following this encounter, Vince deposited my personal belongings, which I had been storing in his garage, on the porch of my new place. By deposited, I mean he threw them. The glass of every picture frame was shattered.

He delivered my personal items in my car, which I had loaned him while I was away. He ended up keeping it for two months after I returned. Legally I could have taken it, but I didn't. To be honest, I suppose I was afraid. He was a raging alcoholic who was in mourning after his father's death and hated himself for not reconciling with him before it was too late, his job was in jeopardy and he felt hurt and abandoned by me. On top of all that, he probably felt deep shame for spending my money. The last bit of hope he had was his new relationship. Leaving him without a car wasn't going to help that, and it might've been the last straw before he did something even more violent than smashing all my things.

He exhibited plenty of warning signs of a mentally unbalanced and potentially violent person, and I did not intend to poke the bear. Was it cowardly or prudent to let the man who stole $10,000 from me and smashed my things keep my car for two months longer than agreed? Either or both, I suppose; you could make an argument either way. But I'd learned a valuable lesson from my sunrise encounter with those dozen angry monkeys: it's better to let the potentially dangerous creature have what it wants if it means getting away unscathed. It didn't matter to me at the time, honestly; my life was moving on, and it was the beginning of what would be the best summer of my life.

CHAPTER 23

Beach Life

I started selling tequila shooters back at the nude beach again, but this time full-time. By "full-time" I mean that seven days a week I woke up when I woke up, usually around 10 a.m. I got ready, cut up limes and ran whatever errands were necessary, like picking up tequila from the liquor store or little paper cups somewhere. I'd get to the beach in the early afternoon and start selling by mid-afternoon after socializing with friends. I'd walk up and down the beach naked with my little bag, delivering my pitch in a sweet sing-song voice: "Tequila, tequila, yummy tequila, Cuervo Gold... Go straight to hell: Drink tequila!"

I'd sell tequila until the sun sank below the horizon. The best sales were in the early evening once people were already drunk on beer; tequila is more of a sunset drink, some say.

There was a community of beach vendors selling beer, coolers, mixed drinks, weed, mushrooms, food, jewelry and clothes. We looked out for each other since selling alcohol or drugs like that is quite illegal. It wasn't right—in my worldview—that people got arrested from time to time, as Wreck Beach was a chill hippie environment. Mostly quiet, well-behaved people having a few drinks at the beach on their day off, maybe a bit of cannabis or a little giggly trip on mushrooms. In addition to being harmless, victimless and fun, it was community-building. But due to its illegality, we went about our work carefully, warning each other if we saw police.

Tyler got back from his winter travel about a month after I did. By that time I had started a fling with one of his friends. I hadn't heard from Tyler all winter, and I had no expectations of us getting back together in any significant way. Yet, when we were reunited, the spark was still there. The affair started up again, but this time he was more interested than I was. I hadn't expected that—and by then knew too much about Tyler's habit of juggling multiple girls at once. I just couldn't take him seriously. He expressed his discomfort with me sleeping with his friend, and I shrugged it off. I told him I would have sex with whoever I pleased, and he decided we should just be friends. I was all right with that. Tyler had boosted my self-confidence when I needed it, and he inspired me to change my life. He put me on a path of figuring out how to live my life the way I wanted. I was eternally grateful, but I was not a fool. Despite being drawn to him, I knew that Tyler was not relationship material.

He and I were great friends that summer. Tyler hosted the best parties at his "Super Pad," a big house slated for demolition that he shared with a few other guys. It was a madhouse: filthy, run-down and cluttered with furniture that appeared to have been liberated from the dump; in other words, it was an ideal party house. He could pack in a couple hundred people, and it did not matter if drinks were spilled, shoes were worn or even if people pissed in the corner, as I'd witnessed.

We had theme parties like pajama parties or "pimp and ho" parties, to which people would come all dressed up. It was a blast.

That summer I easily juggled three full-time lovers as well as a handful of others. Tim, a golf pro and savvy businessman who still loved to party. Craig, the ski instructor and high-rise window cleaner with hair dyed blood-red and a tongue piercing. And Dick. Yes, Dick came back into my life, wounded and vulnerable after having his ego bruised by someone else. The tables had turned, and now I was the strong, confident one. I'm not proud of the way I treated him, but we all have a dark side—and vengeance can be sweet.

I let Dick get close again. We had decent sex, but I made sure he knew he was the last of my choices for lovers. He got the least of my attention. In subtle ways, I indicated that he didn't measure up to the other men. I listened to him moan about the girl who broke his heart, and I didn't hold back when I observed that she was clearly too good for him. After a couple of months, I left him worse off than I had found him. Years later, an acquaintance would confess that he had shown her pictures of me, bragging about having had the opportunity to sleep with such a hot woman, not knowing that she would recognize me. He had become pathetic.

Anyways, back to that magical summer of selling tequila shooters on Wreck Beach, partying and fucking. "Red" Craig, as he was called because of his flaming red-dyed hair, introduced me to the fetish scene in Vancouver. He took me to my first Vancouver fetish party where we did ecstasy and danced the night away. We started to do cocaine too, and I loved it. I felt energized and confident. Craig began to buy it in larger quantities to make it more cost-effective and to share with friends. It wasn't long before he was a small-time coke dealer to friends and acquaintances. It kind of evolved that way.

I had also started making and selling chocolate mushrooms at the beach. I would buy dried magic mushrooms by the garbage-bag full, grind them in a coffee grinder, stir the powder into big pots of high-quality chocolate and then pour it into little happy-face and heart-shaped chocolate moulds. I'd wrap them in tin foil and sell them to people partying at the beach. Most people loved them. It made the trees appear greener and the water and sky more beautiful, and they would laugh until their faces hurt. Others would have uncomfortable trips, and I would shepherd them through it, telling them to focus on something beautiful, to think of something happy and to relax. It was probably because of that interaction that I didn't feel like a drug dealer the way Craig was becoming; I was only selling chocolate mushrooms to people on a clothing-optional beach, many of them hippies who had been playing with psychedelics for decades.

As the best summer of my life started to wind down and fall approached, reality began to set in. What came after the beach? One of my tequila customers offered me a marketing job at his company, and I reluctantly took it. I had dyed the tips of my long, sun-bleached hair teal and had to hide it in a tight, conservative bun. Putting on business clothes after I had blissfully been working naked all summer was hell.

On the weekends I kept partying, usually going on cocaine benders and attending sex or fetish parties. When it was time for Craig to go back to his ski instructor job in Whistler, he asked me to take over the cocaine business for the winter. He only had a handful of customers, so it was simple enough, but one of the first delivery calls I took was a couple with a baby in a car seat in the back of their car. I was shocked. They sheepishly explained that they only did coke once in a blue moon, after the baby was asleep. Convinced that they knew what they were doing, I sold to them.

Over the next few months, I would live a dual life of working a regular 9-to-5 office job while selling cocaine and ecstasy on the evenings and weekends. I would only do drugs myself on the weekends and thought that I was okay as long as I didn't do cocaine every day, but I was wrong. I started to wake up on Friday mornings with my heart galloping in excitement about the fact that I would soon be able to get high again. I was going to weekend-long drug parties where I would consume a variety of uppers, downers and psychedelics, and I was a mess on Mondays.

At some point in there Craig and I broke up, but it was undramatic. Our relationship lasted three months longer than it should have when he started using vibrating tongue jewelry in his tongue piercing. I challenge any woman to part ways with a man with a vibrating tongue ring. Over time, my brain would say, "Things have run their course; you don't love him." Then my pussy would chime in: "But I do!"

The last straw with the coke-dealing business came when the couple with the baby started calling me more and more frequently. They were becoming increasingly desperate. The last time I sold cocaine to them was in a grocery store parking lot. I told them to lose my number and get help. I was done. I realized they had a problem, and so did I. And I couldn't quit it if I kept selling it.

I decided to change jobs. I felt more challenging work would help me focus on not getting high anymore. I started a sales job and poured myself into it. I fell off the wagon a couple of times but was doing well overall. I was selling a lot of advertising space in a magazine even though I wasn't meant to sell anything in the first few months. Apparently new salespeople were only expected to learn the ropes and build relationships with existing customers, but making a sale was my new high.

When they brought me in for my three-month probation review and told me they were letting me go, I laughed. I thought they were joking. That was awkward for my boss. He explained that they had built their reputation on having long-term relationships with clients—"friendships, really." Most of the staff had been with the company for over 10 years. They felt my style was too aggressive and feared that I was only there as a stepping-stone to something else. They felt that I probably wouldn't stay there long, and they preferred to invest their time in employees that wanted to be a part of the family.

I drove home in shock. I hadn't seen it coming at all and felt sick to my stomach. Then I had an idea. I had met a girl at the beach who was a private dancer at a strip club. I was surprised because she didn't look how you might imagine a stripper should look. She had natural, small breasts and was pretty plain in her civilian wear. It dawned on me that I might be attractive enough to be a stripper too. The idea and especially the naughtiness of it thrilled me. I decided to call a strip club to inquire. They told me over the phone that I should come in the next day and meet with the manager. I would be auditioning for her.

I figured it was a long shot, but if I was going to do this, I needed to protect my identity, so I went out that night and bought a dark bob wig. The next day I applied my makeup carefully to match my dark wig and conceal that I was a blond. I blackened in my eyebrows and coated my lids in colour. Smokey dark eyes with heavy black liner. I shaded in my cheekbones and jaw to give my face a more chiselled look and finished with deep-red lipstick. I then packed my black platform stiletto fetish party boots and some lingerie and set out for the club.

The actual audition part lasted about twenty seconds. The

manager asked me to show her how I would dance for a customer and, after I slowly swayed and ran my fingers over my body while making eye contact with her, she quickly said that was fine and that I could start the next day if I wanted. It's not that she was terribly impressed; I didn't suck, and that's all that mattered. Their standards were pretty low, to be honest.

She then explained the rules, the most important being no physical contact in the little private dance booths. No lapdancing, no grinding, no hand jobs. Customers weren't allowed to touch me or masturbate; if they did, they'd get thrown out. And if I touched them, I'd get fired. There were cameras on us for our safety, plus the manager for the night would be sitting right outside the booths.

I arrived early on my first night to find an older, worn-out-looking woman in the dressing room starting to put on her makeup. She was wearing ratty sweats and looked at me in the mirror's reflection with disgust. I now understand that look. The look of seeing a thing that is going to take a chunk of your money. Competition.

As the other girls arrived, I received a similar welcome—which is to say, no welcome at all. They didn't even attempt to be friendly. I was surprised how unattractive most of them were, but by the time we were all under the black lights in the dimly lit club in our makeup, lingerie and high heels, you could barely tell they were the same women. Add a couple drinks into the mix, and in the guys' eyes they transformed into stunning sexpots.

CHAPTER 24

Private Dancing

I was twenty-eight when I started working as a private dancer in a strip club—older than most. But I didn't get on stage and do pole-dancing tricks; I walked around the club hustling guys to go in the booth in the back for a private dance. Once back there, I would slowly strip naked and gyrate in front of them on a little platform while they sat in a chair with a boner they couldn't do anything about. I was good at getting them in there and good at keeping them in there paying for more dances. My aggressive sales skills were finally coming to good use.

Unfortunately, having extensive sales experience was beyond the comprehension of the other girls, and they assumed I was undercutting them to get more dances. I was cleaning up, and they had all suffered a loss since my arrival. More business was coming my way, and they were angry and wanted me gone. They complained to the manager and even had a customer say that I had offered a dance for less. From then on, the customers had to pay me in front of the manager to prove I wasn't charging less. It was humiliating and resulted in me getting fewer tips, but even with that I still outsold everyone else by a long shot. I was competitive and enjoyed being the best, even if it made me hated by all the other dancers.

I also loved the work. I loved being seductive and appreciated. The men were usually well-mannered and complimentary, and I felt sexually empowered. I started seeing a down-and-out musician shortly after I started working there. We had gobs of mind-blowing sex, and I think that made me even better at my job. However, he gradually became uncomfortable with me being a stripper and would get drunk and accuse me of fucking my customers. I think it takes a particularly secure and emotionally mature man to date a stripper. Although he wasn't one of those, it didn't take long for the problem to correct itself.

After I had passed the four-month mark and was starting to wonder how long I would do this work, there was an incident. I was resting my sore feet between dances, sitting on a stool at the bar, when an ultra-muscular young guy tried to hand me a shooter. I didn't drink while working, so I said, "No, thank you." He then rudely shouted, "If you're not drinking, you can't sit there!" Thoughtlessly, I gave him the finger, and as I did, I caught something I had missed. One of those things I couldn't describe but knew in my gut. In a split second, I knew I had made a mistake; this guy was dangerous, and I was in trouble.

I remember it all in slow motion: the loud music pounding, the crowded bar, the dancer on stage. My feet throbbing and the relief I felt when I took my weight off them for a minute. The offer of the shooter and initially not paying attention to the guy offering it to me; then his face changing, the flicker of offense. My first thought that he didn't understand I worked there and that I was in the power position because I was staff. My hand raising and my finger going up as I registered his face—a split second too late. His eyes widening and his lips tightening as he saw my middle finger telling him to fuck off.

I turned away quickly; what I had done was just a glance backward and a quick gesture but so loaded. My gut flipped as my instincts reacted quicker than my brain and I felt the boost of adrenaline that should've fuelled my hasty departure while my body screamed, **"RUN!"**

My mouth went dry, and I'm not sure what I would have done

if a customer hadn't come up to me that very second and asked me to go for a dance.

I grabbed his hand, slid off the stool and quickly started leading him through the packed club to the back where the dance booths were. I kept my eyes fixed ahead of me, thinking, *Don't look back. Don't turn around.* Suddenly, I felt him jerk his hand from my grip, and I turned to see him lying on the floor. The muscle guy had grabbed him, pulled him down and punched him right there in the middle of the crowded club. He continued to punch him and anyone who tried to stop him. We all got pushed to the back, and the bouncers surrounded the muscle guy and the customer who was on his knees begging for him to stop. But no one stopped him. The muscle guy turned to me, took the few steps to reach me, pushed me into a booth and said, "This is happening because of you" before whipping the curtain closed, leaving me inside trapped, alone and terrified. That's a natural reaction though, isn't it? Terrified. I didn't piss myself or anything so dramatic, but who wouldn't be terrified in that situation? Sigourney Weaver?

With shaky knees, I stood up on a chair and looked over the top of the curtain. I could see the bouncers dragging the guy I'd been walking with out the side door by his feet—I'm not sure if he was conscious or not—but I couldn't see where the muscle guy had gone. I only saw the bouncers; his buddies. If he'd decided to put a pounding on me next, there was nothing anybody could have done to stop him (and few that would have tried).

I felt sick. Then the curtain flew open, and my female manager grabbed me. She told me to get my things and get out of there as fast as I could. I later found out that while I was in the change room yanking my wig off and wiping off my makeup she went to the office to tear up the page with my personal information so that they couldn't find out who I was. I grabbed my bag, pulled up my hoodie and walked straight out the back door. I later found out that the muscle guy was high on drugs and had even grabbed another dancer in his blind rage and thrown her so hard she knocked over a table. So why didn't the bouncers stop him? Because it turned out he was a drug dealer who had recently paid for one of their weddings. He also had a junior affiliation with a well-known motorcycle gang.

I had already felt that my stripping days should come to an end, and now the decision was made for me. It wasn't that I didn't love it, but I felt the stigma of society telling me that it was below me, that I was too smart to be a stripper. The money was fantastic, and I had worked hard and saved carefully. I had enough for the down payment on a condo, but the banks wouldn't give me a mortgage without proper employment, so I reluctantly returned to office work. I didn't know it at the time, but it would be the last "vanilla" job I would ever have.

CHAPTER 25

Last Vanilla Job

I started working with a company that made custom hearing protection products for people who work in noisy environments like factories or trains. The shabby little office and production facilities were located in a bland business park in a bad part of town. The employees were mostly painfully dull. My job was to support the owner of the company: a difficult, outspoken, wealthy Jewish man.

The only highlight of my life in the early days of that dreary job was great sex. My hot, unemployed musician boyfriend, Bart, was game for just about anything. I used to get him to role-play a scenario for me in which I pretended I was a wealthy older woman and he was a hired squire. I would imagine I had been at an elaborate party where attractive men and women for hire were identified by a certain flower pinned to their chest. A high-society fundraiser, lavishly dignified and conservative. If you saw someone you fancied, you communicated it to a coordinator who would make the necessary arrangements, and you would soon be in one of the well-appointed bedrooms enjoying the hired help of your choice. I would get him to say, "Is that how you like it, ma'am?" and "Does that please you, ma'am?" while licking or fucking me. Mmmmm.

Working at that job helped me qualify for a mortgage and, using money from stripping for the down payment, I bought a condo for my twenty-ninth birthday.

I reluctantly gave up on the hot, unemployed musician when his alcoholism became violent. He would get intoxicated and accuse me of cheating on him—I wasn't—and always apologize the next day, but when he started throwing stuff, like books, at me, I left and didn't come back.

Well, that's *almost* true. A few days after we broke up I developed a yeast infection: an infrequent and unpleasant visitor. Curious to find a more natural solution than the usual medical creams, I read online—*everything* on the Internet is true, by the way—that a clove of garlic inserted overnight would set things right. Dr. Internet recommended wrapping it in gauze and dental floss so that I could pull it out like a tampon. Since I didn't have gauze, I slid the garlic in bareback and went to bed, figuring it wouldn't be that hard to get it out in the morning.

I awoke feeling refreshed downstairs. No more itch! Sliding my finger into my vagina, I could feel the garlic—slippery little bugger—but I couldn't get a grip on it. *Shit.*

Drawing a warm bath to swish water in there, hoping he'd come out like a baby at a home birth—I started to worry. Ugh. I really didn't want to suffer the embarrassment of going to the emergency room and having garlic fished out of my pussy.

But after 20 minutes of contortionist self-fisting and pushing, I was still no closer to getting that garlic out. Suddenly, inspiration struck: Bart has lovely—*and long*—piano-playing fingers!

I rang him up and was greeted with a grumpy, "What do YOU want?"

"I need a hand with something…" I started, unable to control my laughter.

When I explained the situation, he chuckled and told me to come over.

Thirty seconds after arriving I was laying on his bed, pantiless, with him holding the garlic clove he had easily scooped out of my pussy; despite my garlic stench, he had a raging hard-on.

"Wanna?" he grinned, chucking the garlic in the trash.

"You couldn't possibly! The stink—"

He cut in, glancing at the obvious bulge in his pants. "I clearly do…"

And we had sex, both of us holding our heads as far back as possible from stink-bomb ground zero. Moaning, laughing, gagging. We didn't get back together, but it was certainly a lighter note to end on. I heard through the grapevine that he quit drinking and joined AA—the whole nine yards. I'm not sure what it says about me or the society we live in that I dated so many men with drinking problems.

Single again, I attended fetish parties and enjoyed a juicy social life on the weekends. Occasionally I would slip details about my life outside of the office to a middle-aged, married and perpetually bored coworker. He lived for my stories. I also joined a dating site called Lavalife and met a sexy couple who would become a significant part of my life. I was looking for more experiences with women, but I still wanted cock—without the risk of falling into a relationship. A happily married couple looking for another gal was a fitting arrangement.

Ryan and Candace had money and flaunted it: a flashy car, exciting trips, designer clothes—and when it came to me, expensive hotel rooms set up with every kind of decadent snack and beverage I could want. They liked to spoil. They were deliciously sensual, moving slowly, with purpose, with care, with intensity. Giggling, cuddling, being silly. It was divine.

That is, until one awkward evening when they told me they had a surprise for me. They had learned some new trick they wanted to share with me. It was in the heat of the moment—and a nice moment it was, loving and sexy—when they explained they wanted to teach me how to squirt. I felt sickened, my mother's bedroom walls flashing before my eyes. Mom would point out the splash marks on the walls while folding the heavy towels and rubber sheets used in her lovemaking with Jim. She'd explain how he made her squirt and how amazing it was. I couldn't help but imagine my mother having sex, her juices hitting the wall like a fire hose; my vivid imagination was killing me. Gross. Fuck. *Get out of my head.*

I had no choice but to explain all of that to my lovely friends. The mood was well and thoroughly broken, but they were sweet about it.

On another occasion, for Ryan's birthday, Candace surprised him with fulfilling a long-time fantasy of his. He wanted to be tied up and made to service several women, so that's exactly what we did. He was at first blindfolded and tied with his hands behind his back, kneeling by the bed. He was to lick all four of us to orgasm, then we could all use his cock for our pleasure, but he was not allowed to cum. We had hours of fun, using him. Four gorgeous, sexually liberated women, a lush hotel room and a cheerful, service-oriented, beautiful man.

It was around that time I met Adrian at a fetish party. He was the kind of ridiculously good-looking man who no one takes seriously. He was putting himself through accounting school by dancing at ladies' nights, bachelorette parties and gay bars. He was the most in-demand male stripper in Vancouver. Tall, dark and muscular with a baby face and tanned, touchable skin. He did a cowboy show, a firefighter show and a Matrix show, among others. He would also do shower shows at a gay bar. Those muscles glistening with soapy water were truly a sight to behold.

I didn't take him seriously at first, but as I got to know him, I realized he was intelligent and kind. A gentle giant. A big teddy bear. I had never been into the big-muscle types, but he was a regular guy, using what he had to get through life.

You might think it was serendipitous that I would meet a male stripper at this junction of my life, and a junction it was. I didn't know it at the time, but I was standing on the edge of a career cliff, and I was about to make the final leap.

CHAPTER 26

Crash

Near the end of the year, I was still working in my dreary job when a consultant was brought in to do an overhaul of the office. He was an experienced, shrewd business man in his sixties. He looked like a cross between a bullfrog and Jabba the Hutt. His head attached directly to his body with an invisible neck; all jowls and softness. His tailor must have been a genius to suit his figure, like trying to gift-wrap a live turkey. He spent a week interviewing everyone thoroughly before making his recommendations and was keenly interested in me—my skills, talents and potential value to the company.

At the same time, I had decided to stop taking my birth control pill over frustration and concern about unexplained "spotting." I was bleeding between periods, and my doctor speculated that the pill might be to blame. Unfortunately, I didn't wait until the end of my cycle and stopped abruptly mid-cycle, which caused hormonal bedlam. I was holding it together until I got offered a promotion. The consultant was so impressed with me that he wanted me to take on more responsibility and give me a fancy job title—with a matching salary increase.

As he described the job he saw me best suited for, I felt my anxiety rising. It was hard to swallow, and the smell of his cologne—Polo by Ralph Lauren—burned my nostrils. He looked full of purpose, proud of himself, expectant. His pudgy fingers pointed to the offer on the sheet of paper as he slid it across the table toward me. I remember feeling repelled by that paper coming toward me as though it was diseased. The new job sounded like a nightmare. I realized how miserable I was there, and the tears suddenly flowed—the kind of tears appropriate for the death of a loved one. Unable to contain them, I excused myself and went to the washroom, sobbing and snotting like a child who had just lost her family pet.

I eventually returned to the perplexed and unimpressed consultant and explained that I understood I had blown this, so I might as well be honest. I told him about the spotting, the change in medication, the noticeable impact on my hormones. I stood there, a twenty-nine-year-old woman explaining I was having a hormonal breakdown to a middle-aged male stranger. I even acknowledged that I understood this was career death for a woman trying to make it in a man's world. He stared at me in thinly veiled disgust and didn't try to comfort me.

Nothing more was said, and a week later I was fired. But I did not cry that day; I actually smiled. My boss and the consultant said that life is too short to do a job you hate, and they were giving me the push I needed to find what I love to do.

Without hesitation, I went straight to another strip club, one I knew had no affiliation with the biker gang who ran the other clubs. This one was run by the much more civilized Italian mafia. I joyfully started there the next day and never worked another straight job again. I was a stripper for now and happy with that. And, despite the stigma, I was dating a male stripper too.

Adrian and I started out casually, mostly as friends. We weren't monogamous, but feelings were starting to develop. One night we did a duo performance for a charity event in a gay bar. It was a Western theme, and we both put on an entertaining show in our cowboy hats and chaps. We had some drinks, and the energy was electric. Then a tall, slender, androgynous woman set her sights on Adrian. Before long they were stroking each other in the corner, gazing into each other's eyes and making out.

I didn't know anyone else, so I sat there on my own, drinking, slowly getting more jealous and angry even though Adrian and I were supposed to be casual and open. The plan had been for me to stay at Adrian's so that I could leave my car parked outside of the bar, but since it was clear they would be going home together, I decided that I had no choice but to drive home. Adrian could tell I was too drunk and begged me not to drive and to take a cab instead. But, fuelled by jealous fury, feeling rejected and hurt, I got in my car and pulled out of the parking lot regardless.

I don't remember the accident itself, but the first thing I do remember is the airbag. I'll never forget the way it smelled. It was like nothing else: a unique sharp, musty, chemical smell. It filled my nose, and I seemed to be immersed in it, which, it turns out, I was; a powder shoots out of an airbag when it inflates and that powder, along with its smell, permeates everything. I would smell it for weeks and even years on some of the items that were touched by it. As it started to deflate, I could see the vehicle I'd hit ahead of me.

Nothing made sense. Coming out of a dream, I was trying to figure out what was real. Everything was still for that moment while my mind registered what had happened. "Oh god, I've hit someone. I've driven drunk, and I've hit someone. No. Please. No." Panic was battling with the drive to stay calm, to try to regain some sense of control. I opened the car door, pushed the airbag aside and, without checking to see if I was injured, got out of the car and approached the driver's door of the vehicle I hit. A middle-aged woman got out slowly and looked at me, confused. "You hit me," she said.

"Are you okay?" I asked.

"Yes," she replied, then added, "I smell alcohol. Have you been drinking?"

My knee-jerk was to lie, and I was surprised at how quickly the lie came. "No, I was at a party and someone spilled their drink on me. I'll call 911 and get us some help." While dialing 911 I went back to my car, opened the trunk and found some toothpaste. After I confirmed we needed an ambulance, tow truck and police, I squirted a blob of toothpaste in my mouth. I barely had time to swallow it when a police officer approached me. *How did he get there so quickly?* I was so foggy. Time wasn't moving at the right pace.

The police officer couldn't have been nicer, but I definitely didn't deserve such kind treatment. I had also called Adrian, and he and the other girl arrived shortly, standing nearby, waiting to see if I would be arrested. They watched me take and fail the breathalyzer.

The police only took my license for twenty-four hours—that was it. They didn't arrest me, and I didn't, and still don't, understand why. Adrian took me back to his place, and we held each other and cried. I felt so ashamed of what I had done. I had been so stupid. Even though the other driver only had a bit of whiplash from me rear-ending her, I could have killed someone. Adrian cried because he realized he could have lost me. It brought us closer together in a way that wasn't altogether natural. It created a romantic bond that otherwise would have taken the path of friendship. Despite that, sex never felt right for us, and Adrian was never convincingly interested. We should have been friends and nothing more.

Despite our new bonding and what we incorrectly perceived to be a real relationship, I had already planned a trip to South America. I would be leaving for two months of travel around Brazil and Argentina, mostly on my own.

It was a teary farewell, and Adrian sweetly made me a cake with the Brazilian flag frosted on it. There were no promises of monogamy; a "don't ask, don't tell" agreement. And with that, I was off.

CHAPTER 27

Brazil and Argentina

I travelled rough, staying in cheap accommodations. At one point I arrived alone on an island on the last boat of the day only to find out a festival was taking place and there was no lodging left. Since it was illegal to sleep on the street or beach, I walked and walked with my backpack, asking if anyone had a place for me to stay. The best offer I got was to share a bed in a shack with the ninety-year-old senile grandfather of some locals. No, thanks.

I begged a hostel to let me stay somewhere, even on their floor, but they said it was illegal for me to stay anywhere other than the dorm room, which was already full with eight people on bunk beds in a tiny room with one bathroom. There was no room on the floor between the beds, but there was room under them, and I begged the proprietors for it. I offered to take them all for drinks, and they finally said okay. We all went out drinking that night, and I slept underneath the bed of a nice girl from Sweden. Every time she rolled over the mattress would dip down and touch my nose.

I became friends with her, as well as the friend she was travelling with. I called them "Team Sweden," and we travelled around Brazil together for about a week.

I happened to be in Brazil for Carnival. I hadn't planned it that way, but there I was. I met up with my old lover Tim (the golf pro and savvy businessman), and we partied in the streets of Salvador before flying to Rio to see the parade in the Sambadrome. Ryan and Candace were in Rio at the time with a couple of other friends. I stayed with them, and that was when they planted the seed about going to Burning Man in my mind. I had never heard of it, but they had gone the year before and showed me pictures of costumed people on elaborately decorated vehicles in the desert partying amidst the stark, almost white ground and bright, clear-blue sky. Otherworldly.

"Come with us next year!" they begged with big smiles.

We all went out to a capacious bar in Rio that was full of Brazilian prostitutes—hundreds of them. One of Ryan and Candace's friends was a slick, black man from Vancouver. A carefully groomed pretty boy with a swagger in snug designer jeans, slim-fitting white v-neck t-shirt and white Pumas complete with white ankle socks, he was hot shit. I was drab and decidedly uncool sporting my backpacking garb and figured he wouldn't be interested—especially given the unlimited supply of provocative Brazilian women—so I didn't even bother flirting. So he surprised me when he propositioned me halfway through the night. Was he kidding?

"I'm not interested in prostitutes," he offered by way of explanation. Perhaps he just wasn't interested in *paying* for one.

Not especially flattering, but my tank was running dry, and I knew he'd make perfect eye candy while lying on my back—his total lack of personality wasn't an issue. Off we strolled to a nearby by-the-hour love hotel. Our room was wall-to-wall mirrors. On every surface we saw shadows and reflections of ourselves. The hot tub and vinyl-wrapped mattress were unexpectedly inviting, as were the proudly presented condoms and lube on a shelf close at hand.

In the tub I went about the business of cleaning him to my satisfaction. As I was soaping up his cock, my hand slipped behind his balls, dangerously close to his anus, and his head suddenly flew back as he moaned to the ceiling and perhaps to the gods, "*Oh! How did you know?"* Well, of course I *hadn't* known, but I knew then. I had no intimate knowledge of boys' bums, of man-ass. I had a strap-on which I longed to run through its paces but had rarely approached the forbidden rosebud.

I gingerly slid a coconut-scented, soaped-up finger into his hole. He howled in ecstacy in an unexpectedly feminine tone, and his cock stood at full attention. It was all a bit dramatic, a bit much, but I reminded myself that he was pretty to look at. *Enjoy the view.* The soapy water glistened on his dark, smooth skin, on his washboard abs. His chiseled face, from which emerged his rapturous wails, turned soft and beatific.

We moved to the bed, where we had adequate sex. He loved to look at himself in the mirrors. I took a picture of myself lying on my back while he penetrated me, holding my legs wide and looking up at himself in the ceiling mirror. His striking face, defined chest and arms, and me fully spread, exposed, attempting to keep a straight face.

After a short rest as the sun was coming up, we left the hotel—but not before he had an embarrassing argument with the staff over the cost of the condom and lube we used. He didn't realize it was extra. It was only a few dollars, and I offered to pay, but he insisted on having a stupid yelling match with the staff over it instead.

I chalked the whole thing up as a McDonald's Happy Meal with a chocolate shake. Quick, fun and yummy, but void of any nutritional value.

The experience made me curious about prostitution in foreign countries. A week later I found myself in Mendoza, Argentina, paired with an American fellow for a bicycle winery tour. We spent the day riding around the countryside, sampling wine and local cuisine. By evening he was thoroughly drunk and had acquired a taste for me. I had no interest in him, but I did have an idea. "Let's hire a prostitute," I suggested.

He began to protest, but I stopped him. "I will pay, if I can watch."

Although he considered this for a while with his jaw hanging slack, he came around to the idea eventually.

We hailed a taxi and asked the driver to take us to a brothel. We drove long enough out of town that I was confident our destination was certain death. In hindsight, though, the genuine risk of death was always one of the more romantic appeals of international travel.

To our mutual surprise, we did in fact arrive at the brothel: a bar with a few women and no men. I was received with confusion—they were not accustomed to non-working women in their establishment. But we persevered and ordered drinks. After a moment's hesitation, an Argentinian prostitute approached us. We offered to buy her a drink. After a few minutes of compulsory chit-chat we found out the rates, and the three of us went to a side room.

She sat us down and performed a hypnotic striptease. "Can I take pictures?" I asked. She nodded as she unzipped his pants and expertly slipped a condom on; he looked both excited and horrified. His eyes darted between her and me. She started to stroke a little. His breathing sped up, and he started to squirm. He blurted that he didn't think he could hold on. She shot me a look as she suddenly spun around and sat down on his cock—barely in time for him to splooge. I wondered if she thought she wouldn't get paid unless she technically fucked him? The entire thing lasted less than a minute.

He was deeply humiliated. She and I struggled not to laugh as she quickly tidied up, took her money and ushered us out. The other women looked at us coming out of the room so quickly and did their honest best to conceal their knowing smiles. We knocked back our drinks and left. The taxi was waiting for us, and we went back to our separate hostels. He apologized pathetically the entire ride back, explaining that it was so hot with me watching and now he could last longer with me. I declined.

The next stop on my whirlwind tour was the mountainous northern city of Salta, and the only interesting thing that happened there was another near-death experience.

A few of us were on the way back into town after exploring a tourist attraction by Jeep. Suddenly, the road ahead of us was gone. Washed out. A river of water and mud was rushing over the road so thick and so long that we couldn't see the end of it. It had *just* happened; something had given way. The volume of mud where the road should have been was hard to comprehend. We stared, attempting to understand what we were seeing when we realized the road behind us was starting to flood too. The reality of what was happening hit us with a disturbing blow. We were about to be carried away to the valley below in a rushing river of mud.

The driver quickly turned the jeep around and raced back the way we came as the road was collapsing all around us, Indiana Jones style. We could see the nearby mountain crumbling, mud and water gushing out of places it wasn't supposed to. The driver of the Jeep was panicking but punched the gas and drove through water and mud so high that it threatened to swallow the Jeep. We got through it, breathless, hearts hammering in our chests, and drove through the long night, taking the scenic route back to town; all of us contemplating the lives we had nearly lost.

By the way, the salt flats are a sight to behold, well worth the trip if you manage to survive the journey.

Next stop: the City of Fury, Buenos Aires. The thirty-something Argentinian guy who worked at my hostel was gnomish but friendly. Short and stocky with a button nose, protruding chin and wild ginger hair. I was happy to spend time with him but was not interested in the horizontal tango. Taking inspiration from my experience in Mendoza, I decided to level up and see if I could get a peek into a less-touristy Argentinian brothel.

I made him the same offer: I would pay for a prostitute if he would let me watch. He was confused, but interested. Definitely interested.

We first ended up in the wrong place: a bar with the most beautiful women to have ever passed over my retinas. Scantily clad in stunning evening wear. The patrons were all wealthy foreigners—these women were exceedingly expensive. My little gnome sulked as I explained to him that I wanted to see the sort of place he might go to on his own.

We walked through small winding streets, far from the tourist area, and arrived at a nondescript residential house in a lower-income neighbourhood. I was nervous; it looked like it could have been his grandmother's house. When an older woman came to the door, I was even more confused. They spoke in Spanish, and she kept saying no, looking angry. Finally, she gave me a hard look, a glance around, then ushered us in. She quickly put us in a side room and told us to wait. The room had a bed and a sofa. The lighting was dim and red, and even though I could make out that it was dingy, it was clean enough.

My gnome was sweating and fidgeting. I had no idea if I was about to be robbed, kidnapped into sex slavery, taken hostage or whatever. My heart was banging away in excitement and fear as my stomach performed somersaults. Finally, after what felt like forever, the door opened and a full-figured woman of about twenty walked in, looking shy and uncertain. She had minimal makeup and was fairly average-looking; not gorgeous, not plain. They exchanged some words in Spanish, and he asked me if I liked her. I told him it was up to him since he was the one who needed to find her attractive. He timidly said, "Yes," and it was on.

My gnome showed up the American guy and proved to be excellently skilled in bed. He was gentle with the girl, they laughed a lot and he fucked her in six different positions over nearly half an hour. He enjoyed performing for me, and she soon relaxed into it as well. For such a tawdry situation, it was surprisingly light-hearted and fun.

He finally finished up, and we were all smiles as we left the brothel. I don't recall the cost—maybe forty dollars? On the way home, he asked if he could spend the night in my bed. I laughed and replied that I just paid for him to have sex; wasn't that enough? He pouted and explained that he could go again and would love to have sex with me. What a champ. But I declined; I simply wasn't attracted to him. Little did I know, I'd be on the receiving end of a similar situation when I got back home.

CHAPTER 28

Nude House Cleaner

When my stripper boyfriend Adrian picked me up at the Vancouver airport and greeted me with an awkward hug and a weirdly formal peck on the cheek, I knew instantly that the spark had died. He took me back to his place and gave me a special necklace he had designed for me: a dainty, tear-dropped aquamarine stone on a silver chain. It wasn't the sort of thing I'd ever worn before; the stone was my favourite colour, but it looked like something you'd wear to church.

He had bought a decent futon for me to sleep on in the living room; he would be sleeping in the bedroom. I had moved in after totalling my car in the accident for practical reasons since my condo was far and public transit was unreliable in that neighbourhood. I could have gotten another car, but I didn't think I should drive anymore. My licence should have been taken away—I *wanted* to be punished.

And so after being away for a couple of months, I found myself with a man who cared enough to have a special piece of jewelry made for me but who didn't want to sleep with me, in any way. No welcome-home sex, no "let's break in the futon" sex, nothing at all. After a week of him not making a move while avoiding my advances, I blew up. I demanded to know why he didn't want to have sex with me. He sat on the futon, looking apologetic but saying nothing. He never did tell me.

Meanwhile, I went back to working at the strip club and loved all the male attention I was getting. I felt sexy and beautiful at work but unwanted by the man who could have me any time he desired. Adrian started staying out all night, even when he had to work early in the morning. He had begun a day job by then, and our schedules usually meant that we barely saw each other. I would find out from others that he would be out all night drinking, doing drugs and going home with other women—including other strippers who worked at the same club.

Confusing. So confusing.

Knowing what jealousy and anger had resulted in before—driving drunk and totalling my car—I struggled to contain my rage. Adrian didn't belong to me; he hadn't even fucked me once since I'd been back. I was a glorified roommate.

So I started bringing men back and fucking them loudly in the bathroom and living room when Adrian was sleeping, letting them stay over so that he would see them in the morning when he got up to go to work. Adrian shyly mumbled, "I'm happy for you" on the first occasion and made no further comment after that. He didn't get upset, nor did he want to have a serious discussion about our non-existent relationship. When we saw each other, he was respectful and careful. He looked at me apologetically, with love and sadness, but he would not have an explicit discussion about "us." I finally told him I would move out, and he offered no resistance.

The week before my departure I was frustrated, randy, bored and rejected, so I spontaneously went on the Craigslist "Casual Encounters" section, may it rest in peace. I had never done that before, and I'm not even sure where I got the idea, but I thought that having an exciting encounter with a stranger would make me feel wanted.

As I scrolled through the endless pages of ads by men looking for women to hook up with, an unusual one caught my eye: "Wanted: Nude House Cleaner."

I read the ad and saw that the guy who posted it was a voyeur looking for a woman to do some light cleaning in the nude while he watched. No touching. The idea itself was thrilling enough, but he was also offering money; that sealed the deal for me. I already knew I was an exhibitionist and that I liked men paying to look at my body, so I replied to the ad. A few hours later, buzzing with uneasy excitement, I was walking through the door of an apartment on the sixteenth floor of a high-rise in downtown Vancouver.

I sized up the man as best as I could, gauging the risk to my safety as all women learn to do. He was reserved and pragmatic. An average-looking Middle Eastern man in his thirties dressed in dark slacks, shirt and a knit vest. His apartment was neat and minimally decorated. The wall of windows looked out over the glittering city and into the offices and homes of other high-rises.

He quietly and respectfully explained that he'd like me to vacuum and wash the windows in the nude. He assured me that everything was already clean; it was the voyeurism he was into, not the chores. He promised he wouldn't touch me and said I could leave whenever I wanted.

I smiled as I disrobed and got to work. He sat in a chair reading a magazine, fully clothed, glancing up every once in a while. As I washed the windows, I looked to see if anyone else was watching me; I hoped they were. If so, they weren't standing close enough to their windows for me to see clearly, but with hundreds of people in view, there is no doubt at least a few got a good look.

When I finished, he handed me money and said I could go if I wanted. I asked if I could have a quick shower because I had gotten sweaty doing the cleaning. He asked if he could watch and would pay me more if he could. I made a nice show of it, soaping up my body a few times and rinsing. He stood there leaning against the door frame watching, politely poker-faced.

I towelled off, and he handed me more money. He said I was free to go but wondered if I would be receptive to the idea of him photographing my vagina. He explained that it was another hobby of his, and he showed me other photos he had taken. They were tasteful black-and-white photos of vulvas—extreme close-ups. He said it would only be my vagina, not my face or anything identifiable. And of course, he offered me even more money to do it.

I was starting to feel surprisingly comfortable with him and excited by the experience. I loved being looked at, and I loved all the money.

We went into the bedroom, and he handed me a big metal chain to lay beside my labia for artistic contrast. A few snaps later, and he was done. He showed me the pictures on his camera, and they were great. Again, he handed me money and said I could go... but... if I felt comfortable... and *only* if I wanted to, he would pay me more if he could watch me masturbate. He would sit on a chair beside the bed and not touch me. He'd like to masturbate too. "But only if you are okay with it."

I said yes. His bedroom also had a wall of windows, and I was excited about strangers seeing this scene. Me laying on the bed masturbating while a man sat on a chair beside the bed jerking off, watching me.

I soon climaxed so hard that I'm surprised he didn't have to peel me off the ceiling with a spatula. My orgasm had the power of a herd of charging rhinos. As I floated back to reality, I registered that he had also climaxed and was holding his cum in his hand as he smiled at me. He looked so much more relaxed than he had the whole time. We both did, I imagine. We laughed and got up to sort ourselves out. He washed his hands and did up his pants; I got dressed and headed for the door. He handed me some more money on the way out and said he would email me the pictures.

I later used one of those awesome pics to make "pussy magnets" to hand out at Burning Man, to the delight of many.

This event was so exciting that I went straight home and placed an ad on Craigslist for "nude housecleaning with masturbation show." The tsunami of interest was overwhelming—and thrilling.

My next job was on a yacht. The man was in his early forties, well-dressed and pleasant to look at, with a light personality. His wife knew about our encounter and was turned on by it. His yacht was spotlessly clean. I pretended to dust in the nude for a few minutes as he watched, giddily exclaiming how great it was but how he felt bad about the cleaning part. He loved the naughtiness of it all, me being nude on his yacht.

He offered me some champagne, which I accepted. We sat there sipping champagne, making conversation. He told me about his adventurous wife and their swinging lifestyle. He asked if he could take a couple pictures for her, and I posed for him. He asked what else we could do, what I felt comfortable with. I told him no touching, but he could watch me masturbate while he got himself off. We went into the bed area, and I put on a little show for him while he jerked off. He couldn't stop smiling; he was elated. He asked if next time I'd like to get together with him and his wife. He probed softly, "Would you let her touch you?"

"Maybe."

Most of the emails I received were from men who wanted the masturbation show and not the housecleaning part. Most of them didn't have a place for me to come to, so I got my place set up to receive men there. I had recently moved into a tiny, quaint bachelor apartment in an old character building. It had a unique pull-out trundle bed. My customer would come in, hang his jacket by the door, sit on the sofa while I did a strip show, follow me to the bathroom and sit on a bench while I gave a shower show, then move to a chair beside the bed where he would jerk himself off watching me masturbate.

I customized each show with my words. I would ask what they were into and what kind of porn they jerked off to tease out their fantasies, and then I would incorporate that information into my dirty talk. I'd pretend I was their student, secretary, boss, a friend's wife, sister, a girl they had a crush on in high school. I'd pretend to be their cheating wife and talk about my other lovers. I'd pretend I'm a virgin. I'd tease them with what they couldn't have. I'd tell them what I would do to them, how I'd suck their cock while sucking on a dildo, how tight my pussy or ass would be around their cock while fucking myself with toys. I'd tell them if they were *really* good, maybe, someday, I would swallow their cum or let them fuck me, cum inside me, cum on me... and on and on.

I discovered that my imagination for filth knew no limits; I absolutely loved taking them to another place with my words and body. I'd seduce. I'd tease. I'd control. They would literally drool and give in—moan and cum and cum and cum. The only touching would be at the end as they were on their way out. I'd give them a nice, warm hug. Many of them said that was the best part, and I started to realize how much men craved touch and intimacy.

One of my first customers asked, "Can I write a review of you on Pervland?"

"What's Pervland?"

"It's a place online for guys to share information about escorts, to write reviews or warn others about bad experiences. Escorts advertise there and sort of screen potential clients."

I didn't understand it, but I said he could write a review if he wanted to.

The review was simple. It briefly outlined what I did and said he was happy with the service. Other guys commented that they didn't understand why he would pay to jerk himself off. Paying to be with a woman who doesn't even touch you, let alone have sex with you, was incomprehensible to most of them. This was an escort review board, after all. I was upset by the negative comments, but I loved what I did exactly the way I did it, and my customers loved it too.

Soon after the first review went up, I received an eloquent email from a man who called himself Luther. He claimed to be a well-respected reviewer on Pervland and requested a visit with me to experience for himself the unique service I provided. He informed me that he would be writing an accurate review of the experience: "I like to let girls know that ahead of time. That way you can decide if you want to meet me or not."

Naturally, I agreed.

Luther was a truly fascinating character: a dashing fifty-something Sean Connery lookalike in a crisp fedora, long coat and dramatic walking stick. He had kind, playful eyes and a warm smile. I provided the same service I always did.

Luther was overjoyed with the experience and was excited to write about it. His reviews were famous for being written in an entertaining long-story format. He asked what he should call me in the review. I told him my name was Tracey, and he said I shouldn't use my real name for safety reasons. I'd been going by Sam as a stripper (because I thought it was funny to use a name that could be a guy's name), but I didn't think about going by a different name for these masturbation shows. He smiled and said, "Well, I'll call you 'Miss T' for now, until you decide on a name."

I never did a session with Luther again, but we did become friends. He fell in love with a mature escort he had met as a client; she later left her husband for him and retired from the business. He also gave me a unique antique commode chair that would become a highly valuable piece of furniture. But the best gift he could've ever given me was his review, which appears in full below:

Sweet Miss T – A Naughty Porcelain Doll

Long time, no review. For those Pervetians who don't like the long style review, click away. For those that enjoy a good Lutherization for their wanking material, read on.

I saw a review recently of a new Voyeur experience.

I was intrigued. Why would a Pervetian, even a newbie, fork over $150 just to have a no-touch wank? The thing that got me more than anything, I guess, was that this unique provider lives only a block away from me in the West End. I e-mailed the woman I will now call Sweet Miss T because she signed off her prompt return e-mail with just "T". Somehow, I liked that.

When I talked to her on the phone, I was even more intrigued. She explained the service in reasonably graphic detail and sent me a knockout picture of herself.

I have never had an experience like this where there is no touching involved but the convenience factor was just too nifty an idea and the LuthWallet has seen the canoes and browns floating out of it like I'm watching the dragon boat races lately, so I thought, what's another 1.5?

T's place is one of the funkier, bigger old apartment buildings in the West End but the buzzer is temporarily on the fritz, so we agreed to meet on the street corner. I didn't know which building she would come *out of, but when I saw her, I was shocked. From the photo she sent me, I was expecting some glamorous willowy starlet. Instead, there is this tiny, perfect secretarial cutie smiling away at me. I am 5'11" and as she approached me in a simple black casual dress and no shoes, she seemed to shrink even more. By the time she was at my side, I felt like Yao Ming. My preferred arm-fit woman is about 5'5". As she hugged me, I nearly whiffed on her and passed my arms right over her head. Cute is a really shitty word to describe someone as attractive as this woman is, but when everything perfectly womanly is in miniature, you think to yourself, I'm feeling like Shrek here with the cute Princess before she turns green and gets rolled-up newspaper ears.*

We get up to her weird, wonky little apartment, the obligatory but sane cat greets us and I get a flash like I'm in tiny town. The whole thing is in proportion to T. Living room, bed pull-out from the wall, nifty antiques and a bathroom that is four steps up (yes, up) from the main room. Really charming but somewhat surreal.

I pull out gifts. Donation in a bank envelope. Humongous hazelnut chocolate bar (400 grams, $6.79 at Super-Valu), my only two porno DVD's I never watch (she said on the phone she needed more than the one she had) and my own bottle of lube I bought for a visiting SP from Winnipeg that we never needed because of her natural lubricity (Yes, Ms. Bella, you are slithery like no-one else – stay tuned for an even longer story on that one).

Sweet Miss T gets me going right away by asking if I want the "shower show" or should she just get into the lingerie I requested and leap into the "bed show." Of course, I said, "Both!" She sits me on the teensy couch and pulls up the little black dress slowly and makes me guess what she is wearing. Naturally, being the bum aficionado that I am, I am delighted that she has turned around to do this. The dress goes up slowly but not too slowly and I am guessing, "Panties ... nothing ... thong ... nothing ... uh, ooooooooh! Pink string thong! Yes!!" Before me at eye level is it. By "it" I mean a bum masterpiece. Yes, this may be my bum nirvana. Get on those stair-steppers, Dea, Sabrina, Miranda, Ava, et al. There is a new bum in town and it's gonna win the bumfight down at the OK Corral.

Words fail me for this one. Well, no they don't. You've got lots of time, don't you? This little bum symphony starts at a tiny waist and crescendos out generously to womanly proportions with nary an off-key note. It is, alabaster, um, no, porcelain, um, no, pink-tinged cream. The perkosity of the cheeks is as if a virtuoso conductor were framing a slow rotundo movement with both of his hands for his orchestra. I, of course, being the goof that I am, simply go, "EEE, UHHH! GOFF! VERY, GULP, NICE, ER, THONG!" If you want to know what it kind of looks like, here are some shots of Kylie Minogue's derriere in action. T's is better than this, more voluptuous. Seriously.

She strips off the thong and shoves "it" back at me and bends over and fingers herself. Now, I get to appreciate the perfect smiles of the lower uplifts. The pre-butt cheeks underneath are delectable and I have to restrain myself from my usual nibble-nobble move. Instead, the sight of the whole thing is so wondrous; I just lean back and stroke myself through my shorts.

She turns around and shows me her lacy flowered see-through bra and, somehow, both bra and thong just de-materialize and she stands utterly naked and smiling in front of me. Her tits are perfect and pink-nippled. I can't hazard a size guess because on a woman of her stature (4'11"?, 5' max. and size 4 feet for you shoe fetishists!!), those regular bra numbers and letters don't apply. Suffice to say, when she massages them for me, they squirm out on the sides of her hands quite nicely. They would be the equivalent of a nice 34B/C on a larger woman but they sit nice and high on her no-fat toned upper body.

Before I can start to moan about the "no-touch" rules, she leads me up the little wooden staircase to the bathroom, sits me on a low cabinet covered with a white towel and hops in the bath/shower. She soaps herself up liberally and the whole porcelain doll image leaps to mind. I haven't talked about her face yet but people do tell her she looks like Kylie Minogue sometimes. I don't think so. Yeah, okay, quite a bit.

Kylie is awesome but T is softer and prettier and has a cuter nose. Kylie is all mouth coming at you. T is all aquamarine eyes and sweet smile with tiny perfect teeth. When that face is smiling down at you, looking at your cock busting out of your shorts and fingering herself madly in the shower, the no-touch rule is just not a big issue for the wanker. Then, as the wankee tells you with utter sincerity how much she likes the look of your Luth-tulip and then swings around to insert herself on a see-through dildo that has a suction cup bottom attached to the tub ledge and then starts moaning hoarsely as she plummets all that pinkness up and down at the speed of a hungry ferret, you feel as if you are that dildo. Somehow, I manage to not explode right then and there.

T changes into black lacy garters and black stockings and takes the Luth-tulip doppelganger to the pull-out bed, positions me on a low brown chair with a strategically placed towel on it. I am at eye level to the side bed and she goes to work on the whole extravaganza. I don't even glance at the porno playing on the laptop the whole time. I am transfixed. Her plunging fingers in both holes and her dildo zipping between mouth and pink pussy have me reaching for my warming lube. I last through ten minutes of her moaning and nasty descriptions of what she would like me to do with her, having me in every position and then finally her sucking her juice off the doppelganger gets me to the point of furious wankosity. She starts to grin as she sees my dilated pupils roll back in my head and as my slitted eyes flick back and forth between both pink holes (yes, her butthole is as pink and sweet-looking as one of Barbie's little toy purses), I imagine what real plunging in miniature land would be like. I spray and spurt like a plastic mayonnaise bottle scrunched by a linebacker's meaty paw.

Her grin turns to a huge satisfied smile.

(Excusez-moi, I just had to go to the can for a second there).

Now, you boys that might figure you should sample this prize, a word of warning. She is serious about the no-touching thing but there is no heaviness involved, so guys don't press it, please, unless she changes her menu selection. Remember, I'm only a block away and I've been working out a lot lately. I figure I can take most of you skinny-necked, dough-bummed, high-post guys if you think your fat wallets can convince her otherwise.

If she changes her menu, I have first dibs.

Repeat? Natch.

The day Luther's review came out, all hell broke loose. My inbox blew up with appointment requests.

Guys realized that what I was offering wasn't a rip-off; it was a unique experience that was, in fact, ideal for many. A modern-day voyeur act or a peep show. And for many of my clients, it was a surprisingly perfect fit.

A lot of men struggled with erectile dysfunction or nerves. They worried about not being able to perform with an escort. But with me, they could control their dick. Men who were overly paranoid about STIs didn't have that concern with me. There was no touching beyond the clothed hug at the end. Husbands and boyfriends who didn't want to feel like they were cheating on their wives or girlfriends could do this dirty little thing and feel better about themselves. Fellas who liked going to the strip club but were frustrated by not being able to cum there got a similar experience with me but could jerk off without a bouncer tossing them out. Voyeurs who liked porn but found it lacked intimacy and wanted more connection without actually going all the way with an escort loved what I offered. Also, those who had less money could still afford to see me, as my rates were naturally less than what an escort would charge for full service. Every guy had his own story, but they were all happy.

I had far more clients than I could manage, and many of them wrote reviews because what I offered was so unique. They wanted to share their experiences and felt like writing a positive review was a way of showing gratitude. There were so many reviews that some people claimed I was writing them myself—there was no way I could be *that* good. So other reliable, well-known punters started to come see me to verify what others were saying, and they would write their own reviews backing up what others had reported: "A sweet girl-next-door with a filthy imagination and a mouth like a trucker. Fantastic verbals. Pictures were accurate; even more attractive in person. Safe, sane, smart, drug-free and provided great value for the money."

That's what they reported, and every word of it was true.

CHAPTER 29

Elbow Deep

Even though I made my boundaries about touching clear, I'd still get requests. But not the kind that you would expect; they weren't for sex. Some men asked if I would consider spanking them or if I would let them worship my shoes or feet. Some asked if they would be permitted to dress in women's clothing during the session. Many of the requests were for fetish activities, something that had long been an interest of mine.

I had been reading fetish erotica for years, attending fetish parties in San Francisco and Vancouver, and dabbling in fetish play in my private life. So I said yes to whatever I felt comfortable with, and clients started to bring me implements as gifts to use on them. Fine wooden paddles, leather floggers, leather cuffs, rope. One piece, a long, heavy strip of leather with a wooden handle, was particularly mean. It was about as long as my arm and so stiff that it took a decent amount of effort to get it to snap. I remember thinking, "You could really tan someone's behind with this one!"

Experienced slaves would teach me what I needed to know to cater to their fetish. I started to get reviewed on the site as a Dominatrix. I wasn't qualified for that title by any metric, but everyone has to start somewhere, and the men were happy to "show me the ropes." I had the right demeanour, they said.

It was around that time I ran into Gerald, the fifty-year-old gay uncle of one of my ex-boyfriends. He was a colourful fellow who was open about his sexuality and his HIV-positive status. I felt comfortable telling him about the recent changes in my life and my newest piece of news: that I was becoming a professional Dominatrix! "Oh honey, that's fantastic!" he said. Gerald asked if I had experience with anal play and insisted I come by his place the next day to get a lesson on anal fisting. It's outrageous in retrospect, but he made it sound almost normal.

Shortly after I arrived, Gerald took his time filing down my nails to ensure I wouldn't damage the delicate tissue of his anus. He said that I would be going too deep for gloves because they could slip off, and I would be able to feel what I was doing better without gloves on anyway. He assured me there would be zero smell or mess. He explained his process for cleaning out, the fasting, the multiple enemas. He explained that I was at no risk of contracting HIV this way. Reggie, Gerald's boyfriend, was there too, and they showed me videos of anal fisting and anal punching while they got the bed set up. Gerald laid back in a leather sex swing over the bed and positioned his feet in the stirrups so that he—*my ex-boyfriend's uncle*—was spread wide in front of me. He said he'd never had a woman do this to him before, so he was excited to check this off his bucket list.

I lubed up and, step by step, they instructed me on the technique of safe anal fisting. I ended up with both arms in up to my elbows. Yes, *both* arms in *at the same time* up to *both* of my elbows.

Gerald then discussed how, to be able to handle this, he needed excellent muscle control, not just to be loose. He told me to take everything out except one finger, and then he clamped down tightly on it—after having been stretched five-pin-bowling-ball-wide only moments before. It was an impressive party trick, to be sure.

They also told me that they had recently done a porn vid where one of them pretended to be straight and the other one tied him up and "made" him do gay things. "Apparently it sold well," they said.

"You should meet Webster, the guy we worked with on it. He's made all kinds of other fetish porn vids." I was reluctant but thought there was no harm in meeting him, so I said,

"Okay, sure. Set it up."

On our first meeting, Webster was anxious and jumpy. He was a scruffy Caucasian guy in his early forties. He spent most of the time talking about his successful Dominatrix girlfriend Samara Beatrix and how he had helped her to become so world-renowned. He didn't understand how I didn't know who she was, so I explained that I was new to Professional Domination. "Like brand-spanking new," I told him. "I don't know anyone in the scene."

Webster explained that they filmed fetish vids—trampling, pony riding, clothed facesitting. He wasn't selling me on the idea very hard; he doubted that I was serious. Despite the reluctance on both ends, somehow we ended up scheduling a shoot with me, his famous girlfriend and a slave.

It was a strange time in my life. I realized I was free to do whatever I wanted. I was making decent money and having a blast. The more I said yes to, the more money I made and the more fun I had. So despite the red flags, I moved forward with the shoot.

Samara's apartment was beyond messy; wall-to-wall chaos is more accurate. It looked like Hunter S. Thompson had been vacationing there. Dirty dishes, paper coffee cups, designer clothing and footwear strewn about; shoeboxes were stacked everywhere; and bondage equipment, sex toys and a wide assortment of random garbage covered every surface and nearly every inch of floor. There was nowhere you could walk or sit that was not piled high with stuff.

Samara was still getting ready. I waited suspensefully, feeling like a fool while perched on the edge of a chair covered in fur coats and worn pantyhose. Fifteen minutes later, she graced us with her presence. Samara was slight in stature, with lush, dark, wavy hair that reached past her narrow, corseted waist and almost touched her compact bottom. Her breasts were small, barely covered in a cream lace bra that contrasted dreamily with her sandy skin tone. Killer heels, silky stockings, a six-strap garter belt and panties, all perfectly matched, completed her work uniform. She had an intense

THERE IS MORE TO THE STORY

presence that was both poised and prickly. Devoid of warmth, her detached greeting left me feeling unwelcome.

The slave arrived, and she was dismissive of him. He was a tall, fleshy, dorky man who softly said, "Yes, Goddess" to everything she ordered him to do... which started with clearing away an area for filming. He moved piles of who-knows-what off of an ornate chaise lounge that I could never have imagined was hiding underneath.

Samara asked to see the wardrobe I'd brought, but she didn't approve of a single piece.

"Ugh, come on. Let's find you something."

She had me follow her down the apartment hallway, picking our way around the mess of Starbucks cups and stacks of shoeboxes to her bedroom. She flung the door open, and I stopped right in my tracks. The walls of her room were covered from floor to ceiling with shelves of designer shoes. There had to be tens of thousands of dollars worth of heels and boots.

"Beautiful, right?" Samara asked me. It was the one part of the entire apartment that wasn't filthy.

"Yup," was all I could manage.

"I love them. I masturbate with them," she explained, dead serious. I wasn't sure exactly what that might look like, but I enjoyed the imagery nonetheless.

She pulled corset after corset out of her closet, measuring them against my body, dressing me like a dolly in her clothes. Eventually, she selected an exquisite corset that she made clear was tremendously expensive.

Now that we were appropriately attired, the camera rolled. We alluded to a lesbian attraction and a shared arousal from mutually abusing our slave. She led; I followed. She trampled the slave hard, and he groaned and moaned. She jumped off the chaise lounge onto his big cushy gut, and he cried out as her feet sunk into his flesh. I had never seen anything like it. She encouraged me to do the same, to treat him like a trampoline. To my surprise, it was good fun battering and bruising him for my amusement. She face-sat him until he turned a charming shade of purple. So mean, so extreme. My adrenaline pumping, I did my best to appear cool and experienced. I hoped that my face didn't give away the depth of my shock, the totality of my inexperience.

After the shoot, the slave expressed his gratitude; he was not only completely fine but had loved every moment of it. Samara and Webster were happy enough with my performance, and more shoots were planned.

Now that I had apparently proven my worth, Webster was talking my ear off with advice. He said I needed a website, and I paid them two grand to create it. He took some great pictures of me for the site. Webster was kind to me, but he was difficult to deal with; too paranoid, anxious and scattered.

We had two sets: the apartment where Samara lived and another apartment that had been converted into a dungeon. Both looked like frat houses; the mess and clutter was staggering, the fallout from a steady diet of booze, coffee and take-away junk food. We filmed some smut of an embarrassingly poor quality—it turned out that none of us had any idea what we were doing.

Samara showed me the ropes over a few double domme sessions together. I did my first golden shower with her. She recommended I drink coffee so that it would be easier, and while, yes, it did help, my pee smelled of coffee. We both pissed on the client in the bathtub and when he drank some of hers, I gagged. The combined aromas of our urine and his ejaculate in that cramped space brought me to the edge of vomiting on him, which was more perversion than he could realistically afford.

Although I was saddled with an acutely sensitive nose and an aversion to germs that bordered on phobia, disgust waited around every corner. The reek of clients' dank breath, musty balls, cheesy foreskins, funky butt cracks, armpits wafting onion-like stench—even when freshly showered, I could still smell it all. With the volume of asses I fucked and the amount of ass juice that I had to deal with, the fact that I never puked on a client is nothing short of a miracle.

But I digress.

I was now under the brief and unstructured tutelage of Webster's world-famous Dominatrix girlfriend. Samara introduced me to phone sessions, and I would observe her taking the occasional call.

One frequent client was an eccentric, generous American guy with a shoe fetish named Larry. They would talk for hours. He was the one sending her dozens of pairs of designer shoes and boots. She would take trips and spend days with him in opulent hotels, dining at glittering restaurants in designer fashions perfect to the last stitch. It all sounded titillatingly glamorous.

Samara had a personal slave, "Fat Head," the doughy one I trampled on that first day we filmed. He was always around, doting on her, driving her places, being her film slave. She would sit on his face wearing jeans for hours, ignoring him. He would gently lift her enough to get some air but otherwise would be a perfect piece of furniture. In fact, that's what he considered himself to be: a chair or a carpet; an object.

And being an object, he was silent. But presented with the chance to speak, he could not shut up. He blabbed to me about all kinds of personal things—he loved to gossip—and revealed that another local Domme he had served turned out to be pure evil; she had stalked him and caused trouble for Webster and Samara. That might have explained Webster's frequent paranoia and anxiety, assuming it was true, but the evidence was thin. Fat Head sounded like a loon ranting about what a manipulative, diabolical mastermind his ex-Mistress, Valencia, was.

Then one day Valencia called me herself to warn me about Fat Head. She told me he was a menace and no matter how much money he paid he wouldn't be worth it. He couldn't be trusted. After all these years I still can't separate truth from fiction, but I am certain that all players involved were loopy, each in his or her own unique way.

After a few months of working with Webster and Samara, I hadn't seen a dollar of income from the videos we'd produced. My website was still not finished, and the whole crew became more unhinged with each passing day. I decided to break away as diplomatically as possible. I bought Webster an expensive camera to thank him for the many good-quality pics he had taken of me; this was easily the best thing to come out of our relationship. I gave Samara a fancy bottle of wine and let her keep the $2,000 for the website that was never completed, chalking it up as payment for training. I hired someone else to create a basic website for me, and I focused on doing private Domination sessions. I closed the door on doing videos because it had been a disaster. At the time, I didn't feel that I had the talent for it and didn't think there was money in it. Boy, was I wrong.

CHAPTER 30

Samantha Mack

I was still dancing a few nights a week at The Playhouse strip club. I did short, mini stage shows to promote myself for private dances. I loved being on stage. The Playhouse was a seedy little place with a long history and quirky staff. There was Jake, a twenty-something bartender who had started there when he was only nineteen. It was rumoured that his cock was as thick as a pop can but after the novelty of working in a strip club wore off, he kept it in his pants, so I never saw it. With his swagger and manner of speech, Jake was a watered-down caricature of an Italian gangster from *Goodfellas* or *The Godfather*.

Teddy worked the door, and he was a big teddy bear until push came to shove. One time a guy in the front row reached out and poked my pussy while I was laying in front of him on the stage. Teddy saw it and had him in a headlock lightning quick, dragging him backward, his chair knocked over. I asked him later if he beat the guy up, and Teddy smiled the sweetest smile, chuckling like Santa, and said, "No. We don't beat guys up at The Playhouse." He then flashed a mischievous look like a boy who's stolen a cookie and added, "He might have accidentally hit a wall or two on the way out, though."

Teddy's brother was the DJ, and he watched the monitors to ensure the gals in the private dance booths were safe. No contact was allowed there, and I appreciated that. I liked being watched; I didn't want to be pawed at.

The owner of the club came in occasionally. For an Italian "gangster," he sure was a nice guy. I had been told that despite its history and reputation, the Italian "mafia" in Vancouver now was all about legit business. I was also told that biker gangs didn't come into The Playhouse because they were scared of the Italian mafia. Once again, I could not separate fact from fiction, but The Playhouse was certainly a place of undisputed legend; a bullet hole in the wall was kept as a momento from a famous shooting.

The Playhouse was a wonderful place to work; no one cared about much of anything. It was laid back and had a casual, family-like atmosphere in which I felt safe. The club was hardly bustling, though, and I wasn't making even a fraction of the money dancing as I was with my masturbation shows, where I had more bookings than I knew what to do with. I started working less and less at the club but was reluctant to give it up entirely. I loved dancing, but money is money, and I knew this was the twilight of my time at The Playhouse.

That's when I met Samantha Mack. On her first night there I introduced myself as Sam, and she declared, "That's my name."

"That might be a problem," I suggested.

"Well, I'm not changing it," she snapped back without a trace of humour. I sized her up: big hair, loads of makeup, long fake eyelashes, long fake nails and enormous breasts.

"I've been dancing as Sam Mack, and I'm not changing it." She reiterated. My guts twisted. I was intimidated but attempted to be welcoming; I was the veteran there and didn't want to treat others as poorly as I had been treated at my first club.

I offered, "It's just that I've been working here for months as Sam, and it would be confusing to have two, don't you think?" Eventually she relented and agreed to go by Samantha.

She felt familiar and I wanted to say so, but given her intense unfriendliness, I decided to leave it. I worked in a wig, so I understood if she didn't recognize me. The feeling of familiarity returned a few nights later when friends of hers came in to visit her at work. I knew them from fetish parties and had a flash of a memory; making out with a girl one fine drunken and debaucherous night. Could it have been Samantha?

"Neat friends," I told her. "I go to these..." I started before pausing to see her neutral gaze—not a bad start—"I go to these fetish parties, and I think I've met your friends there. Have I maybe seen you there too?"

"Oh! You probably know Ryan and Candice," she exclaimed, gracing me with the first of many warm Ms. Mack smiles.

"Oh, yes! Yes, I know them *very* well," I boasted.

She laughed, showing her dazzling white teeth, then replied, "I bet I know them way better than you."

Thirteen seconds into our friendship, and we're already having a friendly competition over who's the better friend of a friend. But if that's what she wanted, then I was ready to do this thing.

"This one time after a party we went back to—"

"I was their babysitter for *years*," she cut me off, straightening a few inches to her full height.

And with that, I was soundly defeated.

Samantha was *the babysitter*. The famous/infamous hot babysitter. I had heard about her—*all* about her. She looked after their son when they went out to party. She was a cheerleader in high school and would show up in her cheerleading uniform. Ryan and Candace had a huge crush on her, but she was terribly young. They waited a couple of years for her to be old enough, and for her to make the first move.

It was like meeting a celebrity. I was stunned speechless.

It was some nights later when Samantha was getting ready to leave that I took off my wig and asked, "Look familiar now? Any chance we've met?"

"Nope."

"I think we met on the dance floor at The Lotus at Body Perv," I explained. "We made out to put on a show for a guy you were with."

She finally looked at me—*really* looked at me—and it registered. She started laughing. "Yes! Now I remember!"

Feeling relieved, I offered, "Maybe you were drunk, so you didn't remember? Sometimes I—"

"I'm straight-edge. I never drink or do drugs."

From then on, Samantha and I were great friends. And, before long, more than friends.

The passion that started back at The Lotus bubbled up. I told her about the masturbation shows I was doing, and she wanted to get in on it, so we started doing duo voyeur shows.

It was an interesting contrast. Samantha looked like a brunette Pamela Anderson: busty, tanned, heavily made up, with big sexy hair. I was more of a sweet-looking girl next door: petite, medium natural breasts, fair-skinned, blonde, with light makeup. We were good together, though. We would kiss and make out, and there was a lot of genuine passion and giggling. We did all the "circus tricks," as I called them: fisting, strap-ons, toys and so on. It was a good show, and we were in high demand. We weren't always in the mood for love though, so to speak, and over time began to fake it more and more often.

Years and a lot of water under the bridge later, we would both probably admit that we were better friends than lovers. We certainly had an initial attraction and a lot of passionate moments early on, but that evaporated in short order.

"But wait! Tell me more!" you might be begging of me. Sorry sugar, but that's the end of that yarn. Think of it as orgasm control.

CHAPTER 31

I Never Cum From Blow Jobs

It was the end of August, and Ryan and Candace were getting ready for their second trip to Burning Man. They insisted I come and told me that their friend David would drive me, as they were leaving a week early to camp with their son along the way. Unfortunately, my efforts to meet David before the trip were unsuccessful since he wouldn't return my messages, but Candace assured me that everything was fine. He was a great guy, she told me, and they knew we would get along. The only message I got from him the day before we were to leave was that he had a particularly small car—a Miata—and that I was to bring a little bit more than nothing. Again, Candace told me not to worry; she would have everything I needed, and they would take care of me. I only needed to show up.

I didn't know anything about Burning Man outside of what Ryan and Candace had told me. And I knew even less about David. Samantha knew him, though, and assured me he was exceedingly pleasant, and smoking hot too.

On the morning of our departure, I stood, nervous and excited, on the corner near my place with a small bag. David pulled up in his little car with the top down and said, "You must be Tracey."

"You must be David," I shrugged, tossing my small bag into the micro-trunk. I hopped in, and off we went. Zoom-zoom.

David was a Robert Redford lookalike with a dash of Norwegian heritage. His sandy blonde hair was tousled from the wind and gave him a playful look, despite his resting "I don't have time for your bullshit" face. I guessed his age at around forty. He pushed the peppy Miata assertively, sliding between lanes with confidence, Bowie blaring. I was immediately drawn to him—even though I had the impression that he'd rather be making this trip solo. I quickly realized that this guy possessed a keen wit; the kind of rational intellect that liquifies my sapiosexualism. His words were barbed hooks passing over his lips; no fat, no unnecessary utterances, no room for hollow pleasantries. It made me think more carefully before speaking.

We hit it off, and the conversation flowed that first day as we soared down the highway, the sun shining, the tunes playing. The first night we stayed at some seedy no-name motel. We got a room with two double beds, and it took great restraint for me not to make a move. I wanted him to fuck me as badly as a dying Catholic wants redemption.

Evidently the feeling was mutual: by the middle of the next day I was blowing him while he was speeding down the highway with the top down. As he passed trucks, he chuckled at the looks the drivers gave him. He told me that he didn't cum from blow jobs a moment before his hips jerked and he started struggling to keep the car on the road. I pulled my head up to see what was happening as the first spurt of ejaculate barely missed my face and he came all over his pants and seat belt.

Laughing, we pulled over at the next rest stop so that he could clean himself up. "I never cum from blow jobs," David swore again. "I don't understand what happened there." I smiled. Chemistry happened. That second night of our road trip, in another seedy motel, we had explosive sex. The kind of sex that's so right, so profound, that you feel you've finally arrived in your body for the first time; everything before was just a warm-up. Sex that you crave desperately the instant it stops.

Shortly after, we finally made it to Burning Man: dust-covered interactive art and fire. The theme for 2006 was Hope and Fear. Holding my hand, looking out at the playa full of costumed partiers and decorated art cars, David asked, "What do you hope for and what do you fear?"

"Love" was my simple answer as I kept looking straight ahead even though I felt him turn to look at my profile. Though I was falling hard for David, I was equally terrified of getting hurt. But since Burning Man was a week of life-changing experiences and radical self-expression, I let myself fall.

To say that Burning Man was good would be a gross understatement, and David and I experienced everything together that week: from the incredible costumes and art to all of the people who had let their guards down so that they could open up to each other and connect, accept, share, help, dance and love. It was a feast for the eyes and senses.

In the blazing hot days, the endless, bright-blue sky capped the gleaming white playa as far as the eye could see—except for when the occasional dust storm would kick up and create a blurred contrast. People were dressed in every kind of costume imaginable: Mad-Max-style dusty desert gear with scraps of leather tied together; steampunk top hats and ruffled shirts; naked but completely covered in body paint; human butterflies with wings and antenna headbands; skimpy underwear; fun fur; glittery fabrics; people on stilts—I could go on and on.

It was the same with the mind-blowing art cars and intricate theme camps, which there were more of than you could ever imagine. Giant ships floating over the sand, a huge, fire-breathing steel octopus, and cars made to look like fish, bunnies and countless other animals. There was a vampire camp, where they served red wine out of blood bags; Duck Pond Camp, with a giant water slide; and Angry Birds camp, where they catapulted stuffed animals across the road at The Pig Camp.

There were camps that hosted yoga classes all day, as well as camps that taught pole dancing or lap dancing, meditation, sound healing, tips on navigating altered states, Alcoholics Anonymous meetings, hug camps, compliment camps and lots of boozy party camps with dancing and shenanigans. To describe it all would be impossible, as there were nearly 40,000 people there and hundreds of camps doing what seemed like an infinite number of fun, clever and creative things.

Of course there was also the art, The Temple (a quiet place to mourn loved ones lost) and "The Man" (a giant wooden structure, about three stories high, that looked like a stickman; it's where the festival gets its name). Most of these creations were designed to burn at the end of the week—a pyromaniac's dream—and depending on what they were they elicited a myriad of emotions from the spectators ranging from love to joy to sadness.

At the end of the week, I returned to Vancouver with Ryan and Candace, and David took a side trip to visit friends in Phoenix. When he returned to Vancouver a couple weeks later, I thought we would pick up where we left off. I felt sure that we were great together. But I didn't hear from him when he returned. I reached out, and we had a nice but brief conversation about his trip to Phoenix. I said we should get together, and he agreed, but no plans were made. I figured he was busy catching up with work after having taken time off. I didn't see him again until Halloween, over a month later.

Ryan and Candace had a Halloween party, to which I brought a date—my hot personal trainer. But it was a sex party, and he was nervous—too young and inexperienced. When David arrived, our long, warm hug felt like foreshadowing, so I told my date he should leave. He was uncomfortable and wanted to go anyway, so I let him off the hook. Within minutes, David and I were on the bed passionately making love. It felt *right*. We went back to my place and continued until the sun came up. I was certain we would be together. He was so happy to see me, and the sex was unbelievable.

Hazy and blissed out, savouring breakfast and the still-throbbing ache between my legs, I sighed and commented on how good we are together. He stopped—fork halfway to his mouth—and looked at me, perplexed.

Life is about moments, and this was one I will never forget. Everything froze for a beat, a cue for the tiny paparazzi in my head to pop out his flashbulb and capture a juicy, haunting piece of humanity, with the headline "Two Realities Collide."

At that moment David realized how I felt about him, and I realized how he did not feel about me. Both of us, in an instant, understood that we were standing on opposite sides of a sharp divide. One that we were blissfully unaware of until that moment.

He put his fork down slowly; the first hesitation I'd seen. "I'm not someone you'd want to be with," he said. "There are things about me that you don't know."

"We got along so well at Burning Man, and that sex was so amazing…" I gathered myself. "How can you not want more of that?"

Both of us were trying. Trying not to make things worse, attempting to be gentle. David trying not to hurt me, and me trying to not look like a fool.

We parted ways amicably; warmly, but with a shift that could not be denied. I retreated to my flannel PJs and dozens of episodes of South Park, trying to bury the feelings of disappointment and confusion. How could I have been so wrong? How could it have felt that perfect but not been reciprocated? I replayed the details and moments over and over in my head and kept coming back to the same result: we had a special connection. I was *certain* of it… But if that was the case, then why did he walk away?

CHAPTER 32

Skunked

I didn't hear from David again. Weeks turned into months. In the meantime, I worked, booked solid with Pro Domme sessions. It made me more money than the voyeur shows, but I still did those too. I was mostly done with stripping, but I liked being at The Playhouse, so I worked there occasionally. I was spending a lot of time with Samantha too. Our passion had fizzled, but we remained friends and still did girl-girl shows together.

One time she called a few minutes before a session and sounded totally panicked. "Muffin and I got sprayed by a skunk!" She and her rottweiler had surprised a skunk when she was trying to take him for a quick walk before our session.

I told her the client would be there any moment, and since I didn't want him to give us a bad review, I suggested she should at least show up even if he didn't want us to go through with the session.

The client arrived first, and I explained to him that Samantha had just been sprayed by a skunk. Although she was on her way over, if it was too unpleasant, we should reschedule.

Before he could decide, Samantha walked in, followed by a stench that was so assaulting our eyes started watering. I looked over at my client and waved my hands in front of me. "No, this isn't going to work. Let's reschedule."

The man thought about it—*what was there to think about?*—before saying, "Well, we're all here; might as well go through with it."

I looked over at Samantha, who looked back at me with tears streaking her cheeks from the smell of her own body. She shrugged, "Okay."

What a trooper.

The shower show part went extra long, as I desperately scrubbed her trying to reduce the stench of skunk. It didn't help. I lathered her up over and over. No difference. The show must go on, and we did the whole nine yards with me choking on the skunk fumes and trying to look aroused. How the client managed to cum was beyond me. His eyes were watering too, and it struck me how when a man is horny he'll do anything to cum.

After that night, the smell of skunk would haunt me. It's *incredibly* hard to get rid of. The dog had laid on the furniture in Samantha's apartment while she was trying to bathe him, and now the stench wouldn't come out of the upholstery. When she took him to a professional groomer to try to get the smell out, Muffin infused the truck with a baked-in skunk stink. Samantha couldn't get the smell off of her, the dog, her truck or her furniture. And it was still thick enough to make you gag when we drove to Fort McMurray a couple of weeks later to work at the Fort Mac Girlie Bar.

CHAPTER 33

Loonie Toss

F ort McMurray around 2009 was a booming oil town where men with dirty money and nowhere to spend it dug black gold out of the sand and buried their faces in whatever soft thighs they could buy, without a care for tomorrow.

The ratio of men to women was a staggering 10 to 1. These men were bored, horny and rich, and the only choices available to them were the local Walmart and Girlie Bar. The strip club was a known gold mine for dancers, but things were a little different there compared to other provinces. Laws had been put in place to protect the dancers. There was a three-foot chasm between the dancer on stage and the patrons, so they were not able to lay bills on the stage to tip as they did in other places. As a result, they had to get creative, and this creativity was controversial.

The loonie and toonie toss was a fun game that some argued was degrading to women. Sure, one could look at it that way—having coins tossed at you to knock magnets off your butt or into a poster rolled into a cone at your crotch isn't the most dignified method of getting tips—but it had its rewards. So much money would be scattered all over the stage by the end of the game that you needed a big magnet on a string and a bucket to collect it all. Was it a little demoralizing? Sure. But it was *So. Much. Money.*

That was the stage show part of the gig; the other part was the private dances. Again, things were a little different here. There were four private dance areas, and they were all watched by a mean-looking bouncer who was right in the room. We were allowed to touch the customer, but he was not allowed to touch us. The customer sat with his hands glued to the arms of a big comfy chair, his ass glued to the seat and his mouth closed. He was not to move; he could not touch us, grind against us, blow on us, lick or kiss us. If he did, he'd have to contend with the bouncer.

It was interesting having all that power with a big bouncer behind me for protection, but it was strange for me to do lap dances. Everything I had done before had been without contact; fortunately, the well-behaved men made it easy. It was more like they were going to church than a strip club; perfect reverence. They were careful to wear clean clothes, had perfect manners and gave generous tips.

A couple nights of this, and I figured out what was going on: the club was run by a biker gang. Fort McMurray was a small town, and I'm sure every guy who came to the club knew that the consequences for anything but perfect behaviour would be cataclysmic. As a result, no one got too drunk, no one got into fights and no one disrespected the girls. The place was a house of worship, with strippers in the role of goddesses.

My most loyal customer had a gritty darkness about him. He told me that I could do whatever I wanted to him, and I could tell he wanted pain. I was allowed to touch him any way I wanted, and he couldn't move. It was a powerful situation, and I took advantage of that, kneeling hard on his groin, pinching his nipples and choking him. I did all these things slowly and seductively to the music, so as to not alarm the other customers. He stifled groans of pain and pleasure, struggling to stay perfectly still. His eyes twinkled with delight, and he came back night after night for more abuse.

I worked steadily every night for two weeks: non-stop stage shows and private dances. The club took a heavy cut, and at the end of each week, I was the biggest earner. We were staying in the worst hotel in town, the only one that would allow Samantha to have her dog in the room, and we were exhausted at the end of every night. It was an unpleasant situation for "us," as a couple.

When it was all over, we were once again breathing in skunk and dog while driving home through the Rockies, which were shimmering with fresh snow, and I felt grateful for having done it but vowed to myself "never again." Despite our earnings, Fort McMurray felt dismal. Everyone was there solely to make money. There was no quality of life, no soul, no joy.

Shortly after returning home, one of the other dancers contacted me and made me an interesting offer. Her partner ran the club in Fort McMurray, and he wanted to thank me for making them so much money during my time there. She said that I could stay with them in Mexico for a week; they had a spare room, and it would be their pleasure to have me there. I had thought about booking a trip to Cuba, so I decided to take them up on their offer and spend a few days with them before heading to Cuba for a few weeks.

It was a crazy time. I was still dancing at The Playhouse, still doing masturbation shows at home, still going to fetish parties—and now preparing for another big trip. I'd stay at a luxurious mansion in Mexico, then transition to rough backpacking through Cuba.

A couple of days before my trip I was at a party where people were passing around a mirror with lines and straws. It had been at least a year since I had put anything up my nose. I felt that I had gotten that monkey off my back and one line would make the party more enjoyable—no big deal. I snorted the white powder, and it burned like fire. Something wasn't right. I asked through teary eyes, "What the hell was that?!" and someone replied matter-of-factly, "Rock."

I was outraged and confused—I wasn't even sure what rock was. The host laughed, "If you care so much, you should have asked before you snorted it." Then everyone laughed. I explained that I had expected it to be cocaine, and they said they had moved on to crystal meth a while ago.

"What does it do?" I asked.

"Expect to be up for two days," is what I got in reply.

I didn't think it was funny. I left the party right away and spent the next two days and nights in my apartment watching TV and packing for my trip. With no sleep, I got on the plane to Mexico to spend a few days with vacationing biker gang criminals. An opening to a life that I did not want, a story which could not possibly be my own.

I was welcomed at the airport by the dancer I knew and her boyfriend—let's call him Bruce—who I hadn't met. He ran the strip club and was a long-time biker gang member, as well as an immediately likable guy. They were older than you might expect. She was in her late thirties but looked fantastic. He was in his mid-fifties, a cross between a businessman and a tough guy. He was tall and broad, but his easy smile was disarming. He gave me a big hug and took my bags; a perfect gentleman.

They drove me back to their place, a gorgeous Mexican-style mansion. The backyard was lush with flowering bushes and an inviting pool that flowed under the wall into the master bedroom. I'd never seen anything like it. The ceilings were about two stories high, with gilded chandeliers, and my room had its own glorious bathroom. There were also a couple of servants sporting crisp uniforms who were at our beck and call for anything we might've needed.

We immediately changed into our bathing suits for a swim in the afternoon sun. The servants brought us snacks and margaritas. We splashed around and sat by the pool chatting. I learned that we were part of a large group of vacationing biker gang members, but the older set, those who had been around for decades. Couples in their sixties mostly. We would go out for dinners with them as a group; everyone would dress nice and act normal. Old-world mafia was the vibe; no hint of biker gang. This was the business end of things, not the street-level thugs.

Despite all the niceties, I was warned to watch what I say. The entire group looked like regular people, but I supposed that they were legitimately dangerous.

Bruce explained we were being monitored by police and international intelligence agencies and that I would now be connected with them, but as long as I never did anything illegal, I didn't have anything to worry about. It was still disconcerting. I had no idea this was the situation when I accepted the offer to stay with them in Mexico.

So why was I there? They were so impressed with how much money I made for the club that they wanted to hire me to train the other dancers. They wanted me to work full-time at the club.

I squirmed in my seat. I still felt the effects of the meth in my nose and my tired body after being high for two days. I remembered recently crawling all over men, naked, rubbing my boobs in their faces, showing them my pussy. I remembered being on stage, surrounded by money and having coins thrown at me. I remembered all those unhappy people, the oil patch workers, the employees at the club, the other dancers. I looked at this friendly man, who I suspected had spent time in prison, and I didn't want to offend him. My stomach churned with a mixture of fear and dread.

Here I was again, being offered a "promotion" that I didn't want. A big jump from that shabby office job to a busy gang-run strip club while relaxing in a stunning pool at this luxurious mansion in Mexico. Things had gotten more spicy, that's for sure, but it was another door opening to a life that was not right for me. Still, part of me was afraid to say no.

I told Bruce the truth: that I couldn't teach other girls to do what I do. I didn't know why I made him so much money. I didn't know why men lined up for me, why they paid for dance after dance and came back every night to see me. I was so busy I didn't even have to hustle there; there weren't any "techniques" to teach.

He thought about that for a minute as I held my breath.

It was similar to being back at the first strip club where I did so well, and everyone thought I was gaming the system somehow. Whatever I have that draws men in is not immediately apparent to most people. I am not the best-looking woman out there. I don't turn heads on the street. If I were, people probably wouldn't be surprised by my success. Honestly, I don't know what it is that I possess that has this effect on men. Talk about imposter syndrome. I feel like there's been some magical sex spell cast on me that makes some guys go bananas around me when it's time for me to make money using my sex appeal. I truly don't understand it.

After a long silence, Bruce nodded slowly. I think he was expecting a list of tips and tricks to get men to part with their money. Some specific things I said or did, something other girls could learn from me. I don't think he expected me to say that I was as much a mystery to myself as I was to him and everyone else. After all, my success at Fort McMurray wasn't a one-night fluke. It was every single night for two weeks. I made more money than anyone else, by a long shot. I wasn't the hottest woman; I wasn't the best stage dancer; I was neither the most experienced nor a young rookie with that newbie appeal. From Bruce's perspective, there was no reasonable explanation for why I made him so much money.

His girlfriend sat there listening. She had seen me work. She too thought that I must have some special skill for the game.

I apologized. "I would help if I could," I added. "But I honestly don't have anything to teach your other dancers."

I sat there in my boring wet bikini, aware that my body wasn't nearly as nice as his girlfriend's. With my wet hair plastered to my head, I probably looked like a drowned rat.

Bruce finally sighed, had a drink of his margarita and said, "Okay, let's forget the whole thing. Let's just have a great vacation." He was grateful for the money I had made him, and he wanted me to enjoy myself. We spent the next few days going out for nice meals, swimming in the pool, shopping and getting drunk. They *loved* to drink.

Dangerous men came and went from the mansion and quietly talked business by the pool. I was advised to say nothing, to not even look at them. We went out for a couple of lavish meals with a large group of influential heads of organized crime, mostly normal-looking couples with grey hair. One older gentleman took a shine to me because of how tiny I am. He said I was like one of those little pincushions his mother used to use for sewing. That's how I got the nickname Pin Cushion, which sounds bad if you think in terms of intravenous drug use.

My hosts were wonderful. We talked a lot about biker gangs and organized crime. They explained that it was the young hotheads that gave the gangs a bad name and that it was all about making money and running businesses, including legit businesses, not about hurting and killing people. I finally felt comfortable enough to talk about the incident in the other strip club where the "prospect" came after me and beat up my customer. They knew about the incident but hadn't known I was the dancer. They told me that he had been an out-of-control roid monkey off his head on drugs. What he did was not okay, and he was disciplined for it, but he continued to spiral out of control until he stole a bunch of money and was never seen again. Without thinking, I blurted out, "He got away with all that money?" Bruce looked me steadily in the eye and said that I'd never have to worry about him again.

On our last evening together, Bruce and his girlfriend took me to an exquisite restaurant high up on a cliff overlooking the town. Nearby was an infinity pool, which I'd never seen before, and the blue water disappearing over the edge blew my mind. Bruce told me that he was happy that I wouldn't be working for him; he liked me and knew that I could do better in life than work in a strip club in Fort McMurray. Although the pay would be great, he also felt it wasn't the life for me. He was simultaneously one of the nicest and scariest people I'd ever spent time with.

CHAPTER 34

Taxi

From Mexico, I went to Cuba to meet up with Tyler. In a moment of gratitude for his role in changing the course of my life and inspiring me to do what I wanted, I offered to pay for his flight to travel with me somewhere. I was curious to know what it would be like to travel with someone who liked to party all the time and mix with locals at the same time. I anticipated a unique adventure.

We hadn't had sex in a couple of years and Tyler had a girlfriend, but for some reason drinks on the first night ended in sex. Disappointing sex. It will never cease to amaze me how relations can feel one way with someone at one point in life, and then change later on. The brain is certainly the biggest sex organ. It was the last time we ever plowed.

Tyler and I travelled across Cuba staying in "casas particulares," private homes that were Cubans' version of bed and breakfasts. We didn't want to do the all-inclusive resort thing; we wanted to experience the real Cuba.

The Cuban people were beyond lovely. Warm, friendly, relaxed. I loved the classic American cars and the crumbling old buildings; time had stopped decades ago. People gathered in the evenings in town squares, to chat with neighbours, to let their kids play and, for young people, to flirt. At night they danced, and I have never seen anything like it. In a place without much in the way of entertainment, music and dance was their lifeblood. From toddlers to the elderly, *everyone* danced. With smiles on their faces and well-oiled hips, they moved to the music joyfully. Young people danced intensely with each other—gracefully, sensually, making love standing up. Shamelessly, they celebrated the naturalness of sexuality.

I have never been as curious and aroused as I was watching those beautiful Cubans dance. Naturally, I needed to know if they also fucked with the same freedom, joy, coordination and intensity.

Tyler and I were trying to travel from one place to another by bus, but we didn't plan ahead. We arrived at the bus station expecting to hop on a bus only to find out they were full for the next couple of days. I saw a group of taxi drivers standing around chatting, so I approached them to inquire about getting to where we wanted to go. It was the strangest thing—you might not believe it unless you saw it—but among a gaggle of completely ordinary taxi drivers, plain-looking men in their forties and fifties, stood an Adonis of a man. Thirtyish, tall, Paul Bunyan muscular. A sex god straight from the cover of a Harlequin romance novel. He could have easily been a model with his chiselled jaw, flawless coffee-coloured skin, perfect teeth, strong nose, sparkling brown eyes framed by thick, dark lashes, a full head of neatly styled dark hair and a body that was obscene in its perfection. His short-sleeved dress shirt strained to cover his defined biceps, wide shoulders, chest and narrow waist. His tight jeans encased thick, strong thighs and God knows what else.

I tried to address the crowd of taxi drivers as I inquired about travel to another town, but I couldn't help looking at him. I felt that there must be some mistake; he couldn't possibly be a taxi driver. He must be a famous actor or model. The Adonis professionally and dispassionately answered my questions. It would be a six-hour drive overnight, and he could do it. Since the cost wasn't much more than what the bus would have cost us, Tyler and I tossed our bags in the trunk and got in the back.

We drove silently for the first hour. It was dark, and I couldn't see much, so I stared at the back of the driver's head and thick neck. I watched his shoulders move as he drove. The thin cotton shirt disguised little.

We stopped at a gas station to fuel up and all went in to buy some food and drinks. Adonis didn't speak to me; he barely looked at me. Tyler left the shop first, and as I pushed the door open to leave, the driver was right behind me, his hand lightly touching mine on the door. I turned and looked at him. He calmly asked, "Is he your boyfriend?" I smiled and said, "No." In that split second his demeanour changed, and he suggested I sit in the front.

My heart was dancing and bouncing in my chest as my tummy did little flips. My pussy hadn't fully registered what was actually happening yet, but the signals were being sent and received. Tyler looked confused when I got in the front, but I said he would have more room to sleep, and that's exactly what he did.

From my new vantage point, I could properly take in the driver's beauty. His muscular thighs, impossibly thick; his chest; his shoulders; his arms. We didn't talk much. His English wasn't great, and we wanted Tyler to stay asleep. It wasn't long before he reached over and touched my thigh with his big, meaty hand. I was wearing a long, red summer dress. He inched the hem up to put his hand directly on the warm skin of my thigh. All the while he drove. I could see his face as the lights of oncoming traffic cast their spotlights on him. He would glance at me, look back at the road and smile. I ran my fingers up his arm and felt his biceps. His skin was like butter. So smooth, so hot. I slid my hand into the neck of his shirt, undid the first button and felt his chest. It was rock solid and lightly damp with sweat. I brought my fingers to my lips to taste his salt.

At a stop light, he leaned over and kissed me. The feeling of his lips on mine, feeling him inhale me as he tasted my lips, was indescribable. By the time I heard him groan, my pussy was well caught up, and wetness was flowing like one of those chocolate fondue fountains you see at weddings and special events.

He kept smiling and looking at me with lust. His hand pulled my dress up higher as he grazed the sensitive flesh inside my thighs. He found that I wasn't wearing panties, and he grinned widely as his eyes sparkled.

With one hand on the wheel and one hand on my thigh, he manoeuvred the car along quieter countryside roads. I lifted my right leg and put my foot on the dash. My dress was pulled all the way up by now, and his fingers were probing the wetness that was increasing by the moment. My breath quickened, and I pulled the neck of my dress aside to access my nipple. I reached across and felt the hard bulge in his pants. His moan was almost a growl. I stroked his smooth, muscular arm as he thrust his fingers deeper into me. He started working my clit, and it didn't take long. As far as I know, Tyler was asleep in the back seat the whole time, yet the fantasy that he wasn't in fact asleep but secretly watching this whole scene, an exquisite Cuban god, me with my leg up, exposed, cumming, added to the ambiance.

CHAPTER 35

Forbidden Sex

Tyler and I spent about a week in Santiago de Cuba and out on the beaches of Sancti Spiritus before deciding to part ways. He'd met another girl who was travelling back to Havana, and I wanted to keep making my way up the coast.

I met Miguel in the quaint town of Trinidad. He had dark, curly hair and a friendly smile. After a couple days of him playing tour guide, taking me to explore the fishing villages, markets and dance halls—and flirting—I proposed we take things further. He said it wasn't possible; that it was forbidden for tourists and locals to have sex. The government had implemented strict laws to eliminate sex tourism of Cuban prostitutes, and the rules covered both genders.

He explained that there was nowhere we could go; anyone who was caught allowing tourists and locals to have sex in their home or hotel would be in big trouble. He explained that neighbours spy on each other and report anything unusual. I suggested that we could go into the woods or to the beach, but he told me that men watch for this sort of thing and follow... that women get raped that way.

If I was interested in sleeping with him before, knowing that it was forbidden only made Miguel even more appealing. I encouraged him to find a solution. It took him another day, but he said that his sister and her husband had said we could use their place, but we had to come late and leave before the sun came up.

Even though it was dark when we arrived, I could see that it wasn't the Ritz Carlton. Women love romance novels that describe opulent surroundings, castles, high-end hotels or apartments overlooking the city, fancy mansions or villas with the ocean waves crashing outside the window.

But this was a small town in Cuba. No one has mansions or castles there. Miguel's sister's house was small, basic and grubby. Cockroaches scattered when we entered the room. The sheets on the bed were old and worn out, but clean enough. A filthy, rickety fan cooled us as we had sex, and the sex was good. I don't mind a gritty setting; it can make sex feel dirtier, more primal. Most importantly, I got my answer: Cubans *do* fuck like they dance. Those well-oiled hips are made for effective thrusting.

We tried to repeat things the next night, but Miguel's sister's husband turned us away at the door. He said a neighbour had reported them and an inspector had visited that day with a warning. They were being watched, and so were we. We had to leave. I was disappointed and shocked at the thought of being spied on and reported—that neighbours would rat on each other. I just couldn't understand their culture, the world that Miguel lived in.

On my last night in Cuba, the host at my casa particulare took me out dancing to a local spot. I was the only tourist, and it was wonderful to see the sexy Cubans dancing and enjoying themselves. My host had invited his handsome son to join us. He was self-assured and looked so mature puffing on his cigar that I was surprised to learn that he had just turned eighteen. I was not surprised, however, when later that night he quietly slipped into my room and my bed. He had been flirting with me all evening. I asked if he was a virgin and he laughed, saying that he certainly wasn't. The bed was squeaky, and I knew his father could hear us. His father had been interested in me, and I knew this was an awkward situation. We moved to the floor and tried to be as quiet as possible, but his father sulked in the morning and didn't see me off.

On my flight home, I couldn't help but laugh. For a place where sex was forbidden between tourists and locals, I certainly got a lot of action. Of all the places I've been in my life, Cuba had the sexiest people by far.

CHAPTER 36

Goddess Caviar

Back home after Cuba, I was again inundated with Pro Domme session requests. It no longer made sense for me to dance at The Playhouse. I had become, without question, the most popular Domme in Vancouver.

I turned thirty-one at the end of April and thus ended the most eventful and transitional year of my life. I had finally pushed over the soda machine of a vanilla life after rocking it back and forth a few times. I had given up on working for other people in the mainstream world, climbing the corporate ladder, following other people's rules and caring about what people thought of me. I was following my own compass, figuring out what I liked and what I was good at, and that, in turn, ended up being more lucrative than any work I'd done for other people.

My days and nights were filled with catering to the kinky desires of paying customers. Strap-on anal play was the #1 request. I popped a lot of cherries. I wore out many slender vibrating toys warming up virgin asses. I went through boxes of gloves, hundreds of condoms, buckets of lube, many cans of air freshener and boatloads of cleaning products. That leather strap-on harness I had custom-made in San Fransisco years before ended up being very well used.

I did a myriad of other things too. I went through yards of rope tying up cocks and balls, impressive volumes of clothes pegs, hot wax, duct tape, plastic wrap and more cleaning products. I was constantly washing towels and wiping down everything in my apartment.

I had many forgettable clients. A handful were unique, I suppose, and stood out more than others. One good boy used to come by on his lunch break and bring food and dessert to lick off my feet. I'd lay out a plastic sheet and smash the food up with my bare feet, and he'd lick it off. The strange part was that he acted like a dog and wanted me to treat him like one. He'd whimper and pant, lap up the food and woof. He liked to be called a good boy, to be ordered to sit, to clean up everything. I ruffled his hair and petted him. Often being a Professional Dominatrix wasn't as much about Domination as it was fetish fantasy fulfillment.

Another guy created a whole fantasy about his wife sending him to a Dominatrix. He started emailing me, pretending he was his wife in the beginning. I played along, and after a few sessions—after I locked him in chastity and wrote "slut" on his balls with a black marker—he panicked and confessed that his wife knew nothing of this. He had lied and made the whole thing up. He meticulously scrubbed his balls clean before he left so that his wife wouldn't find out what he'd been up to.

I turned down a lot of requests too. If I didn't know how to do something or if I felt uncomfortable with it, I'd say no. But I also tried a lot of stuff, and I was always honest about my lack of experience to the client.

One of these was a request for a full toilet session. If you don't know what that means, it meant he wanted me to shit on him. The client was sweet, polite and patient. He wasn't creepy or pushy. He offered fair compensation for me to try, so I made a plan. I told him that he would need to be there as soon as I woke up in the morning, as that was when I went regularly. He was to be in my neighbourhood, a block or so away from my building. When I woke up, I would text him to ring my buzzer. When he entered, he was to say nothing—just disrobe and lay down with his face under the antique wooden commode chair. He could start stroking himself, but quietly and gently. I would sit down, read my book and try to pretend he wasn't there. I asked him to not swallow, for health reasons, but he could have it on his face or his mouth while he finished himself off, and then I would help him clean up.

It worked. I didn't think it would, but it did. In the early morning light, with the slight sound of a creaking wooden chair, my bare feet resting on his warm chest, I managed to relieve myself onto his face. I watched him stroke and ejaculate a few seconds later. I sprayed air freshener and jumped up to grab the plastic bag to collect my "Goddess Caviar" off his face like an owner scooping up her dog's doo-doo. I wiped up his cum and directed him to the bathroom where he scrubbed his face and carefully rinsed his mouth with strong mouthwash. He then got dressed and left, without saying a word the entire time.

We repeated this every few weeks for a long time, always exactly the same way.

CHAPTER 37

Shoe Weakness

The activities and men from these sessions should have stood out in my memory, but instead I experienced a strange forgetfulness. I could not even recall the details of a client's face after he left. I would remember big things—if he was younger or older, for example—but not much else. After doing a few sessions in a day I found it impossible to remember what they had consisted of. This became problematic when clients returned and reasonably expected me to build on our last scene. I would have to cleverly try to get them to tell me in the form of a confessional or a report on their feelings after the last session.

Many of the activities were the same. I've said before I fucked a lot of asses, and that by far was the main thing I did. There were a few other common themes, like pain sessions and foot worship, but my restrictions were so high that there wasn't much left. I wouldn't give hand jobs or allow the client to touch me above the knees, no nude facesitting, no ass worship. Certainly no intercourse or oral sex of any kind. So when a unique request came in I was thrilled to have the variety. A guy wanted me to walk on him wearing high-heeled shoes. I hadn't trampled anyone since Samara's slave Fat Head, so this was an exciting request for me.

Chris was specific about not wanting platforms like strippers wore; he wanted regular shoes with slender high heels, which I didn't have. I have an unusual shoe size, slightly smaller than most women's footwear comes in. I had worn platform boots when I stripped, even though they were too big. I put thick insoles in them and wore thick socks, but I couldn't do that with shoes. My dressy shoes were conservative-looking; I had bought them from a shop that catered to rich old ladies. Not super sexy like he wanted.

Years before I had seen an image by the famous kinky photographer Roy Stuart of a woman wearing sexy heels standing on a man's chest. That image burned into me: the look on her face of lusty excitement; the look on his face strong and confident even with her standing on his chest, her heels digging into his flesh. She still looked slightly vulnerable too—or perhaps enraptured? An exercise in Dominance and control? Whatever it was, it left a powerful impression. I had enjoyed trampling that furniture slave. Even though it wasn't at all sexy for me at the time, it was definitely fun.

I took the session and told him that he didn't have to pay if he didn't like my footwear. His communication was polite, and he explained that he didn't want to be Dominated, abused or humiliated. He requested I wear regular clothing, not fetish attire. It was all about the shoes. This was his fetish.

He looked about my age, early to mid-thirties, handsome in a clean-cut and well-mannered way. His twinkling blue eyes were endearing. He was shy at first, but I figured out that it was because he was trying to hide his crooked teeth. He unbuttoned his shirt and laid on the floor. His torso was toned, tanned and smooth. He wasn't a Chippendale dancer, but he was easy on the eyes. I stood on him like I'd seen in that photo, and I felt sexy. He smiled up at me, but then looked a bit disappointed as he looked at my boring shoes on his chest. They were standard black but shorter heels. The session went okay, and he left. I didn't think I'd hear from Chris again.

However, he contacted me a couple days later, asking if I'd be okay with him getting me a pair of shoes to use for another session. He said he had done some research online and found a gorgeous pair of size-four heels. I said it was fine, and the next time he showed up he brought the most spectacular pair of shoes I had ever seen. They were Stuart Weitzmans: a gorgeous dark shade of cherry red with a gold, slender six-inch heel, ending in a sharply pointed toe.

This session went much better. We clicked, even though I only walked on him and jerked him off by rubbing the shoes against his cock. He called it a shoe job, which I'd never heard of before. Chris was so enthralled with the shoes that his excitement was contagious, plus he was nice to look at and had such sweet manners. I looked forward to seeing him again.

The next time Chris brought a bottle of wine. We opened it after the session and had a drink together, getting better acquainted. I asked how he had developed a fetish for trampling. He said he didn't know, but he blushed and looked away. I didn't push it.

The next time he brought wine again and asked if we could drink it during the session. For safety, I had a policy of avoiding drugs and alcohol during a session, but this felt innocent enough. After all, we were just doing the same thing as before. I sipped a little, but it was a challenge for Chris to drink while flat on his back, which is how he spent the whole session. I tried pouring some in his mouth but ended up spilling it all over his face. I nearly fell trying to stand on his chest while he coughed and laughed.

Before our next session, I found a glass with a pouring spout in a second-hand store. I used it to pour quite a bit of wine into Chris's mouth. He loved it. We ended up going way over time. He always booked as my last client of the evening, so it didn't matter. We got tipsy and laughed a lot. I noticed his cock for the first time—really noticed it. It was an impressive cock, and I suddenly wanted him. My boundaries had been made clear from the start—no oral sex or intercourse—and he had honoured them. Though Chris never tried to kiss me or cross a professional line, I knew he liked me.

The next session went similarly to the last, but it was an extra-steamy session. I had edged Chris the whole time but did not let him cum. After the hour he paid for had passed, when I felt like I was technically off the clock, I looked him in the eye and asked him if he wanted me. Chris looked puzzled, not sure if this was a trick question. I made myself clearer, "Do you want to fuck me? This is off the clock. No extra charge. This is just me, a real person, not the Domme, asking you Chris, not my client, if you would like to have sex with me."

He replied, "Yes, but I feel like you should know my name is actually Carl. I used a fake name, 'cause that's what you do. Ya know?"

We both laughed. I joked that I had kept him on the edge for nearly an hour, so it was unlikely he would turn down an opportunity to have sex—"Unless you don't like sex and only want to be jerked off with shoes?"

Carl assured me that he liked regular sex too, and it was on. I pulled my trundle bed out from the wall, and we started to kiss. I could feel my heel marks on his chest with my fingertips. I could tell he was nervous and unsure of what to do in this situation, so I took the lead. I would have loved more of a warm-up, but I didn't want to instruct him to lick my pussy in case he thought I might have an STI. I understood the stigma attached to sex work; even though I didn't have sex with my clients, we are still often viewed as being "dirty."

If this doesn't sound hot and steamy, that's because it wasn't—not yet. It was clumsy and awkward at first, both of us unsure whether we should be doing it at all. Unsure also of what it meant. I kept thinking about that nice cock though, and I hadn't been with anyone in a while. I craved closeness. So I put a condom on Carl and straddled him. He was sitting with his back against my headboard, so I rode him like that, kissing him, his lips, his neck, his shoulder. I took him hard and fast, like the hungry woman that I was. I expected him to cum quickly, with that level of intensity, but he did not. He stayed rock hard while I used his cock for my pleasure until my legs gave out.

On our first non-work date, I explained that I felt strongly about non-monogamy. "Full disclosure," I told Carl. "I will never be happy in a traditional monogamous relationship." I asked him if he thought he could deal with a non-monogamous arrangement. Carl reluctantly said he would try.

We started spending a lot of time together. I still trampled him but much more casually. We didn't have structured paid sessions anymore, and we went out drinking a lot. I don't know why Carl drank, but he was a happy drunk. We frequented a gay bar for its fancy cocktails and great music even though Carl was completely heterosexual. We went to nice wine bars and got a taste for rough California Zinfandels. My favourite was called *Seven Deadly Zins*, which I was sure tasted like the filthy, mouldy vinyl backseat of a 1960s car on a hot summer's day. If the wine didn't kick me in the face and put up a fight on the way down, it wasn't meaty enough for me.

Drinking became such a hobby for us that there was barely anything beyond drinking, hangovers and work. I took fewer sessions so that I could hang out with Carl more. We didn't have much sex, but we bonded quickly. When, a month into the relationship, I received a message out of the blue from David asking if I wanted to go to Burning Man with him again, it should have been a difficult decision. Things were still new with Carl, but we were certainly involved.

I wanted to go. I had loved my first Burning Man and not just because of David—although I knew by the way I reacted when I heard his voice on the phone that I was still infatuated with him; my body heated up, and I started to perspire. I felt short of breath, and my knees felt weak. I said yes. Carl didn't take the news well, but I stood my ground. Burning Man was about a month away.

It was around the same time that Larry contacted me for the first time. He was the wealthy, eccentric guy who Samara used to talk to on the phone all the time. Larry told me they were through, and he was interested in serving me. I felt suspicious, but then he said that he knew I was a size four and had already found some beautiful designer shoes he'd love to send me. "I just need your mailing address." *Dammit.* For every person, there is a bait which they cannot resist. Carl was desperate for me to trample him in sexy shoes and boots, but they were nearly impossible to find in my size. So I gave Larry a chance, reluctantly, even though my gut told me he was trouble.

The first box arrived: a half-dozen pairs of the most exquisite footwear I had ever seen, and most of them fit me perfectly. They were all by high-end designers like Gianmarco Lorenzi. Carl was like a kid at Christmas. He kept having me try them on and trample him. So, for Carl, I let Larry into my life. He would call and talk for hours about nonsense. He would mostly ramble to be heard and didn't need me to say much.

Larry gossiped about Samara mostly, sharing all kinds of personal details even when I told him it was inappropriate and none of my business. He talked about how perfect her ass was and how on their trips together they would sleep with his face right against her ass so that he could lick her asshole whenever he woke up in the night. He said she loved it. I was shocked. I was still under the impression that Pro Dommes didn't allow oral sex of any kind. But I was sheltered; the only other Pro Domme I'd met was her.

When he went on about her perfect ass, Larry didn't hesitate to point out that my ass was bigger than he liked. Actually, he didn't find me particularly attractive; he was serving me hoping to make Samara jealous. I should have ended it, but the shoes and boots kept coming. On the heels of all that, it was time to leave for Burning Man.

CHAPTER 38

Temptation

The trip began eerily similar to the year before. David picked me up on the corner in his convertible, and we drove across the border and south to Vegas, where we would rent an RV. David refused to tent it again. We got along like a house on fire, chatting about everything under the sun all day as we drove. We awkwardly had sex the two nights on the way down, but something had certainly changed. It was good, but we were both holding back.

When we arrived at Burning Man and met up with Ryan and Candace, the most adorable little kitty hopped out of their RV and changed everything.

Her name was Tess, and she was the twenty-year-old plaything of Ryan and Candace. She wore pink fuzzy cat ears, boy shorts, sneakers and not much else. Cute didn't even begin to describe her, as she had a devilish smile and endearing giggle that pulled at your heart and groin at the same time. David and I both looked at her like some apparition.

When I say Tess was cute, I mean she was truly adorable. She could flash a wide-eyed look like a kitten, and any resistance would melt. Petite with a perky bubble butt, tiny waist, small pert breasts that she loved to show off, curly brown hair cropped a little past her ears, a little turned-up nose, pouty lips and big, brown eyes. Those wide eyes turned ever so slightly down on the outside edges, giving her a steadily pleading expression. People gave her whatever she wanted. All the time.

She flirted with us both unabashedly; the damage was swift and complete. The next morning when we woke up I initiated sex with David, and he obliged, but he wasn't into it. That was the last time we ever had sex.

David and I both fell completely under Tess's spell. After Burning Man we both started dating her, which meant that we spent a lot of time together. Carl wasn't happy about that, but at least David and I weren't having sex. Carl had been so devastated by me going to Burning Man with David that I threw Tess at him. I encouraged them to have sex. I even took pictures. I wanted him to see that non-monogamy had its perks for both of us. It was like pulling teeth though, and he cooperated only reluctantly.

I bought a book on polyamory, a kind of "how-to" book for introducing non-monogamy into your relationship. The chapter that tackled jealousy explained that a healthy poly relationship is not defined by a lack of jealousy, but by healthy processing of uncomfortable feelings. Carl had a sour look on his face. I may as well have been explaining astrophysics to a five-year-old. We read it together, but he didn't want to. Carl's possessive, jealous nature was showing, but I chose to ignore it.

The furniture slave who had served Samara reached out again and begged to see me. He said he'd been driven off by Webster during one of his psychotic episodes. I agreed to see him, which meant hours of sitting on his face in yoga pants or jeans, but he served me with minimal enthusiasm. I understood that I wasn't his first choice. He preferred a Mistress who was meaner, colder, more sadistic.

For all of his fearmongering of his former Mistress, he was clearly addicted to the thrill of being involved with someone manipulative and dangerous. A lot of slaves are, the way some women are attracted to bad boys—they want a woman who is dangerous, unpredictable, unhinged. They're excited by it. Those slaves found me too nurturing, too safe, too boring. They might stick around for a while because I could fake it to a point, but they didn't fall for me like they did the others. I did not *truly* control them.

The furniture slave would come over for extended sessions in which I just ignored him and used his face as a chair. His goal was to be so comfortable as a chair that I would forget he was even there. He did have a big, squishy melon of a head, but chairs don't have noses. Despite him flattering himself with the nickname "flat face," I could never forget that his mouth was pressed against my crotch, carefully stealing sips of air. I'd trample him in bare feet or with socks too, but mostly I sat on him.

He was also a gossip who shared way too much information about his previous Mistress and Samara. When people think, "Oh, if the furniture could talk!" they don't think that a slave who quietly pretends to be a chair is listening with both ears and could blab about all that he heard.

He would often tell me that I should give Heel Guild a chance, that he felt I had a talent for video. Webster had warned me about Heel Guild, a fetish film production company in town. He said they were bad people. Besides, I'd tried video, and it didn't work out. Nope, no more filming for me. It wasn't in the cards. I took his advice about as seriously as I would have listened to a kitchen table.

I was still doing in-person sessions. Many of my friends needed money, so I tried to help them out by creating sessions where they could participate. I did girl-girl voyeur shows with Tess, as I had with Samantha. I did sessions where Tess was my submissive and guys could watch me do things to her. I introduced her to Larry over the phone, and he started sending Tess footwear and other presents. He was more excited about serving her; she had the figure he preferred, thinner with a smaller bum, but she wasn't Dominant, and at twenty years old she was so naive … or so I thought.

I created a glory hole in my apartment through which another girlfriend would suck a guy's cock while he looked through the peephole at me. Carl and I would put on a fuck show for the guy to watch. The glory hole got loads of attention but not many actual bookings. It was one of the dirtier, more creative ideas I tried out.

Meanwhile, I was getting many session requests from exciting cities, and one was particularly appealing. A guy wrote one day that he would send me $100 for me to take his phone call. I accepted and got my first introduction to Financial Domination and cuckolding. I admit, I had to Google what it was. He told me he was a paypig and got off on women making him spend a lot of money on them. He wanted women to make fun of his small penis and tell him about fucking real studs. He encouraged me to come to his city so that he could take me shopping.

When I mentioned to Larry that I was thinking of going for a work trip, he said that Tess and I should come to Philadelphia to visit him. He would put us up in the highest-end hotel, and we'd dine in the nicest restaurants. He'd cover our airfare, all expenses, plus a generous tribute.

Larry had come to Vancouver a few times to see me; we had gone for lunch one time, and another time I brought him back to my place briefly and pissed on him in the bathtub. He had tried to lick my pussy without permission, so I knew Larry was one to push boundaries, but I felt I could control him. I made it clear that there would be no sexual contact between him and I or him and Tess.

In the big city, I had a handful of sessions lined up at two different dungeon-for-hire places: Cleopatra's, which was a dark, cold and gritty place that smelled of ammonia, and Lyceum's, which was a classier and friendlier establishment. I met up with the paypig cuckold, and we went shopping for lingerie.

He was a small, tightly wound, sarcastic man that displayed no sign of being submissive. He ran a huge, successful company and was filthy rich. When it was time for him to pay for the lingerie, the bill came to nearly $1,000; I expected him to tell me to go fuck myself, but he shrugged, laughed and paid. I couldn't tell if he thought what we were spending was a lot or not enough. He was difficult to read but talked constantly about his fetishes.

He explained what about cuckolding turned him on—the idea that a beautiful woman would have better sex with another man and rub his nose in it. He loved the thrill of humiliation, knowing that his little cocklet couldn't satisfy a woman. He liked being used for his money because his dicklet wasn't good enough.

The next day I told him to take me shopping again, this time for a video camera. I had made a deal with a friend back home who wanted a specific one that if I could get it for free, I'd sell it to him for 25% less than retail. The camera was pricey, and again he laughed when I told him to pay. He did though, and as we left the store, he said that was the most any woman had got out of him in one go. It was exhilarating. I couldn't believe this guy had just bought me something so expensive—and I didn't have to do anything for it.

Then he requested that I make him a personalized vid; I didn't have to, but he'd love it if I filmed myself having sex with my boyfriend. It was important that I also looked into the camera lens and addressed him, that I made fun of his small penis. He said it would be especially amazing if I did a snowball, where my boyfriend came in my mouth, then showed it to him (to the camera) and pretended to spit it into his mouth. The idea of him having to swallow my boyfriend's cum would be extra degrading.

I felt a little guilty about spending so much of his money, so I wanted to create that vid for him.

As well as things were going in some regards, the wheels were coming off on the whole Philadelphia part of the trip. I was supposed to go to Philly in about four days but had heard from Tess that Larry had changed her flight to get into Philadelphia two days before my arrival. He wanted two days alone with her. I called him and asked what was going on. Did he think that he was going to take advantage of young, naive Tess without me there?

Larry confessed that he hoped to seduce her but wouldn't have made her do anything against her will. I blew my top. David had trusted me to take care of Tess. He wasn't comfortable with the idea of her going in the first place, but I insisted that I would ensure she would be safe. I cancelled the Philadelphia part of the trip and told Larry neither of us was coming. He accused me of being jealous. He said that he and Tess had been talking a lot and that she wasn't as innocent as I thought she was. I felt sick to my stomach. Larry was insane, and I had come close to exposing my girlfriend to someone who was clearly manipulative, entitled and disrespectful. He was the type to push and push boundaries for the thrill of seeing how much he could get.

I had felt confident that I could hold my boundaries firm, but Tess was a different story. She needed money, and I could see her being tempted to do things she wasn't comfortable with to get it. A poor twenty-year-old girl and a rich, manipulative, crazy old man... what a horrible combination.

The rest of my trip went well despite Larry blowing up my phone the whole time, leaving horrible messages about me owing him for the flights and hotel—that I had screwed him over and if I didn't pay him back, he would get revenge.

Back in Vancouver, I was happy to have a boyfriend to return to. Carl had become my best friend, and he was fascinated with my business. It was fun and reassuring to share my life with him. He was game to help create the vid for my cuckold paypig and helped me with the technical aspects. That's when I filmed my first sex scene, for an audience of one.

We had sex, and then I jerked Carl off into my mouth, which was extremely challenging because Carl took forever to ejaculate, and I hated both the taste and smell of cum. I did it though, and the vid turned out surprisingly well. I sent it to the paypig, and he loved it. I then sold the camera to my friend and figured that was it for my porn film career.

CHAPTER 39

Vengeance

Carl and I decided to go to India for two months after Christmas, but he wanted me to meet his family first, so we drove to Saskatoon with his sister for the holidays. His family loved me, and I had finally found what I had been longing for. I didn't get to enjoy it for long, though.

Tess phoned me on Christmas Day and said, "Larry called my parents' house last night."

"What?" I stammered. "Why would he do that? How did he get their number?"

"He must have figured it out from our conversations about what my father did for a living, and he had my real name from booking the ticket," she explained.

Fuck.

"So what did he say? What happened?" I asked.

"He told my mother that her daughter was involved in pornography and prostitution in Vancouver," Tess when on.

I gasped, "Oh my god! What a fucking psycho. What did your mom say?"

"She hung up on him and then asked me what was going on. I told her that he was the crazy ex-boyfriend of one of my friends trying to cause trouble and to hang up on him again if he calls back."

I was shocked and impressed with her quick thinking and told her so. "Wow, I don't think I could have come up with a lie that fast. Did she buy that? Are you okay?"

"Yeah, I'm fine. A bit shaken up, but that's got to be the worst thing he could do. Hopefully, it's over now. So glad we didn't go to Philly to meet him."

I felt guilty. "I'm so sorry I got you tangled up in this."

"It's okay," Tess said warmly, even giggling. "It's all pretty interesting, and a learning experience."

What a fucking nutter, though. He called Tess's mother again a week later, but she hung up on him. We never heard from Larry again.

CHAPTER 40

How Did You Do That?

India with Carl was unexpectedly different from when I went there on my own. He wanted to continue to drink as we had in Canada, but India isn't set up for it. Alcohol was harder to find, and when you did manage to find it, it was expensive. If we ordered a few drinks in a restaurant, they were served with disapproving looks. And being hungover there with the heat, stink and noise was unbearable.

Things kept going wrong. We got scammed several times, and we ended up on a nightmare houseboat where we both got food poisoning. Carl struggled with it and hated it. Finally, after about a month, he snapped and suggested we fly to Thailand to get a break from India. Off we went, and we spent a week partying in Bangkok and on the island of Koh Phi Phi. Carl was truly happy there, but I felt obligated to go back to India. We hadn't done the camel safari in the desert yet. That had been one of the highlights of my first trip, and I wanted him to experience it. Carl reluctantly agreed.

The camel safari was great, but the rest of our time in India was challenging. Every step of the way someone was trying to scam us out of money, always telling us things were more expensive than they were. It went beyond haggling, which I was used to doing. Cabs would drive us around and around, never actually taking us to our destinations yet still trying to charge us the full fare. Hotels would try to charge us for nights we didn't stay there, and so on.

This wasn't the India I had loved four years prior. I wasn't sure how much of it was the place and how much of it was me; had I become a princess? Looking at India through Carl's eyes made the flaws more prominent. Despite the many frustrations, our relationship sparkled. We laughed and pulled together during the difficult times. In any case, Carl and I were both glad to board the plane back home.

I went straight back to work taking Pro Domme sessions. The furniture slave was still serving me, and he continued trying to talk me into at least meeting the people who ran Heel Guild to discuss filming with them. I finally said yes and was surprised by how warm and welcoming they were. Gaspman appeared strong on the outside but soft on the inside. By that I mean he looked like he could move a boulder, but he would kiss a lady's hand with the gentleness of a butterfly. Dickie, in contrast, was a wiry fella, slight and tightly wound.

We discussed what had happened with Webster and how that put me off the idea of filming.

Gaspman carefully and respectfully explained, "Our site is made up of a variety of Goddesses. Our vids cover FemDom themes: foot worship, trampling, pony play, ass worship and facesitting. You only do what you're comfortable with." He delivered that last part without expectation. It was simply an invitation. "Maybe we can start with a simple foot worship scene where you show your feet to the camera and talk to the viewer who will be jerking off to your feet. Do you feel comfortable with that?"

I sat in the chair wearing regular clothes and socks and imagined one of my clients who had a thing for socks and feet. I talked to him, teased him, seduced him. It felt silly and simple, but when I finished and looked up, they were all staring at me as if I'd levitated. There was complete silence for a solid minute before one of them asked, "How did you do that?"

I shrugged. Having never seen a video like that before, I genuinely didn't understand. I had nothing to compare it to; I just did what I thought they wanted me to do. The furniture slave started grinning ear to ear. "See?" he said to them. "I told you."

Heel Guild booked me for a full shoot after that. Photos and video. We filmed a couple of vids where I played the role of a young, mean girl called "Princess" who dominated my "Uncle Ernie." We did pony riding and facesitting with panties on.

These vids shot straight to #1 on clips4sale's Top 50 list—whatever that meant; I had no idea. I really thought they were trying to boost my confidence. I thought the scenes were fun but silly. Other than what little I did with Samara and in sessions, I didn't have an understanding of what these vids were supposed to be about.

We shot a few more "Princess and Uncle Ernie" vids, and the Heel Guild people were going wild for them. Every time we released a vid, they would clamour for three more. They were paying me a decent amount, so I was happy to oblige, but I had no concept of the business. I never even saw the finished product. I was told all of my vids were getting into the Top 10, often going straight to first place, and that was enough for me.

The private session business was booming, and I had befriended a few other local Dommes, as well as trained one who was renting my space to do sessions. I felt it was time to expand, so I rented a bigger space. I went from a tiny bachelor suite with a pull-out trundle bed where I lived and worked to a palatial two-bedroom apartment with a large solarium, storage space and two bathrooms. My plan was to open up a "Domme House" styled after Arena's in New York, a rental space for other Dommes and a place to hold kinky parties.

I held the first foot worship parties in Vancouver there. They started out small, with about a dozen Dominant women. Some were escorts, some were Pro Dommes, and some were friends— vanilla women with a kinky side. We had about an equal number of slaves, and though the parties were excruciatingly awkward at the beginning, they were always fun after folks loosened up. They were also profitable enough to motivate me to have more.

As soon as I moved into the bigger space, the other areas of my life took a dip. Carl and I weren't doing well. I craved more variety in our sex life, but he was becoming less receptive to non-monogamy than ever. We went to an open-minded counsellor who specialized in working with couples "in the lifestyle," which is another way of saying "non-monogamous." After a few sessions, she told us (in the kindest way possible) that we were doomed and that we might as well call it a day.

It was a lack of alignment, she explained; I had been on the racetrack for a while, experimenting and liking non-monogamy, but Carl wasn't even in the stands. "And he doesn't want to be," she added emphatically. It was an odd analogy, but the message was clear. It wasn't long before Carl and I broke up, after being together for a year.

CHAPTER 41

Full Service

Since Carl and I called it quits, I decided it was a good time to try "full service." After all, I was single and horny. I had developed friendships with some high-end escorts, and I was curious about that end of the business. I figured it was similar to what I had done, a cross between the voyeur shows and fetish sessions, but with intercourse. Men had been begging me to offer full service, especially on the escort review site where I, the only non-escort on the site, was so frequently discussed. So I set my rate high and made the announcement.

A mix of excitement and outrage followed. Yes, outrage that I would set my rate so high—above what most men could afford—when I was essentially a novice escort. I didn't offer anal or allow men to cum in my mouth, and my bed skills were unproven. It amused me to see how angry it made some of these men to think they might finally have a chance to fuck me but then realize they couldn't afford it.

My first client was an older professional gentleman in a wheelchair. His legs didn't work, but his cock definitely did. My place wasn't wheelchair accessible, so I had to go to his home when his wife was out. I was his esteemed guest, and he couldn't have been friendlier. Unfortunately, I could find nothing about him to be attracted to. We had sex twice in the bedroom; he had a lot of stamina and certainly wanted more than I was able to keep up with. When we took a break, he asked me to go to the bathroom to get his pee jug. I did, he urinated in it and I took it back to the bathroom to dump and rinse. As I was doing so, I concluded that this had to be the unsexiest sexual experience I had ever had.

He offered me more money to stay longer and keep going, but I politely declined. He gave me a rave review on the escort site, but I didn't know why. I was as nice as I could be but doubt that I remotely faked arousal well enough to be convincing even to the most hopeful, delusional man.

My next client was also well-mannered. This time, he was more of a down-to-earth, blue-collar type. Not bad looking, a little heavy with a big cock. Again, stamina. He fucked me for an hour straight and was charging straight into the second hour when I had to interrupt him. I simply could not go on and told him that I would be happy to refund half of his money. I didn't mention this fact, but I was raw. I was convinced he was fucking me with a blowtorch. He was so sweet about it and said that he was happy to cuddle and chat for the second hour. No need to return any money. Again, he gave me a rave review, and I didn't understand why.

I told my escort friends about my first two experiences, and they called it unusual bad luck; the guy is not paying for intercourse the whole time, no matter how much he pays. In fact, usually the higher the rate, the more they're paying for quality companionship, conversation and intimacy. One of these escort friends, Vicky, said she would bring me on a date with one of her regular clients to show me the difference. "I should warn you, though," she added. "He is a bit eccentric."

Vicky and I met up with Magnus for lunch, and right away I could tell that "eccentric" was an understatement. He was a tall, pot-bellied man in his fifties clad in a loudly patterned designer shirt, the sleeves rolled up to display his flashy rolex. His protruding forehead and wide-spread buggy eyes gave him an almost alien look. Magnus was keen to come across as intelligent, sharing his opinions loudly, trying to get a rise out of people.

"Waitress, get me a sparkling water with a slice of lemon in a tall glass half-filled with ice. Tell the manager the music in here is shit and if he wants to drive away customers, he should keep playing it," he rudely spat at our server in an abrasive German accent.

Vicky was nonplussed by his behaviour. He had been her client for years, and I suppose she was used to him. She argued with him over politics, world affairs and even the smallest things. They both enjoyed the debate. Neither took any of it personally. I listened politely, trying to give off an air of reserved intelligence. Better to keep my mouth shut, I thought.

We went back to his place. Magnus wanted to show off his mansion. He had mentioned something about hoping his wife would be home. I thought he was joking, but when we arrived, she was indeed home, sitting in her office. We could see her through the window while he was giving us the tour of the backyard to show off the fancy pool he had specially designed and installed.

Vicky and I were dressed discreetly and casually, but we were still attractive women, so I couldn't imagine what his wife was thinking. Magnus fixed us drinks and gave us a tour of his antique weapons collection in showcases all over his house. I learned bit by bit that he and his wife were in the middle of a messy divorce and he had brought us to their house for the sole purpose of making her angry. I looked around at all the weapons and couldn't help but see the humour in the situation. It was so horrible it was funny... as long as she didn't kill us.

Over the next couple hours, we drank while Magnus played the piano for us, until eventually he decided that he wanted to have sex with me on the dining room table, right where his wife ate her breakfast every morning. There had been nothing sexual up to that point, so I was taken back by the idea, but I remembered that I was there for sex; that was my job.

It was mechanical and absurd: I was a prop, a thing to upset his wife. I took off my clothes and laid back on the table in this opulent room surrounded by firearms, antique daggers and hatchets. Vicky had undressed and was reclining on a chaise by the table, watching. Magnus got undressed, put the condom on his smallish penis and penetrated me. He was humping away, assessing the situation in his stern, Germanic manner, "Sehr Gut!" when suddenly he glanced past me, and his face shifted into a look of gleeful satisfaction. His wife had entered the room with a video camera and was recording us. I didn't want my face filmed, but I didn't want to look away in case she did something violent. She didn't say anything. Magnus laughed. He thought it was hilarious. What a lunatic.

I took my cues from Vicky and Magnus to play it cool, but inside I was shaken. Vicky and I left shortly after.

That was near the end of my experiment with escorting. I had sex for money a handful of times after that, and they were not bad but not terribly memorable either. Overall, it simply didn't suit me. To be a good escort, you must be genuinely service oriented. The client is paying you to satisfy them sexually. They may be nice about it, and they may even make a big deal about wanting you to enjoy it as well, but at the end of the day you're selling a service, and that service is sex.

Pro Domme sessions are slightly different in that you can be firmer, you can assert your boundaries or even change them in the moment, and it's more acceptable. Slightly more respect is granted to a Pro Domme. It's also a lot less intimate giving a hand job than being penetrated. The differences might seem minor to most people, but I knew my direct manner was better suited to Professional Domination than escorting.

CHAPTER 42

Open Your Own Clips Store

I missed Carl. I missed his companionship and the laughs we had. I didn't miss the sex and the possessiveness, but I was lonely. I didn't want to be single and alone, and I became a bit depressed. After six weeks Carl called me and asked if I wanted to go for a drink. "I feel like we could at least be friends," he added. I met him at one of our old haunts, and I learned that in the last six weeks Carl had launched his own online shoe job clips store featuring various pretty women jerking him off with their shoe-covered feet. He had bought a camera, learned how to edit, had hired a few amateur models and was already making money. I offered to help him out by doing a few shoe job vids for him. It was fun filming, watching him edit and then seeing the sales roll in. It wasn't much money, but I could see the potential.

Carl and I started hanging out and filming more. After a few weeks, I made a proposition to the folks at Heel Guild. I asked how much they would pay me if I filmed scenes for them on my own and gave them the raw footage to edit and release on their clips store.

They said the max they could pay would be $600/month because their business model was about having multiple performers and, even though my stuff sold the most, they needed to keep an even mix of other Goddesses. "What you ought to do," they advised, "is open your own clips store."

I was surprised to hear that. The team at Heel Guild surely must've understood they risked losing me and the impact that could have on their numbers. No performer had ever received so much fan mail and no one else's vids sold as well, but I didn't know that yet. They would tell me later, but at that point I had no idea how well-received I was. Opening my own clips store had the potential to do extremely well and could certainly make me significantly more money than Heel Guild could ever pay me. I was surprised by their integrity. They could have kept filming with me and not advised me to go out on my own. I respected that, so I told them I would continue to shoot for them as well.

I asked Carl if he would help me start my own clips store. It was at that time that I received an eviction notice. It had somehow been discovered that I was holding "sex parties" in my apartment, and my landlord wanted me out. However, that wasn't exactly true—they were just foot worship parties—but still. I could have fought the eviction; I wasn't doing anything illegal, but my business plan of renting out dungeon space wasn't taking off as I'd hoped. I decided to move into a smaller place and abandon the dungeon rental idea. I wondered how they had found out about the parties, though. I had been careful and discreet. Someone had betrayed me.

Carl and I filmed a few scenes in the old place and continued in the new place. We opened the clips store with ten vids all at once and released one a day while filming more content. Some of those first vids were cuckolding scenes with a cool older guy from the US nicknamed Toy. The first time I jerked Carl off into my hand and fed it to Toy, it was completely unrehearsed; we hadn't even discussed it beforehand. But the spontaneous risk played well. The scenes had a raw amateur feel since we were still figuring things out, and this gave them an air of authenticity.

Our first month, my store climbed to fourth place overall on clips4sale. With less than forty vids in my inventory, that was a remarkable accomplishment. Several of them rocketed into first place. Our first cheque for our first full month from clips4sale was US $12,176.31. With the exchange rate at the time, that was over $14K Canadian. It's like we had won the lottery!

From that point forward, we put all of our energy into filming content. I barely took any sessions. I tried to keep things from getting serious with Carl. He didn't want non-monogamy, and I did, which was a recipe for disaster. Between shoe jobs for his clips store and hand jobs and intercourse for mine, Carl was kept thoroughly milked. I, on the other hand, was increasingly frustrated by hollow sex devoid of satisfaction.

Filmed sex is not intimate, especially when you're also shooting it yourself. You're always thinking about camera angles, dialogue, sweating under the blazing lights, etc. I had few opportunities to take other lovers because I knew it would upset Carl, plus filming and editing took up so much time, but I did manage the occasional tryst.

The big city was calling again, and Carl was keen to go. He hadn't done much travelling before he met me and, like a lot of people who all of a sudden start making a lot more money, Carl was eager to spend it. We took a few clients to pay for the trip; most notably, my cuckold paypig who paid us $1,000 for me to jerk Carl off in my mouth and then snowball the cum into his, just as I had done in the vid. That was it. In and out in about twenty minutes. Carl and I literally skipped down the street to the first bar we came to and started drinking. Oh yes, the boozing never stopped.

He and I unofficially fell back into a relationship after a few months. I knew it was a bad idea, but things were going so well with the business. Carl and I took a romantic trip to Europe and decided to move in together so that we could get a bigger place that was better suited for filming.

I opened a paid members-only site and hired David to manage the project. David and I had grown into close friends while he was still with Tess, and then even closer after she was out of both of our lives. She had turned out to be a skillfully manipulative sociopath. Tess used her charms to get what she wanted from people, and if she didn't get what she wanted, she had a temper tantrum. When people were no longer useful to her she tossed them aside callously. She only took, never gave back. Had Larry seen what I had not been able to? I wonder what would have happened between them in Philadelphia?

No sexual tension remained between David and I, but a strong bond had taken its place. I felt vindicated; I had been right about our special connection, but it wasn't a romantic one as I had imagined.

David offered helpful business advice, including setting me up with a great accountant and ensuring that I listed myself as the sole owner of the business with Carl as a contractor. David was always kind to Carl, despite Carl being venomously jealous of him, but David made it clear that I should protect myself, "Just in case things don't work out, Tracey."

Around this time I sort of came out to the family that hadn't been kept in the loop that I'd changed from regular jobs to sex work. My mother knew everything as it happened. My father knew some details, but he wasn't the type to ask a lot of questions. He never wanted me to feel like I was being interrogated or judged. That was actually how I would describe most of my family on both sides. Despite my coming home for annual visits, the topic of my work just didn't seem to come up for a while, but some of them noticed I seemed to have more financial security, bought real estate and took a lot of trips. My family has always struggled financially and never really travelled, so they notice things like that.

One day I was visiting my aunt and uncle when they very gently broached the topic: "We want you to know that we get you're different and living a different life. We want you to know that we love and support you, no matter what you're doing. You can tell us if you want to."

I was a little surprised by the intervention feel of the conversation, but I did feel safe telling them. "I'm a Dominatrix, and I make fetish porn films."

They looked at each other and smiled. My uncle left the room and returned with a set of BDSM nipple clamps and something that looked like a stainless-steel syringe, but almost the size of a soda can. I immediately could see how the stumpy tip could be used to insert lube into an anus to aid in anal insertion. I later learned it was a veterinary syringe for administering medication.

My uncle handed the items to me, explaining, "Some of the family thought you were escorting, and if that was the case, it was fine, but I guessed you were a Dominatrix, so I got you these things. I just picked them up at Value Village to give to you in case I was right. I wanted you to really feel that we celebrate whatever you choose to do with your life. We love you."

Touching, right? A little weird, but touching.

Explaining to both of my Christian grandmothers was slightly less touching. I got just enough of an explanation out for them to stop me and say they didn't need to know much. They could see I was healthy and doing well. As long as I was being safe, it was fine.

You see, I come from people who have mostly never left the slow-paced rural communities they'd been born into. They get low-paying jobs or collect unemployment, get married, have kids, take care of their parents in their old age, and that's about it. The bar is set pretty low. Unwanted teen pregnancies are common, and after that, alcoholism, drug addiction, domestic abuse and gambling problems are a part of most families at some point. That I had never asked them for money or help counted for a lot. They figured whatever I was doing across the country in the big city must be okay, and it was none of their business to judge.

CHAPTER 43

Classy Filth

Carl had little to do with the business and marketing end of things. He ran the camera, performed and did some editing. I enjoyed editing, so once Carl showed me how to do it I ended up doing it myself. I paid him 25% at first and 35% later, and I performed in his shoe-job vids for free.

I was still filming with Heel Guild and had grown close to Gaspman. He was part-owner of Heel Guild and also the slave I facesat and rode like a pony on video. He was "Uncle Ernie" in the first scenes I filmed. A true gentleman-warrior: strong, well-mannered, intelligent, thoughtful, generous. Passionate about music, cooking and wine. Gaspman was loved by everyone who encountered him. The shoots with Heel Guild didn't feel like work. We'd film, drink, chat and then film some more. In the first hundred scenes or so that I filmed with Heel Guild, I was at least tipsy if not completely intoxicated.

With the launch of my members-only site, I delved into one of the most extreme things I'd ever done: scat content. The demand was there, and since the obscenity laws around it were unclear, I was motivated to go for it.

At first I produced vids of me alone, pooping, while talking to the guy viewing the vid about him eating it, about him consuming my Goddess chocolate. Poor Carl had to film these scenes half-awake in the morning with a face mask filled with coffee beans to cover the smell. These vids were both fascinating and disgusting. Having a bowel movement is an entirely natural thing, yet it's something most people consider to be a private and dirty act—hence the demand for it. Most people have never seen what it looks like when a person takes a shit: what the anus does, how it moves throughout the process. As I said, fascinating and disgusting.

I thought I could sell these vids on my members site. My webmaster assured me the payment processor he chose was fine with it, so I put these vids on my site, and business exploded.

Through my popularity spike, I crossed paths with Dahlia, a woman who was famous for catering to this fetish, especially in person. My only in-person experience was with that one repeat client. Hardly extensive in variety. I was excited to meet her and pick her brain.

Dahlia was an eccentric character. Outspoken, loud, opinionated and assertive, she was passionate about scat play and probably knew more about it than anyone else alive. She ended up coming to Vancouver and filming a bunch of scenes for me and with me. I was blown away by her comfort with poop. When she knew she needed to produce, she ate in anticipation. She was a strict vegetarian and ate like a 17-year-old football player. I have never seen such a slender woman pack in so much food, but that's how she produced impressively large quantities of Goddess Caviar.

We even filmed a scene with Gaspman where she covered his mouth with cellophane and shat on top of it. She pushed it into his mouth so that he could feel the warmth and softness but not taste it. He could certainly smell it, though. Then she reached through her poop and made a tiny hole with her fingernail and started pushing her poop through it so that he could taste it a little.

I had seen vids Dahlia produced where the guys ate ALL that she offered them, but most people haven't had the pleasure or misfortune of seeing such things.

There were a few of us there that day, and we all gagged through this scene. Gaspman had reluctantly accepted the challenge of doing this scene; he loved to serve Dominant women, but this was taking things to the most extreme level.

Together, Dahlia and I produced the highest-quality and, dare I say, classiest and most legendary scat content anyone had ever seen. The money train was short lived, unfortunately. There had been a misunderstanding with my payment processor, and I had to remove the content from my site.

I was grateful in a way. The type of customer that it attracted was unlike my other fans. They were more extreme—and often totally unhinged—men who had gone so far down the rabbit hole of depravity that they no longer had a grasp on reality. Obviously, they're not all like that, but the emails I got from scat fans were more disturbing and more persistent than others.

CHAPTER 44

Hustle Pays Off

Over the next couple of years, Carl and I focused solely on the business. Well, to be honest, I focused on the business and pushed Carl to keep pace. There's no way to sugarcoat it, and I'm sure he would remember it differently because he worked hard, but he had a more laid-back personality. We wouldn't have accomplished as much if I hadn't pushed. I'm not sure where I got the energy, but I was driven. I lived and breathed the business.

We were putting out a new vid every day on my clips store, a couple of vids a week on Carl's, and I was still filming with Heel Guild on a regular basis. We held several crazy Goddess Parties where all manners of debauchery took place between drunken Dominant women and brave slaves. We'd play games where the women would head-scissor the slaves to see who could hold out the longest. (That means squeezing a neck and head between your thighs, for the uninitiated.) We'd mete out punishments for the one who tapped out first and give rewards to the guy who was the most resilient. We'd use slaves as human toilets, and they would nearly drown in piss from all the women drinking and needing to pee frequently. We'd egg on guys to jerk each other off for more prizes or punishments. There'd also be pony riding, using slaves as human furniture and so much more.

Carl and I made numerous trips for work and pleasure. Through all of it, we drank way more than we should have. Bottoms up!

Despite all of the excitement, I was dissatisfied sexually. When Carl nagged me enough I would give in to having sex off camera—I didn't understand how someone could have that much sex drive—but I now wonder if it was more of a neediness for reassurance than sexual impulse. I would usually have sex with him on my side, facing away, so that he couldn't see my face. I winced in pain as he ploughed away for far, far too long. He always took forever to cum, on and off camera. I would feel completely disconnected, an animated blow-up doll. It didn't matter to him that I got sore or that I didn't enjoy it.

When filming hand jobs, I would sweat and pray for him to cum, the muscles of my arm and shoulder burning and aching. With shoe jobs, my leg and hip would cramp up. With sex, I would be raw. In all those cases we edited out many minutes of stroking or fucking, but after the cut I would look significantly more dishevelled with my hair sticking to my sweaty, glistening face, and my makeup running.

I tried to open things up so that we could both have more sexual excitement outside of the relationship, but Carl was still resistant. I paid for him to sleep with escorts. I set him up with my open-minded, horny friends. We went to swingers clubs. Carl resisted every step, especially when it came to me being with anyone else. He just couldn't handle it. Not only did he not want me to have sex with anyone else, but he also worked subtly to isolate me from others.

When Carl suggested we move to a tiny island just outside of Vancouver called Bowen Island, a move that would have isolated me even further from anyone else, David finally spoke up.

"Carl's possessiveness is unhealthy," he cautioned me. "And it's getting worse."

I was stunned. I didn't understand how I had allowed myself to get into this situation. I told David how sexually dissatisfied I was and how I had been trying to pretend, even to myself, that everything was fine.

David understood that more was at stake now. The business was booming, and Carl wasn't all bad. He did love me intensely, though it was perhaps not the healthiest kind of love. "Look," David suggested, "there's a way to get your needs taken care of on the side. Have your cake, so to speak."

But I wasn't so sure. On the one hand, it might be what I needed to stay in the relationship. On the other, I had been dead set against cheating on Carl. I wanted to have complete honesty in the relationship, but there was no way he would consent to me having sex with another man, even though he had sex with several other women while we had been together.

"I might have the solution for you," David offered.

"Oh, yeah?" I gave him a little smile. "What do you have in mind?"

David set up his plan for the next week when he was out of town. He asked me to look after his parrot. It meant going twice a day to feed the bird and hang out with him for an hour or two. Parrots are social creatures, and it's cruel to leave them alone for several days. David also had a friend who was in a similar situation as I; happily married with kids but not sexually satisfied. He arranged to have us meet at his place at a certain day and time. We didn't have each other's contact information, so there was no way we could get caught.

"Just don't forget to actually care for the bird," David laughed before hanging up.

My "date" was beautiful: tall, muscular, smooth and sexy. We didn't talk at all, both knowing exactly why we were there, and we had limited time. We kissed, explored each other and ripped our clothes off quickly—the mutual feeling of a stranger's skin against our own after going hungry for so long. He kissed down my neck, collarbone and breasts. He paused at my nipples, licking them, growling a little, continuing down to dive his tongue into my already-dripping pussy. I felt alive in a way I'd forgotten that I could feel.

My vagina pulsed and gripped, seeking a phallus, wanting to be filled. It didn't have to wait long. Putting a condom on, he sat on the edge of the bed and pulled me on top. In the mirror, I could see us side-on. His tanned skin, muscles rippling, beautiful shoulders; me pressed against him, straddling him. He lifted me and plunged in. I gasped, and the parrot went wild whistling and laughing in David's voice.

We tidied up afterward, and he kissed me goodbye: a nice, long, sensual kiss. He looked at me with what I perceived as reverent gratitude. I figured I would probably never see him again and probably shouldn't, but a part of me hoped I would.

I felt light and elated on the walk home. I called my mother to tell her what I had done. She was the one person I could say anything to, and I did; I told her everything. Unsurprisingly, she was supportive, even encouraging. My mother was morally bankrupt when it came to fidelity. I thought I would feel bad about cheating on Carl, but I didn't—I was reclaiming my independence. I felt entitled to it. I was angry that he would not permit me the freedom to get the sexual pleasure that he was unable to provide elsewhere. He didn't care if I was sexually satisfied, with him or in general.

Life went on as usual after that, but something subtle had changed. In the back of my mind was a ticking clock. I couldn't keep going like this, but I also couldn't jeopardize the business; it was like a child I had given birth to and was raising, growing.

Carl kept talking about Thailand. We had such a nice time there, and he desperately wanted to go back for a longer visit. We were making a lot of money and could afford it, so we pushed even harder, built up enough content to cover us while we went away and booked a two-month trip. We gave up our apartment, deciding we would get a fancier place when we returned. We packed all of our stuff together in one storage unit, and off we went.

Carl and I explored Cambodia, Vietnam and Thailand for the first month. During the second month, his parents came to visit us for two weeks. We rented a sprawling, luxurious condo where we could all stay; it cost as much as our apartment in Vancouver. I wanted his parents to be comfortable. Before they arrived, we spent our afternoons drinking, listening to music and reading. I hoped the trip would bring back the spark in our love life—sex had been about work for two years. Before his parents arrived, Carl and I had sex a couple of times in Thailand, but it didn't click. I wasn't sure if it ever had; trying to remember the fun sex in the earliest days seemed like such a distant memory.

Carl's parents' visit turned out to be a disaster. His mother complained the whole time and was nasty to me. She held a grudge that I had hurt her son, and she didn't trust me to not do it again. At the same time, she pressured me to give her a grandchild. I kept telling her I would never have children, that I had no desire to and neither did Carl, but she was relentless. Eventually, she capitulated and asked at least for a wedding. I didn't care about getting married either, but I said fine.

I didn't think Carl cared about getting married, but he looked positively gleeful when we discussed it. Deciding to marry someone to shut their nagging mother up might almost be acceptable if the other person is on the same page, but this wasn't the case. Carl acted like a teen girl who had been asked to the prom by her crush.

It was about that time, our last couple weeks in Thailand after Carl's parents left, that I got the email that would change everything. Another one of those pivotal moments that changes the trajectory of life. The email was an invitation from the biggest FemDom fetish site in the world, asking me to be the VIP at their FemDom ball in two months. They also wanted to film me and were offering generous compensation, including covering travel expenses to bring my partner and me to England.

It came out of the blue. The only contact I'd had with The FemDom Authority was helping each other a bit with piracy, letting each other know when we found each other's content on free sharing sites. Despite years on clips4sale's Top 50 list, I still regarded myself as an unknown in the international fetish porn world. Me? A VIP guest? It didn't make sense.

The FemDom Authority wanted an international guest for their ball, and as far as they were concerned, I was one of the most well-known Dommes in the world who fit with the style of FemDom on their site—sex on film. They had one odd condition to the offer: they required exclusivity. I was not to film with any other producers while in England. I laughed, thinking they had made some amazing mistake about how popular I was.

I accepted their offer, and Carl and I decided to take advantage of the free flight to England by making a trip to France and Italy. This left us only six weeks in Vancouver between Thailand and Europe.

My tenants had moved out of my condo, so we camped out there, left our things in storage and filmed and edited like crazy. Despite all of the exciting things happening, this wasn't a good time in our relationship. Carl and I were both sluggish and often irritable with each other, but we blamed it on the dreary Vancouver winter weather.

CHAPTER 45

Ka-Boom

After a long flight, Carl and I arrived at Heathrow Airport. We were being picked up by Blake from The FemDom Authority. Blake and I had frequently corresponded, but I didn't understand his role. I didn't know if he was a slave, the owner or something else entirely. I certainly was not mentally prepared to be approached by a punk rocker in combat boots, ripped jeans and a mohawk.

Blake was reserved and polite. He spoke softly with a thick British accent, and I had trouble understanding him. We made small talk on the ninety-minute ride into the countryside, with me in the front seat and Carl in the back. I learned on the trip that he and Audra, the site's founder, were a couple. Carl barely said a word the whole time, only responding when Blake tried to engage him in the conversation. By the time we arrived, Carl was in a deeply sour mood.

When the lady of the house came out to greet us, I wasn't sure that it was really her, the larger-than-life Head Mistress Audra Handler of The FemDom Authority. She was so petite and looked completely different in her casual clothes. She could not have been nicer, welcoming us into her home. The view from the balcony of her mansion was a waking dream: a private sunken garden backed by a field and rolling English hills. We walked through the house passing film sets and many closed doors to finally reach our well-appointed quarters at the far end of the home. It was late, so we retired for the night. Filming would start early the next day.

The first scene was supposed to be a cuckolding scene with Carl and me. Audra had thoughtfully booked a cuckold that we had coincidentally worked with on our first trip to London the year before. Carl was nervous. He had never had to perform sexually in front of a film crew. He wanted a bit of liquid courage to settle his nerves, but I was told they preferred performers to stay sober when filming.

Carl never, ever had trouble getting an erection before, even under the most bizarre situations: literally fucking on top of slaves, having three slaves watching and jerking each other off in a contest to see who would earn the coveted creampie cleanup, a slave lying beneath him with a funnel in his mouth waiting to catch Carl's cum... I could go on and on. Carl was called "Ever-Ready" for a reason. He took forever to ejaculate, but he was always erect, and he always eventually produced the money shot.

Today, however, something was different; Carl could not get hard. Lights, camera, no action. The slave was there, as was the cameraman, the lighting man and me working his cock like my life depended on it. Dominant woman be damned. I sucked and stroked that cock as I had never done before. He was under a tremendous amount of pressure to perform, but I suspected it was Blake that was throwing him off. Something subtle had been brewing since the drive from the airport the day before.

Eventually, after a painfully long time and a lot of work, we managed to get the scene done. I felt nauseous with stress. I was vibrating from the adrenaline of the shoot, but I didn't have time to rest. We were now running behind schedule, so we had to move right into the next scene. It was meant to have some water sports, but I didn't know that in advance and hadn't been staying hydrated. On top of that, I was taken aback by Blake's cock, which I saw for the first time when he slid it through a glory hole for the slave to suck. It was so thick that I thought it was fake. I squeezed it and tried to look around it through the hole to see if it was truly attached to him. I was intensely aroused by that cock, so when it came time for me to pee I couldn't do it for a long time, and the pause was awkward. I felt like an amateur; these people had paid all this money to film with us, and we were complete and total fuck-ups.

Carl and I both would have benefited from a drink, but I didn't want to seem like a raging alcoholic by begging. And we weren't anywhere near a store; otherwise, I'm sure Carl would have gotten a bottle anyway.

We broke for lunch and sat at the table discussing the scenes that were coming up. I learned that I'd be doing more scenes with Blake. Things hadn't gone well with Carl, so they were giving him a break until the end of the day. Blake had been professional and reserved all day, but there was something simmering under the surface. Audra kept teasing him subtly, giggling, and Blake kept scowling playfully. The tension was building. Good and bad tension.

In the next scene with Blake, he was restrained in a bondage chair wearing a leather hood with concealed eye holes. Tiny perforations allowed him to see, but I couldn't make out his eyes clearly. He was like titanium; I'd never witnessed such a solid erection. Audra was in the scene with me, and she briefly instructed me on how to tease Blake most effectively. How he loved his nipples squeezed, but not too hard. How he responded better to a soft touch on his cock.

I could hear him breathing in the leather hood, but I couldn't tell if he was looking at me. We did the scene, teasing him, tormenting him and eventually bringing him to climax and feeding his cum to another slave as punishment. I was dripping wet; my cunt reacted to Blake in a way that startled me. He was a tied-up slave! I couldn't even see his eyes, and he didn't even touch me.

For the last scene of the day, Audra decided to do a duo boot job on Carl to try to ensure a cumshot. She figured if we did the one thing he loved the most, it should be easy. Sadly, it wasn't. Though we eventually got the pop shot and Audra was gracious throughout, it took Carl even longer than usual; by the end, both Audra and I were visibly sweaty and fatigued from stroking his cock with our boots. It was hardly "FemDom."

Over dinner, they finally broke out some wine, which Carl dove into with gusto. There was no hope of cheering him up, though. He quietly drank and sulked while the rest of us got to know each other. I felt immediately at ease with Audra, Blake and the rest of the film crew and slaves. I experienced a sensation of arriving home, to people who accepted and celebrated who I was.

Audra continued to playfully tease Blake about how erect he was in the scenes that day. He didn't say much, but I felt drawn to him and emboldened by Audra's encouragement. The topic of non-monogamy came up, and Audra vaguely indicated that they didn't play by traditional rules. Blake visibly blushed.

It was then that I learned the reason why they had required exclusivity: a competitor with unethical business practices and a personal vendetta had a habit of scooping their talent. He had become an annoyance in numerous ways, and it reduced their stress if the talent they hired didn't work for him. Fair enough.

That night in bed Carl was sour and critical. He was clear about his dislike for everyone and everything. He felt embarrassed by his performance that day but blamed it on the pressure and on me for not doing enough to make him comfortable. I suggested that there might be an opportunity for a swap. I hoped that if I could have him look at Audra as a possible sex partner, something novel, he might find something to be positive about—but no. He was too preoccupied with the idea of Blake and I having sex even to consider whether he was attracted to Audra. We went to bed; Carl slipped into a fitful sleep simmering with anger, fear and bitterness. I barely slept at all, thinking about the connection I felt with Blake and Audra. I liked them both, strongly. In contrast to Carl, I felt like I had found water after walking in a desert for days.

The next day of filming went well, but it was exhausting. Audra was a shrewd businesswoman. She meant to get the best scenes out of me. There was a lot of pressure on everyone, but I was the star of the show and was expected to perform like one. To say it was stressful would be underselling it. Carl wasn't supportive and made things worse by being needy and sulky all day. He and I only had one scene, and it was created to be as fail-proof as possible.

Carl was a prisoner, chained naked and hooded, lying on a mattress on the floor. I was his captor, nude except for a sexy leather trench coat and thigh-high leather boots. It was just him and me in the scene, and I was to use him for my sexual pleasure, sitting on his face and having an orgasm using his mouth, then riding his cock. All Carl had to do was lay there and stay hard.

The hood kept him mostly in the dark, so he wasn't distracted by the film crew. We managed to pull off the scene well enough, but I hated having sex with him. I kept imagining punching him in the face instead. I felt resentful of the obligatory babying he demanded, while what I needed was his support. I felt angry that he would behave this way over something as unimportant as me possibly having sex with an attached man who lived on the other side of the world.

My last scene of the day was with Blake. It was a latex fetish scene with tease and denial and an eventual release. I decided to have some fun with it, even though I knew Carl could hear the scene from the next room. Part of me desperately didn't want to hurt him, and part of me absolutely did. I felt resentful that he was making this situation more difficult for me. I was embarrassed by his behaviour from a professional standpoint too. After all, Carl had received payment via a free flight to be there and was benefiting greatly from the experience. The exposure our business would get from being associated with The FemDom Authority would be massive.

So in that last scene, I dove in and enjoyed it. I savoured the chemistry that had built between Blake and I over the last few days. I made it a mind-fuck scene where I told him that if he managed to resist my teasing and not ejaculate, I might use him for sex later. The idea was to have him cum eventually anyway and ruin his chances of actually getting his greatest desire, which was to fuck me. It was a made-up story for the scene, but it worked a little too well. Blake did want to fuck me, badly, and once the seed was planted that he might have an opportunity as long as he resisted cumming, there was nothing I could do to get him to pop.

In the scene, I put a condom on his cock and pressed it against the entrance to my pussy but did not put it in. I teased the tip of his cock with my wet pussy, and both of us nearly said "fuck it" to the scene and everything else. How we found enough restraint to not go for it right then and there is beyond me. Anyone who watched that scene would have seen the palpable mutual arousal. We both broke character subtly several times out of sheer frustration. The camera operator had no idea where the scene was going, and when I could not get Blake to ejaculate, I had to make up a new ending that implied later he would be used for my pleasure. Maybe. This left him frustrated but hopeful—both in real life and in the scene.

After the filming had ended, Carl and I had some time alone before dinner. He had heard some of the scene and thought that I had fucked Blake. He said it didn't bother him as much as he thought, so I took the opportunity to say that if there was a possibility of it happening that I wanted to. Carl had several other experiences with my friends and escorts, I explained, and it was time for me to have an experience too.

It was the perfect opportunity. Blake was in a happy relationship, and he lived in another country. He was no threat; it was only sex. Carl and I were leaving the next day for a few weeks in Paris and Italy, then returning for the FemDom Ball at the end of the trip. Carl reluctantly agreed that if the opportunity came up, he would try to deal with it. He wasn't sure if he was interested in Audra, but he'd consider that too. I already knew that Audra wasn't interested in him, and although she was excellent at masking her feelings, I think she wanted to punch Carl in the face as much as I did. She had gone above and beyond to make him feel more comfortable, both professionally and personally. All he could manage in return was unwavering sulkiness, social withdrawal and ungrateful whining.

After dinner, the four of us were soaking in the hot tub, chatting casually. I steered the topic to non-monogamy and boldly inquired as to the possibility of Blake and I going off together. I directed my question to Audra out of respect, with the side question of Blake's interest. Audra gave an enthusiastic green light, assuring me Blake was keen. With my stomach in knots, I checked in with Carl but in a way that left little opportunity for him to pump the brakes.

And with that, off we went. Blake was inexplicably calm. He sat on the bed with a towel around his waist; there were condoms on the bedside table. He asked me to sit on his lap. I found this an odd request, but I did so. His movements were slow, careful, controlled. He stroked my hair and back in a nurturing way. He placed his hand between my thighs, close to my pussy. He told me to kiss him, and it was at that moment I realized he was in fact more Dominant. It was a welcome change after being around so many submissive men for so long.

We kissed, slowly, and Blake controlled the speed. He made me wait. He touched me carefully, slowly, skillfully. He put his hand around my neck and squeezed gently, testing my response. I liked it and wanted more. He told me to open my mouth, and he spit into it. I was disgusted, but it felt exhilarating to do something I didn't like for him. I understood the desire to please a Master, but I hadn't had much experience being on this end of things.

Blake took his time, not saying much. He explored my body but kept me away from his cock. He wanted the focus on me but was acutely rigid the whole time anyway. He didn't need any help. Finally, when I was sopping wet but hadn't yet cum, he slid on a condom, looking into my eyes the whole time. He didn't rush. He held me down firmly but painlessly and slid his cock in so slowly I thought I would scream. He was massively thick at the base, and it hurt a little when he was fully inside me.

As he started sliding all the way in and all the way out, I suddenly got teary; a flash flood of tears. I did not feel them coming, but they came from deep within. I sobbed as he fucked me. Relief—a meal after near starvation—and pain over having gone so long without it. No clear thought, only raw emotion. Blake held me and kept slowly fucking me as I wept.

We were in there for a long time. Hours. When we finally came back to reality and realized how late it was, we knew that the world had changed. Blake knew Carl wasn't okay with what we'd done; we both knew that I would suffer for this pleasure. Blake didn't enjoy hurting Carl, but he wanted me. Badly. And the feelings were obviously mutual.

I scuffed along the dark hallway back to our room on wobbly

legs, my pussy throbbing. I didn't want to turn on the light, in case Carl was asleep, but I needed a shower. I couldn't go to bed with him in my current state—smelling of sex with another man. In the dark I couldn't figure out how to get the water hot as I fumbled with the taps, so I had an ice-cold shower in the dark. I felt like I needed to suffer for what I'd done, so I took my punishment. I later found out that Carl was awake and knew I was showering in the dark and that I wouldn't have been able to figure out how to get hot water. He didn't try to help; he let me freeze.

I came to bed, a human popsicle, and Carl curled into me and sobbed. He said nothing, only cried. I held him, stewing in pity and anger. Why was my sexual pleasure not important to him? Why did he not care if he pleased me? And why was he so hell-bent on ensuring no one else did either? Why was he so threatened by someone else giving me sexual pleasure? We had a good relationship otherwise, and the business partnership was great... but this war on my sexual pleasure was driving a wedge between us. Carl's selfishness, possessiveness and jealousy were poisoning everything else, but somehow I still felt guilt for hurting him.

The next day I thanked Audra, and she thanked me. Blake had come to bed and fucked her so thoroughly that she wished I were around more often to spice things up. The contrast between her reaction and Carl's left me deeply resentful. Carl's sulkiness reached its climax; he wouldn't even come out of our room for breakfast. He wanted to go, so Audra drove us to the train station. She understood that it was best Blake kept his distance.

Carl and I travelled to Paris for my birthday. We spent most of our time in our hotel room arguing and crying. Carl had taken to the bottle in earnest and was now drinking every waking hour. As soon as he woke up, he reached for wine or whatever else he had on hand. It was alarming.

We did a little filming with a sweet, thoughtful French slave on the evening of my birthday. He brought me lovely presents and treated me like a Goddess or celebrity. But it is evident from the pictures and video taken that day that I was beaten down emotionally. I had bags under my eyes from lack of sleep and crying. I started to get physically ill from the stress.

We continued on to Rome, Tuscany, Florence and Venice for the next few weeks, arguing and crying the entire time. Several times we almost broke up. Carl threatened to fly back to Canada and begged me to come with him, to not go back to The FemDom Authority for the FemDom Ball, but I refused. I had a professional obligation to attend, and it had been advertised that I would be there. It was a tremendous opportunity and would benefit our business enormously. Even more importantly, I wanted to. Blake and I had been in touch over email, fanning the flames of passion from afar. I was desperate to fuck him again.

Those few weeks were the most stressful and painful I'd ever experienced. Carl often clung to me and sobbed, begging me to not break up with him. He drank the whole time, and it was like trying to manage a toddler with his frequent outbursts and breakdowns. I drank more as well, trying to numb out my feelings, but I couldn't keep up with him. Carl was a freight train.

We did a bit of filming here and there. I thought if Carl came, it would help his mood, but the thought of fucking him disgusted me. At least with filming, I could detach. My anger came out in our FemDom scenes. As I jerked his cock and looked into the camera, I took out my frustration out on the viewer, humiliating and degrading them with vigour. My disdain was palpable. I became colder and less empathetic; I'm not proud of how I handled the situation. In hindsight I was cruel, even though at the time I was making the best choice out of several lousy options.

We tried to enjoy the sights, but we bickered and talked about the relationship while at the Vatican and the Coliseum, while driving through vineyards and exploring cities. I probably should have let Carl go back to Canada on his own, but I didn't trust him not to do something crazy. We were staying at my condo in Vancouver, all of our stuff was in storage together and the business was all tangled up between us. I had already decided that the relationship wasn't going to work out, but I needed to save the business I had worked so hard to build. I also suspected that Carl might attempt to commit suicide, so I decided I would break up with him during a session with our relationship counsellor to help prevent that.

We returned to The FemDom Authority on the morning of the ball. It was buzzing with activity, and there were dozens of people setting things up. Our help was needed, so we were kept busy and focused. When the slaves started to arrive, I was part of the inspection committee. Each slave was given special FemDom attention by Audra and me as we inspected, interrogated, spanked, toyed with and teased them.

There were games played and much frivolity. I met dozens of other Pro Dommes and slaves. Far too many to ever remember. Carl got to flirt with a few of the ladies, so he was distracted most of the day. We both drank non-stop and ended up in the hot tub with a handful of other deviants. I made out with several ladies, putting on a spicy show, evidently. The party was a huge success and, as things wound down and people left, Blake and I had an opportunity to connect. We planned a rendezvous after everyone was asleep.

The mansion was full of people in nearly every room and possible sleep space. All was quiet. Carl was intoxicated but in a good mood. He had a lot of fun that day—we both did—and it was badly needed after weeks of so much heaviness between us. I told Carl that I was going to go off with Blake for one last quickie and that I would probably never see him again, so there was nothing to worry about. Carl capitulated. He was so afraid of me leaving him that he would agree to anything—hardly enthusiastic consent.

Blake and I met in a storage room. This wasn't quite the glamour of the first night in a well-appointed bedroom, but those were all taken by esteemed guests. We had a small mattress on the floor among wardrobes of clothes and props. Things moved a little quicker this time; the passion had been building over the last few weeks as we emailed each other back and forth. We kissed passionately, embraced and quickly disrobed.

He was intent on taking me more aggressively this time. Blake's hand slid up my neck and into my hair, grasping it and giving it a little tug. As he kissed me, he wrapped his other hand around my neck and squeezed a little harder while looking into my eyes. He reached for the condom, and my heart rocketed. I wanted this; I needed this. He started to fuck me, and I fucked back. Suddenly, we heard a pounding noise, and my stomach lurched. Carl was banging on the door, trying the doorknob and finding that it was locked, demanding to be let in.

I jumped up and opened the door, fearful that Carl would wake the others and we'd be found out. He was holding my laptop and had an email opened. He said he read that I had told Blake I was going to break up with him when we got back to Canada. Carl was furious. I grabbed the laptop from him, closed it and set it aside; I didn't know how much he had read, but there was far worse in there had he dug further.

Carl entered the room and dove toward Blake who was on his knees on the mattress, the condom encasing his cock standing at full attention and shining with my cunt juices. Blake ducked and avoided Carl's clumsy punch, and I pulled Carl back. Blake smirked and said, "Is that all you've got?" It seemed unlike Blake to say something so cruel, and in doing so he revealed his disdain for Carl. I picked up my things and told Carl to go back to our bedroom. As I left, I looked back at Blake still kneeling naked on the mattress, still fully and magnificently erect, and I felt a deep sense of loss. I would have done anything to fuck him right then, but it was not to be.

Carl and I went to London for a week to take private and filmed sessions. The never-ending demand for content didn't cease, even when our private life was falling apart. If I had felt like I was pushing a car before, now I was pushing a cement truck. Carl was in full-on self-pity mode, drinking and depressed, now certain we would be breaking up. I kept telling him that we would go to the counsellor when we got home and see if we could figure it out, but I knew that we were done. I couldn't tell him that, of course, out of fear that he would kill himself if he didn't have any hope left.

The last weekend before we left there was a big fetish party that I had committed to going to with Audra, Blake and a couple of other high-profile Pro Dommes. We had all agreed to share a hotel room to keep costs down. Carl wasn't happy about it, but he thought at least nothing could happen with all of us sharing a room.

At the last minute Audra decided not to come, so it was five of us. The party was on a ship, and there were many rooms, stairways and hidden dark corners. It was easy to lose people, and that's what Blake and I did. We ended up tucked between a curtain and a sofa in a place so dark we could hardly see each other. Neither of us had condoms, and no one else nearby did either. The cruelty of the situation was maddening. We messed around for as long as we dared, and it was intoxicating. The ultimate tease. Like being thirsty and getting tiny sips when you want to gulp. I have always been adamant about safer sex practices, and as desperate as I was, I wouldn't risk my sexual health for a few moments of fun. No condom meant no fucking.

Back at the hotel, I volunteered to sleep on the floor. I hated sharing a bed and was happy to have a break from Carl. Blake and I barely slept. In the dim light of the room we looked at each other, so close, yet so far.

In the morning we had breakfast and parted ways. Carl was relieved that he wouldn't have to see Blake again, and Blake and I were in utter disbelief that all that intensity had led to nothing. Unfulfilled wanting.

CHAPTER 46

Parting Ways

Carl and I travelled back to Vancouver. The highest drama of the breakup was behind us. We were both beaten down and exhausted after weeks of being at the climax of the end without relief; a situation most people would never find themselves in. Our second day back we went to the counsellor, and I finally had to say it out loud, to him and to the counsellor: I was done. I didn't want to work things out. The counsellor spent some time with each of us alone and then together. He advised us to not return to the same place and to go our separate ways immediately. Out of guilt, I let Carl stay at my condo, and I spent the night on David's sofa. The next day I rented a temporary furnished place for a few weeks while I figured out what my next move would be.

The apartment I rented was owned by a man who gave off a strange vibe. It wasn't until I paid and he was leaving that he mentioned, "Oh. And I have an extra key to the apartment, so if you lock yourself out for some reason, just call me."

I spent the first two nights sleeping in the closet with a kitchen knife, fearing he would come in at night and try to harm me. After that, I slept in the bed but kept the knife tucked under the mattress. Most men have no idea how often women fear violence from men.

I had been warned about rape and abuse since I was too little to even understand it. I had mentally prepared myself to fight off an attack and had even taken several self-defence courses. I had also mentally prepared myself to *not* be able to fight off an attack and knew I would need to call the police, go to the hospital for a rape kit and get counselling to help me process it even though it would impact me for life. This is how every woman I know also thinks.

Over the next couple of weeks, Carl and I negotiated the separation of the company. He got all the equipment and all the shoe-job footage, and I got all the other footage for my site. I bought a camera, tripod, lighting and editing software. I already knew how to edit, so I started working on the content we had filmed in Europe. There was enough there to get me through at least a month.

The camera sat in the box for two weeks; I had anxiety about learning new technology, and for some reason the new camera paralyzed me. Blake and I had been in touch. He finally forced me to go on Skype with him, set up the lighting and pull the camera out of the box. He walked me through it step by step as I held the video camera up to the webcam, showing him the buttons.

Carl and I had worked out most details amicably until it came to a dollar amount. He felt he was owed a buy-out equalling the amount he had earned the year before. I was outraged. I knew that he was getting bad advice, probably from his mother or a shady, scam-artist pal. I legally owed him nothing but had offered him a generous amount. Enough for him to live on for at least six months. I begged him to be reasonable, reminding him that if we could work things out amicably, we could still work together, and I would help him grow his own business.

But Carl grew bitter. He was hurt, heartbroken, humiliated and fearful of the future. He was angry, and this was his last stand. I'm sure he had people egging him on and no one attempting to help him see reason. I encouraged Carl to seek legal advice, feeling sure that a lawyer would tell him that my offer was more than fair and that, since he wasn't legally owed anything, he should take it. But he managed to get some shyster lawyer who thought they could get a lot more out of me. It wasn't true.

Blake was cautioning me to get an airtight agreement signed in front of a lawyer to ensure Carl wouldn't try to come after me later for more money.

Carl and I met for lunch to try to come to an agreement. His smile was tight, his jaw tense. Snide remarks were all he could manage—his hatred for me could not be concealed. We discussed making arrangements for him to move his things out of our storage space. I told him to take anything he wanted. I didn't care about sofas, coffee tables or chairs. When it came down to the payout for the business, Carl told me that he planned to sue for more money.

At that moment, something inside me snapped. All hope of us being friends vanished, and any compassion that I had left for him was gone. I felt that his sense of entitlement to that money ran parallel to his possessive entitlement to my body for the years we had been together. Adrenaline kicked in, and I experienced razor-sharp tunnel vision as I looked into his eyes and with barely contained rage said, "If you sue me, you will not be fighting for this amount versus that amount. You will lose, and you will get nothing. If you sue me, you will get what I legally owe you, which is nothing. Not a cent. Or you can take what I'm offering now and sign the agreement."

Carl's face scrunched up into a scowl as it registered that if he lost, he wouldn't get less money, he'd get none. I knew he had been careless with his money and had no savings. In other words, he had nothing to pay a lawyer with and now needed my money to live on. He finally responded, "Okay, I'll take it, but after I never want to see your fucking face again."

I've sacrificed myself on the altar of truth by telling the story as it happened, knowing that I come across as a sadistic villain.

We met at the lawyer's office the next week and signed the paperwork. On the way out I told Carl that if I could help him with his business, I'd be happy to and, as improbable as it was right then, I hoped we would one day be friends. He laughed and walked away. Later that day he sent me an email calling me a few derogatory names and making it acutely clear that we would never be friends. He was likely drunk.

CHAPTER 47

A Crack at the Big Leagues

Carl moved out of my condo soon after and pulled his things out of our storage space. I moved into another furnished apartment, unsure of what the future held and not feeling up to dealing with a big move. I needed to figure out how to run my business in a new way, on my own. I had to learn how to film all of my scenes with the camera on a tripod, without a camera operator. I needed to recruit guys to perform in the vids, to take Carl's place. I was overwhelmed by the idea of doing it all on my own, but I somehow trusted that it would all work out.

Gaspman from Heel Guild was incredibly helpful and supportive. And Blake and I were in constant contact—too much, in fact. I leaned on him. When we feel like we're drowning we grab for something, anything to hang on to stay afloat. In times of desperation, I haven't made my best choices.

Rather than taking the time to heal from the trauma of the breakup in a healthy way, I poured myself into my work. I decided to set my goals higher, to try to become "famous." I knew I needed to crack into the LA porn scene to do that, but I had no idea how. I did some research and set up appointments in Los Angeles with agents and publicists. David and I once again headed to Burning Man in Nevada, and on the way back I met with as many people in the industry as I could. Samantha flew down for a few days to go to some of the meetings with me; she wanted to be famous too.

The agents and PR people were discouraging. The main problem was that we were Canadians, and it was illegal for most big porn companies to hire us for US porn shoots. I wanted to continue to do the FemDom fetish stuff, which involved a little bit of sex, but had no interest in doing assembly-line vanilla porn for big porn companies. No, thanks.

One of my most fascinating meetings was with "the" agent, Culver, the guy who managed the best girls. He was an infamously eccentric man, and everyone knew who he was. If you were one of his girls, you were guaranteed to be famous. His brand was your golden ticket. When he asked me to come to his home, it struck me as suspicious, but when Culver wants to set a meeting, you go to the meeting.

It was a normal, slightly cluttered apartment in an unassuming cluster of apartment buildings. He was wearing a shabby tracksuit; apparently, personal grooming wasn't the top of his priorities. He made a big deal of showing off his cat. Could this really be the guy managing the most successful ladies in the LA porn world? I was unsure until he started to rattle off advice. I could barely keep up with my notes. He said he wouldn't take me on and that I didn't need him anyway because he had looked at what I was doing and I should just keep doing it. I'd be happier and wealthier than if I had an agent.

"If you want to branch out and work for other people," he advised, "you can contact the production companies yourself. You don't need someone to pick up the phone for you." Culver said I'd need a US ID to work legally—no one could hire me without it—which I could get, but it was tricky. He told me how and gave me the contact names for places where he thought I'd fit in. To lubricate things, he encouraged me to drop his name when I reached out to them.

That evening I was having a drink on the rooftop of The Standard hotel in LA. I had been swimming in its glamorous pool and was now standing at the building's edge, looking out over the city as the sun was starting to fade. A mountainous, visibly nervous man walked up and stood by me. He tried to play it cool, looking out over the city casually, while repeatedly stealing shy peeks at me. I decided to put him out of his misery and start a conversation. "So what brings you here?"

His voice broke when he responded, "I'm going to a tech conference nearby and decided to come here for a drink on a whim. I live in LA but have never been here."

He was looking at me strangely, so I just asked him point-blank, "Do you recognize me?"

He lowered his eyes and said, "Yes, Mistress. I'm sorry; I couldn't help myself. I just can't believe it's you."

I asked him to act normal in public and to buy me a drink. We sat and chatted, and he profusely sweated and shook the whole time. He said he and his wife were huge fans and that watching my cuckolding vids has inspired parts of their healthy and kinky sex life.

Many of my fans live in a fantasy world, so I wasn't sure if he was telling the truth, but I felt I could trust him. When he offered to serve me in any way possible during my stay, I suggested he drive me to a meeting the next day. I had no other plan on how to get there, so it was fortunate for me that I ran into Arnold.

The next day, Arnold picked me up from my hotel, and we drove for nearly an hour to the set of Cruel Chambers to meet with Gus, the owner, to discuss the possibility of working together.

On the way, Arnold told me all about his wife and their fascinating relationship: "I have a thick cock that my wife loves, but I cum too quickly, so I made a replica of my cock and wear it as a strap-on to fuck her longer."

It sounded preposterous, but then he shyly reached into the back seat and pulled out a rubber dick sealed in a ziplock bag and handed it to me.

He said with a cautious smile, "You see that nib on the end? That's because I ejaculated as soon as I put my cock in the mould. That's how quickly I cum."

I laughed nervously, torn between my persona of making fun of premature ejaculators, two-pump chumps and minute men, and sincerely feeling sorry for this guy who struggles with it daily.

Arnold didn't want sympathy or humiliation; he simply thought I would find it interesting and felt safe sharing something deeply intimate with someone open-minded and experienced.

When we arrived at the Cruel Chambers studios, they were in the middle of filming a scene with another model and slave. She was a cliche LA star: a tanned, bleached-blonde, busty bimbo in a fishnet body stocking. After a few minutes she asked if we could step out while she finished the scene. From the next room, I could hear her faking her orgasm as she rode the guy's face and jerked him off. He came out, sweaty and covered in cum, bad-mouthing the model to us complete strangers: "I didn't think I was going to be able to cum, she was such a lousy performer, but mind over matter." Then he gave me his card, which stated something like "Professional performer for hire," and said I should call him if I needed his services while I was in town. It was all relatively bizarre to me.

Gus introduced me to his friendly, down-to-earth crew and showed me around his tiny but functional studio. He said he would love to film with me, but I needed a US ID for him to do so legally. He promised me work if I could get that sorted. It was a brief but friendly meeting. Arnold and I drove back to downtown LA, and he chatted away, telling me about his kinks and asking me questions. I felt at ease with him.

David and I drove to San Francisco next. My target was FetRoyalty, the biggest US-based fetish site. Their FemDom site was called Royal Dommes, and that's where I would best fit. Culver had given me the direct line to a hiring manager there and told me to drop his name.

I showed up at The Armoury, the home of FetRoyalty, for my appointment with Andrew, the person tasked with interviewing and hiring new talent for a few of the FetRoyalty sites. The imposing building was constructed as an armory and arsenal for the National Guard in the early 1900s and designed with a castle-like appearance.

I was left waiting in an ancient room with grey rock walls, beamed ceilings, comfortable brown leather sofas and a plain glass coffee table on a threadbare persian rug. Andrew started the meeting curious to understand how I had come to know Culver without being one of "his girls." I explained the situation, and he was both fascinated and confused that Culver would help me without any benefit to himself.

It also took a while to explain who I was, as Andrew hadn't even looked at my site. He was stuck on the fact that I was Canadian and they couldn't legally hire me. He was immediately dismissive. I explained that I knew of a way to get a US ID to make it legal for them, but he was not convinced. At the end of the meeting, as if sorry for wasting my time, he offered me the consolation prize of getting a little tour of The Armoury film sets. When we bumped into Marcella, the director of Royal Dommes, she squealed like a fan girl, "Oh my god, Mistress T! What are you doing here?"

I laughed, shocked, and explained, "I'm hoping to work with you."

She smiled and excitedly said, "Yes—YES! Andrew, make it happen!"

Poor Andrew looked a little shell-shocked. He asked if we'd met before, and I said no. "Marcella must have seen my vids or something." Andrew's tone was entirely different now, and we left things as being 100% certain as long as I got my US ID.

I walked away from The Armoury hoping to flag a cab back to my hotel. I was practically floating, totally euphoric, replaying in my mind what had just happened. Was I more famous than I realized? Why was the great Marcella from porn giant FetRoyalty so excited to meet and work with me? Standing on the corner in the sunshine, half-looking for a cab, I didn't even see the limo sitting there until I heard, "Can I help you?"

I looked in the direction of the stretch black limo and noticed the back door open to reveal a man reclining in the backseat smoking a joint. He was in his mid-fifties, with a long, white beard and hair, a slightly rumpled suit and weathered sandals. He looked friendly, so I told him I was hoping to flag a taxi.

The thin fog of smoke accentuated the rays of sun streaming through the open sunroof and windows of the limo. The man's teeth were bright white as he smiled disarmingly and asked, "Where are you trying to go?"

I told him the part of town, and he offered to drive me if I'd toss him a few bucks. It was then that I realized he was the driver of the limo, relaxing in the back seat. He explained that his primary business was weed delivery, but he'd be happy to help me out. His name was Forest.

As we drove along in the sun, I felt the whole world shining on me. It wasn't the most glamorous limo experience—there were tie-dye pillows tossed in the back and it was a bit worn out—but I was in a limo, dressed in my best heels and sexy business dress. It was what I deemed appropriate attire for something of a job interview at a porn company.

I was feeling generous, so I asked Forest if I could take him for lunch to thank him for helping me out, and he accepted. We went to a local diner where he knew the owner, and I told him about my day. He applauded and thought it was groovy. He told me his life story and then dropped me off at my hotel. David wasn't back from his adventures, so I grabbed a mini bottle of champagne and drank it alone in a nearby park, hoping that my career was on the edge of taking off.

CHAPTER 48

Hunting

A week after returning from California I flew by myself to Honolulu to get a US driver's licence. It was the only place in the US you could still get US ID without a social security card. I had found a loophole, but it was legal. I spent three lonely and boring days in Honolulu, but I got my precious US ID.

When I returned, I went out to celebrate with David. We went to a fetish party, and I was feeling powerful, confident and sexy. I was on the hunt. David spotted a tall, shirtless man standing at the bar and stated that he was probably the best-looking guy there. He also mentioned that he recognized him from other parties; he was a Dom.

I strolled up to him and said, "Hi, I'm Tracey." He responded with one of the biggest smiles I'd ever seen. The kind of smile that lit up his whole face, expressive lines breaking out all around his eyes. A smile that was closer to a laugh.

I bravely said, "My friend thinks you're the best-looking man in the room. I'm inclined to agree." As I handed him my Mistress T business card, I continued, "I know you're not into this yourself. But as it happens, I'm interested in exploring the other side of things in my personal life. Why don't you drop me a line?" I thought his smile couldn't get any bigger, but it did; he laughed as though I'd told the funniest joke in the world. He then looked at me warmly and said, "My name is Donovan. I'm with a friend tonight. She's not my girlfriend, but it would be disrespectful to desert her. I will call you, though."

I continued my hunt, drinking, dancing and cruising around the room looking for fresh meat. I was kissing and choking a beautiful young woman when out of the corner of my eye I spotted a brawny guy dressed like a gladiator wearing a small leather eye mask. He was standing on the edge of the dance floor watching me. I dropped her and strode over to him. I paused with my lips an inch away from his mouth, and he didn't move, so I kissed him. His hands went around my waist and pulled me in firmly. I liked it. I ripped off his mask to get a good look at his face. I saw strength and lust. I led him onto the dance floor, where we grinded hard and made out. I realized Donovan was also on the dance floor watching the spectacle with a big grin.

At the end of the night, I dragged the gladiator along with David to get a bite to eat. I told him, "I'm taking you home to fuck, but I need to eat first." It was halfway through the meal when he carefully told us that he was straight, and I realized he had been confused about David. We laughed as I explained that David wasn't joining us for sex. Just food.

The gladiator did not disappoint. His long chestnut hair hit the top of his broad, muscular shoulders, which flexed powerfully as he thrust into me, looking at me groaning with hunger. This man was built for fucking. In another place and time, he would be considered prime breeding stock, or a sexual servant to royalty. These thoughts crossed my mind as I took in his square jaw and grazed my fingers along his sturdy back.

Donovan called me the next day, and we made a date for the day after. We met in a dingy hole-in-the-wall bar in the middle of the afternoon. It was empty except for a couple rock-bottom alcoholic regulars sitting at the bar arguing about hockey or something equally irrelevant.

It was immediately obvious that Donovan was incredibly intelligent. He had been a successful criminal lawyer for many years before deciding it wasn't what he wanted to do with his life, so he was now studying yoga. Realizing how intimidatingly confident, open, inquisitive and sharp he was, I felt I was out of my depth. But there was something rough about him too: his vocabulary consisted of as many curse words as it did byzantine words I couldn't comprehend. Donovan was unabashedly dominant, and I could feel his grip on me without him even laying a finger on me. It was thrilling and terrifying at the same time. Donovan was one of the most intriguing people I had ever met.

He held my gaze, compelling eye contact like a chokehold. It was painful, but looking away would show weakness. Though I fought to stay afloat, I was drowning. Donovan growled deeply, "I like you." I wanted him to like me, but I was afraid of it too.

We went back to his place, and Donovan asked me if I was willing to open myself up to him. I could barely see over the walls I had carefully constructed to protect myself. I wasn't sure there was even any place I could open; I hadn't thought to build in a door. I knew that I would disappoint him, that he wanted to connect on a level which I simply couldn't reach. I went through the motions, and he sensed it; he didn't even get erect.

We called it a day, and I left an utter and complete failure. I vaguely understood that Donovan was in a place spiritually that I couldn't even imagine.

Filming was booked in San Francisco and LA. I asked Blake if he would join me in California. I thought it would be interesting for both of us to see how other porn companies worked. Let's not bullshit, though: I was nervous about going alone, and Blake and I wanted to see each other. Audra gave her blessing.

I was pouring myself into work and fucking, living in a furnished apartment to avoid confronting the storage locker packed with junk and broken dreams. The wise choice would have been to not spend a couple of weeks with Blake in California, but my brain was taking a back seat to my emotional impulses. Lingering raw vulnerability, exposed by the breakup with Carl, tangled with my feelings for Blake. Making wise choices from that position would have been like escaping from a straightjacket.

Blake and I flew into San Francisco and had a few days together in a hotel room before filming for FetRoyalty. We also shot for my site and took innumerable photos; it was a work trip after all.

"If you want to get hired, you're going to have to prove to me you want the job," I smirked as I said the clichéd lines of one of my own personal fantasies.

"Yes, ma'am," Blake mumbled, kneeling to service my pussy.

I loved filming office scenes; my skirt hiked up, him fucking me on the desk in our hotel room. It was different than the more intimate lovemaking off camera. Him sliding his cock into my pussy so slowly, stretching me, until he was all the way in, the thick base of his titanium cock filling me. Sliding in and out impossibly slowly as we looked deeply into each other's eyes. Sexual chemistry with friendship can feel like falling in love if you're in a vulnerable place. When dopamine and serotonin come into play, common sense goes out the window.

Blake and I moved into The Armoury the day before filming. They put me up in a posh room on the upper floor. It was well-appointed with antique armoires, luxurious tapestries and a decadent four-poster bed. I felt like I was in a royal castle.

On the day of filming, my face was painted up like a common whore, with so much light foundation and dark eyeliner that it looked like two piss holes in the snow. They dressed me in standard-issue sexy Domme attire; a black lace top, black leather corset, black leather skirt, black stockings and black leather boots. The outfit was fine, but I hated my makeup.

When I arrived on set I was blown away by how gorgeous it was. There was a huge painting of a muscular man entangled with an anaconda, and my strapping, oiled slave was standing in front of it being wrapped in heavy chains by Marcella. "I know they're heavy, but you can take it," she cooed at him sensually. Marcella cheerfully greeted me and introduced me to the slave and crew.

"I'm excited to work with a real Domme who knows what she's doing! It will make my job so much easier today," she exclaimed. "I'm usually directing regular porn girls and having to feed them every line."

"What will we be doing today?" I asked.

Marcella replied deviously, "Whatever you want," before shooting the slave a sly smile. "Dutchy here can handle a lot of pain. He'll take it in the ass, drink piss, lick boots... What would you like to do to him? We're going to call this scene 'Mistress T Is What You Crave', so it's about you having fun, doin' what you enjoy."

I was still extremely nervous. I was used to winging it and had never worked with a script or much direction, but a little more structure would have felt comforting in this situation. I couldn't think of anything creative at that moment, so I said, "Great. Let's do all of that."

Filming went smoothly, but it wasn't my best performance. The stop/start style of filming was new and challenging.

"Freeze!" Marcella shouted. I blinked and glanced at her. I stayed frozen mid-thrust with the strap-on while the camera girl moved and framed up another angle.

"Go!" she'd then say. An assistant would read out the last thing I had said, and I would be expected to keep going as if I hadn't paused, trying to make the action flow realistically.

I understood it created a more cinematic and finished product, but my verbals are a key part of my appeal, and the constant interruptions made it difficult for me to weave the story verbally as I normally would.

The next day I asked the makeup department to dial my look back to more of a pin-up style. They still went heavier than I preferred and insisted on fake lashes, which look ridiculous on me, like a camel. Wardrobe put me in a similar look as the day before, only this time it was red.

I knew I'd be filming with Fox Holden and had creeped his Twitter page the night before. I had seen a vid where he danced to a Michael Jackson song skillfully. I found him attractive and was happy for that because this was going to be a cuckolding scene, and we would be fucking. This part of porn, actually having intercourse on film with someone I had just met, was all new to me.

I was nervous at first, but Fox was zen-like. A seasoned professional, he had done this dozens, maybe hundreds of times; it was just another day at the office for him. I would have liked a little more interaction to build chemistry, but he mostly kept his distance. Blake was there, and perhaps Fox was being respectful.

Filming was intense for me, but everyone was chill throughout, which made it easier. The starting and stopping format was a little easier for me on the second day, but it was still annoying.

There was a cuckold slave in the scene who I teased, tortured and fucked in the ass in front of Fox. Then it was time for the sex scene. Multiple positions, including right on top of the cuckold slave. Fox had a great sense of humour and performed perfectly. He was professional to the point of detachment, which gave the sex a mechanical feel. I didn't sense that he was attracted to me; he was simply doing his job. I decided that day that this was likely the most positive experience I could expect to have fucking a stranger on film, and it didn't feel great. Doing porn like this, being directed by someone else, fucking a stranger who may not even be attracted to me; this was not what I wanted.

I felt deflated; FetRoyalty was the giant in the industry, but their style wasn't for me. I thought that this was my big opportunity to break into the larger mainstream porn world, my chance to become a bigger star. Yet I felt the scenes would not showcase me well—I didn't like the way I looked, and my verbals suffered from the interruptions. More importantly, I didn't want it anymore. I didn't want to work for other people. Wasn't that what took me down this rabbit hole in the first place?

Luckily, Blake was supportive throughout the entire experience; he was truly a gentle, nurturing person. It was a vulnerable time for me, and his company was a soothing balm.

Next stop was LA, for a shoot with CruelChambers.com. I was impressed with how organized, yet relaxed, the environment was. Gus had storyboarded the scene and directed me like it was my first time. I didn't mind because he was respectful, and he didn't treat me like I was stupid. He explained everything clearly, like he was used to working with women who had never done any Domination before. Everything went smoothly, and we wrapped early.

And just like that, my foray into the California porn industry was done.

I didn't bother cashing the paycheques from those gigs, as I didn't know how to deal with the accounting. I also didn't care, expecting the cheques to be peanuts compared to the increased sales and fame from the exposure. I thought it would lead to other big things, but it didn't work out like that.

I didn't get any emails from fans saying they discovered me through those big sites, and there wasn't a noticeable increase in my traffic or sales. No one else contacted me asking if they could feature me on their site, and I didn't even hear from Marcella again; it was like the whole thing had never happened.

Don't Cum in My Hair

B lake and I had less than a week left together in California. We continued to film and enjoy each other's company. We played sexy games, and it was a relief to have someone else in control. Blake took me from behind with me on all fours facing a full-length mirror, gently choking me with his belt around my neck. It was intensely sensual and intimate for me to give someone else control.

Later on, we were having sex in bed when without warning Blake pulled out, straddled my head and ejaculated on my face. It was a Dominant move—marking his territory, I suppose—but something inside of me snapped, and I pushed him off. The submissive side of me switched off, and I was angry. My hair would need to be washed now, and it was a lot of hassle when all I wanted was to go to sleep. It was late. Blake tried to maintain Dominance in an attempt to save the situation, but I wouldn't have it. That was the last time we played like that.

I realized that giving up control to someone else was something I could play at in the right circumstances, but my natural Dominance and pathological independence would not let me do it for long. For better or worse, this is how I was hardwired.

Blake went back to England, back to Audra, and we kept in touch. I didn't know until much later that he returned confused about his feelings. What we had was exciting, but what he had at home was a real relationship. I hadn't meant to cause problems for him and Audra, but I had.

I went back to Vancouver, where I continued to avoid my feelings and put off straightening my life out. I went on trips to Maui and home to Nova Scotia to visit my family. In December, I moved out of one furnished temporary apartment into another. I considered the possibility of moving to England to be with Blake and Audra, but I wasn't thinking straight.

Something drew me back to Donovan. I was looking for an excuse to explore our connection further. He had mentioned before that he was a trained martial artist and that he could teach me some self-defence techniques if I felt it would be helpful in my line of work. People think that sex work is dangerous and suggest various protective measures, like hidden cameras, pepper-spray, a security person and the like, but in fact violence is much more common in street-level sex work. Independent sex workers experience remarkably little. The reality is that women are in greater danger dating men in their regular life. Online dating in particular is high-risk, but most violent acts are committed by a man that a woman has made the often fatal mistake of trusting: a partner. Anyway, I liked the idea of sparring with Donovan, so I reached out and asked him if his offer was still on the table; he confirmed it was.

I met Donovan at his apartment a few times and practiced getting out of holds, targeting pain points, blocking properly, punching and kicking. Every time we came into contact, despite his professionalism, my body reacted. It was hard to focus. There was no denying I was attracted to him. Donovan didn't make a sexual move, but he did give me focused attention. He asked a lot of questions and listened to my answers; he genuinely wanted to know me. He convinced me to come to yoga with him, and I immediately loved it. He cooked for me. After a couple of weeks of spending a lot of time together, I finally asked him if he wanted to have sex with me.

"I would love to have sex with you—but not if you're unable to open up to me," he replied confidently.

I wasn't sure what he meant, but I wanted to know.

What transpired next was some of the strangest, yet pleasurable, love making I'd ever had. Donovan threw himself into the act, taking control. Holding my eyes so that I couldn't look away, his face contorted dramatically from animalistic growls to wild grins. He broke eye contact to drag his gaze over my body, to press his lips against mine, to sink his teeth into my flesh nearly hard enough to break the skin. I would like to say that I made love with him, but the truth is that he made love to me. I was more of an observer than an active participant, so enthralled by his performance that I couldn't let go. When he climaxed, he growled and howled like a beast and then laughed like a madman. I'm sure he could be heard three blocks away.

Whatever he was hoping to get from me in terms of "opening up" I was sure I had not delivered.

Despite my inability to meet him on a spiritual level, things got serious quickly anyway. The sex was addictive in its uniqueness, and we shared some darker fantasies that I had not been able to explore with many others.

Donovan saw the possibility of me, the person I was at the core. No one had ever spent so much time trying to get to know me on a cerebral level. He could see over my walls, but he couldn't crack them.

It was close to Christmas, and Donovan and I were spending more time together. I loved his complex mind. He was one of the most well-read, intelligent and colourful people I'd ever met. He consumed documentaries and books the way some people eat. He was constantly feeding his voracious brain.

I remained in regular contact with Blake, and there was still some discussion of me moving to England. But I was on the fence, knowing I would need to make a choice at some point: to stay or go. On New Year's Eve, while I was drunk and out dancing with David, the song "Home" by Edward Sharpe and the Magnetic Zeros played as the clock struck twelve. We hugged and cried, and I told him that I would stay. David had become the closest person in the world to me, and I couldn't imagine leaving him.

Donovan was only a part of the equation—I stayed for David—but Blake took it differently. It was as though I closed the door on anything more happening with us. But what could have happened? Blake was devoted to Audra, and they had a great relationship. I, meanwhile, was a reputed man-eater, incapable of having a healthy relationship. Even in a three-way relationship with Audra, Blake and I would eventually be doomed; my track record was all the evidence any rational person would need to see to verify that.

CHAPTER 50

Venus in Fur

found an unfurnished apartment and finally moved my stuff out of storage—the emotionally daunting and draining task of closing the most recent chapter of my romantic misadventures—which I'd expertly avoided for as long as possible. Months earlier, Carl had been in that gloomy storage space, pulling things out, sorting through our belongings, things we had acquired together, things that smelled like me. It must have been horrible. I could barely stand to unpack and by the middle of February, on Valentine's Day, I still had a living room full of boxes. That's when I received a curious email from a fan. It read:

Have you seen Venus in Fur? I haven't yet, but I'd like to; just need to find someone suitable to take. Any suggestions? ;) PS Happy slightly belated Valentine's Day!

I was in a cranky mood but resisted sending a snarky response about living in Vancouver, so of course I hadn't seen a play in New York. Instead I replied, "Moi?"

His quick reply said, "Good thinking. How should we arrange that?"

I was annoyed. I got so many bullshit emails every week, and I was tired of fantasists. But it was Valentine's night, and I was sitting alone in an apartment full of boxes feeling sorry for myself, so I kept things going as a distraction: "You tell me."

His answer to that wasn't at all what I expected:

"I'd be delighted to fly you to and from New York (first class of course, to and from anywhere in the world), to put you up at any hotel you'd like there, to take you to the theatre, and, if you would do me the honour, to take you to dinner or drinks anywhere you'd like as well. The one and only thing I'd prefer not to pay for is your time; that's something I'd like to have if you choose to give it to me. I can promise you it'd be worth it... I'm smart, sane, stable, mature, single, free, kind, obscenely successful (I don't know how I got so lucky?), young (your age), and pretty ok to look at. And I think you're truly fabulous. What do you think?"

Privacy was a concern, he confessed, as he was a higher-profile person. He hadn't even watched my vids to avoid any scandal associated with him being a fan of freaky fetish porn. He had only read my blog and seen my photos. I decided to take him up on his offer.

I flew to New York, first class as promised, and his driver met me in the arrivals area. He took my bags and led me to a limo with tinted windows. I stepped inside and met my wealthy, famous suitor, Max. That's obviously a made-up name, as I already explained; discretion was and still is required. He was smiling calmly, but his eyes gave away his excitement. Max was a clean-cut, younger-looking guy in his mid-thirties. His casual but fashionable clothes didn't immediately scream "money!" but on closer inspection the quality was certainly top-notch; a man who valued quality but didn't like to be flashy.

We chatted nervously at first but soon settled into a comfortable place. I learned that Max was extremely intelligent, and that's how he had accumulated his wealth. He had an interest in BDSM, but due to his high profile, he hadn't had an opportunity to explore it.

After the play, which was outstanding and had a BDSM theme, Max and I went back to the luxurious hotel room he had gotten for me (he booked his own room in a different hotel) and played around a bit with light Domination. Like many men of power, he enjoyed giving up a bit of control, but it was new to him, and he was cautious. He mostly wanted to talk. I was curious about him, and though Max was happy to share, he was eager to hear more about me and my experiences.

The next day we walked around Central Park talking before we parted ways. It had always been planned that we would only spend the evening and next day together. Max had other commitments after that, so I would be on my own for the last night and next morning before flying back to Vancouver. Before he left, Max asked what I planned to do with my remaining time. I told him that I would be going to Christian Louboutin for a pair of shoes. He offered to buy them for me, but I said, "No, thanks. This is something I want to do for me." He accepted that and left without probing for the full story.

A couple of years before, Carl and I had been in New York. We had stumbled across the Louboutin boutique. I'd never heard of it before, but when we went inside I was awestruck—I had never seen such exquisite shoes in all my life. They even had a pair that fit me, which was rare with my unusually petite feet. They were $1,000, more than triple what I had ever paid for a pair of shoes. Carl had desperately wanted me to buy them and jerk him off with them. His insatiable fetish for shoejobs resulted in me having more shoes and boots than I wanted or needed. But $1,000 was out of both of our budgets at that time. I "could" have afforded it, but it was a stretch, and it felt too extravagant, especially as a tool to jerk him off with.

Yet here I was in New York City just two years later, and business was solid. I wanted to get those shoes to symbolize my success. I wanted to get those shoes just for me. The rush of buying $1,000 shoes was exhilarating, and after I'd flown back to Vancouver on a first-class flight, I realized Max had sent the extra $1,000 anyway with a note: "I enjoyed meeting you. Thank you for coming to New York, and please accept this gift. The idea of treating you to special shoes gives me a great deal of pleasure."

CHAPTER 51

Attempted Eviction and Successful Ejection

O ver the next few months, I worked hard at my business. Most of my belongings stayed in boxes, as I avoided dealing with them. I was only half-moved in; the only usable spaces were the sets.

I ran into one of my neighbours in the hall, and it was an old acquaintance from years before. He knew through a mutual friend what I did for work, or at least what I used to do, and soon the gossip mill was churning with talk that a Dominatrix had moved into the building. Panic ensued as the older, more conservative neighbours imagined all sorts of horrors befalling their humble abode. I got a call from my forty-something landlord asking to meet.

He explained a building meeting had been called, and everyone had looked at my website. They were pressuring him to evict me, which he was reluctant to do. I assured him that evicting me was highly illegal under these circumstances. I knew my rights well. I ran a completely legal, tax-paying, incorporated business.

He nervously mumbled, "It was rather shocking seeing your website. I took some more time at home to study what you do, and I would like to discuss it with you further if you would be receptive? I'm recently divorced and curious..."

I interrupted, "No. We will not discuss it further."

"But the neighbours insist you cease all business activity in the suite, as there is a strata bylaw about running a business from a residence," he stammered. "They are nervous about crime and want me to pay for security cameras in the common areas if you refuse to move out."

"Again, I'm not moving out, and I'm not going to cease business activities. I'm not going to pretend that I am either, as you will be able to identify the inside of your suite in the vids I'll be releasing in coming months. I assure you that you have an excellent tenant who will always pay the rent on time and who will take good care of your suite. The neighbours will not hear me, and there will not be a parade of weirdos or riff-raff coming and going from my suite. You'll see. This is a moral issue, and they'll have to get over it because I'm not leaving." I then ended the meeting before he could clumsily try to hit on me again.

I continued as usual, never knowing if there would be further action or confrontation, but nothing else ever happened. I assume they looked into what they could legally do to get rid of me and figured out it was hopeless.

In the meantime, I travelled often. That winter and spring I spent a month in Bali with friends, a portion of it at a luxurious estate belonging to one of my fans. When I blogged about an upcoming trip to Bali, he wrote and insisted I stay there since it was sitting empty anyway. He arranged to have servants there who cooked and cleaned. They even put on a traditional dance performance for us. It felt surreal lounging in our private pool surrounded by manicured greenery and an imposing, sprawling marble Balinese mansion with servants waiting to serve us. I had never even met this fan before. In fact, to this day I have still never met him in person, although we kept in touch over email occasionally.

Despite my frequent absences, my relationship with Donovan intensified. Our sex games became twisted rape fantasies that were taboo and thrilling at first, but eventually became a little repetitive. He was highly emotional and occasionally during sex would become too rough, and I would reluctantly use my safe word, which I hated to do. Donovan certainly pushed my limits.

Then one night, in an unusual, irrational drunken outburst, Donovan kicked me out of his apartment in the early hours of the morning, yelling "Get the fuck out if you're in love him and want to be with him!" He was referring to one of my exes from years ago whom we had randomly run into at a party. Donovan swiped his arm across the bathroom counter, sending everything that was on top of it flying to punctuate his rage.

I calmly left, telling him he would regret his actions when he sobered up and dismissing his unusual behaviour as momentary drunkenness. But as I stepped into the street at 3 a.m., the cool air hit me, and rage overtook me. I was humiliated to be in a relationship with a man who would treat me that way. I had done absolutely nothing wrong in this case, yet I was being punished, pushed out on the streets in a rough part of town in the middle of the night. I called David and had an angry meltdown. I yelled, ranted and cursed barely coherently for at least ten minutes as I walked quickly down the street. I did not recall ever feeling such overpowering anger; it carried me away.

Donovan and I somehow patched things up, but things weren't the same. Something had closed in me, and I couldn't trust him anymore—even though he tried to counsel me through one of the hardest and most vulnerable times of my life while I was agonizingly ending things with Carl and recklessly falling for Blake, learning to run my business in a new way and trying to figure out where I wanted to live.

Years later I would see how Donovan kicking me out after I had built so much trust in him echoed another pivotal event in my formative years: Jim, my mother's husband, kicking me out. It explained the consuming rage and the detachment that followed. Jim and I never recovered from that incident, and I never forgave him. In a way, I never forgave my mother for allowing it to happen either. Donovan didn't have a prayer after my unconscious connected him to that shit.

CHAPTER 52

Little Red Riding Hood

In the spring of 2012 I took a trip to Europe to film in Budapest, Paris and England.

One of my most unpleasant filming experiences happened in Budapest. I had accepted the invitation from a woman I met at a party in London. She and her husband produced fetish content from a luxurious estate in Budapest, and I was excited by the idea of visiting an exotic location. Despite my efforts to determine what we would be filming prior to my arrival, the details were vague. A slave from The FemDom Authority, one that I had worked with and liked, was also booked. We arrived the night before filming and were still not told what we would be shooting the next day. They were disorganized, and it was disconcerting.

The next morning we were finally presented with the list of scenes planned for the day. I sat there listening, mortified. In one scene they wanted me to fuck myself with a shoe—like actually penetrate my vagina with as much of the shoe as I could ram in there. In another scene, they wanted me to dress in a cheap frilly

Little Red Riding Hood costume for some reason. They also wanted me to be dominated in a lesbian strap-on scene.

The worst was that in several of the scenes they wanted me to fuck the slave, which I had no desire to do—he was not a fuck slave in the first place. I knew his cock barely worked, as he had erectile difficulties. He wouldn't be able to perform sexually, even if I did want to fuck him. They wanted me to wear a mask in some scenes, and I thought that was a foolish idea—to hire a semi-famous performer and then cover her face—but I already felt that these films would be such an embarrassment that I might actually prefer my face to stay hidden. This company wasn't interested in collaboration; they expected us to do what we were told without question.

They had already paid me, and I had come all the way to Budapest. Their estate was also far away from anything. The slave and I looked at each other as if we were about to face a firing squad. I felt trapped and started to panic, so I asked for a drink.

I pulled the woman aside and explained that the slave's cock didn't work and, even if it did, I would not fuck him. They certainly should have discussed that part before we agreed to come. I also expressed my hesitation to do everything else on their list. I explained that I had a brand to protect and that I couldn't do scenes where I played the part of a submissive. They didn't even try to hide their annoyance.

I self-medicated with wine to get myself through the day. The slave was comforting, and somehow we got through it. I'll be honest: I was so intoxicated that I don't even recall what we did in some of those scenes. Later on, I saw photos of me dressed in that ridiculous Little Red Riding Hood outfit and the slave in a hentai wolf costume and had no recollection of what had taken place. In one lesbian scene I wore a cute, pink and frilly latex nurse's dress. I recall another lesbian leather fetish scene where we licked each other's leather jackets and gloves, and another woman fucked her pussy with a shoe. The whole day was a blur, and when filming was done, we went to our separate rooms. The next morning they drove me into town without a friendly word. The whole experience solidified my feelings about working for other people: it just wasn't worth it.

After a couple of days touring around Budapest on my own, I

took the train to Paris. I felt incredibly lonely and raw, traumatized from my filming experience in Budapest. Trying to relax in Paris, I explored the museums and spent some time with a fan that I met and felt comfortable with. He was young and eccentrically cool. He made me smile, which I badly needed. The last time I had been in Paris, Carl and I had been breaking up on my birthday. Being back in the City of Lights, I had to be honest with myself and admitted that I had been keeping busy to avoid dealing with my feelings about that whole episode. While it's obvious in retrospect, until that moment I couldn't admit I'd been walking wounded.

I took the train to England and stayed with Blake and Audra at their new estate. It felt like a big warm hug to be with them again. They were so welcoming, accepting and loving. The English countryside was charming and relaxing with its rolling pastures and quaint little towns full of ancient rock buildings. It was exactly what I needed.

Audra mothered me. We talked endlessly about my breakup with Carl and my new relationship with Donovan. She offered me valuable business advice. She told me about her stress from ongoing drama with her ex, which sounded genuinely horrific; I couldn't understand why anyone would want to hurt Audra. Then I remembered with guilt that there were moments when Blake and I considered running away together—even if it was only pillow talk— and how that would have hurt her. I never wanted to take him away from her, and I didn't think of it like that in the heat of the moment. I just desperately wanted someone to cling to; I wanted to be saved, and in those dark moments Blake was an island in a sea of nothing.

Blake and I had moved on to a deep friendship, with enough passion remaining to still have some fun and to create some fantastic FemDom sex scenes. My feelings for him had cooled, and he may have been hurt by that, but it was for the best.

We filmed some sizzling content that trip. We worked collaboratively, and Audra never requested I do things I was uncomfortable with. She carefully created scenes that showcased the best of me and used my unique skills and talents. Audra is an unparalleled FemDom genius. Our business relationship was solidified: I was good for The FemDom Authority, and they were good for me. I gave them unique, valuable content, and they let me use their sets, slaves and equipment for my own content. The exposure and traffic they sent my way was invaluable.

After a couple of weeks, I reluctantly went back to Vancouver. I wanted to stay at The FemDom Authority, a place where my soul was fed and my business would flourish, forever. But I had already booked a surgery for the following week.

CHAPTER 53

I Love Sam Mack

———

I had made the decision months before to have a subtle breast augmentation. I was thirty-six, and my breasts looked okay, but they were deflating. Age and gravity are unforgiving. I had gotten into the adult film industry later than most—at an age where many adult film stars are already washed up or burned out. I had to keep up. It went against my personal feelings about growing old gracefully and the cosmetic industry's ongoing assault on women's self-esteem, but it was a business decision.

I tried to choose the smallest, most natural look. I showed the doctor pics of my breasts from my twenties and asked him to try to recreate them. I didn't want women who looked up to me to be influenced by my choice. I decided not to announce the surgery, as some performers do, but rather to wear bras for a couple of months before and after the surgery to hopefully camouflage what I had done.

Samantha took me in for the procedure. When I awoke after, she was standing there holding a bright-blue t-shirt that read "I love Sam Mack" as a gift for me. Half-stoned, I was confused by the gift; she had an odd sense of humor. Samantha took me home, got me set up with everything I needed and left. I slept for the first day or two. I wandered around my apartment, avoiding the mirror. I felt regretful of what I had done and resentful that I worked in an industry where I felt obligated to have surgery. I had cut into my body and inserted foreign objects, for what? To make my breasts appear more youthful? To give the appearance of fertility to arouse men I'll never meet?

On the third day, I reached out to Donovan to see if he would help me bathe. We had discussed the surgery, and he had offered to help before our last disagreement, which was about nothing in particular. There was a rift between us, and any small thing—anything at all—could widen it. While he probably was surprised that I actually took him up on it, Donovan was a man of his word and showed up to do his duty without any warmth or love or humour or empathy. He was just doing his job, which stung. I felt abandoned in a time of need—I didn't want to ask for any more help even though I needed it. Donovan was cold, done and fed up, so I let him go without telling him how I felt. I knew it was over, and I couldn't help feeling that I'd missed something. Something huge. Something right in front of my face that I somehow could not see.

During my recovery I came across a fetish blog. The most recent post featured an image of a painting and asked, "Is this a cuckolding scene?"

By the light of a television a half-dressed woman straddled and embraced a man, while another man sat beside them looking disinterested—or maybe annoyed? The painting was dark, gritty, rich and highly textured. The style provoked something visceral inside of me, so I looked up the artist. I could hardly believe it when I discovered that he lived in my city! The blog was by a guy in Europe, which made the coincidence especially unusual, and the artist's portfolio website mentioned that he took commissions, so I reached out about having my portrait done.

"A dark horse, this one," I thought as Drew Young stepped into my apartment. He was almost thirty, slender, of average height and had tousled brunette hair; everything about him communicated that he wasn't trying to impress me. He had a face that didn't lend itself to smiling. Probably a nihilist. On second thought, definitely a nihilist.

I had explained how I had found him in the email I had sent to arrange this meeting. So the first thing he opened with in person was, "Um, what is cuckolding anyway?"

Well, that settled the blogger's question.

After I explained he laughed and asked, patronizingly, "Didn't you, like, see the cocaine on the table in front of the sofa? The painting is entitled 'The Usual Lengthy Visit.' It's just a typical image of people who stay up all night doing blow, you know?"

I opened my laptop and looked again at the painting from the blog. Indeed, right there in plain sight was a little mirror with neat lines of white powder.

"Sometimes cocaine is glamourized, you know?" he continued. "Ummm, but in the real world it's often just, like, people sitting around kind of bored doing lines. Nothing to do with cuckolding. Like, that's not his wife or girlfriend. He's probably not getting off on it, you know. I don't think he cares. I dunno, there wasn't any deep meaning to it. Just, um, regular people doing rails sittin' 'round. It's funny how it ended up on that blog, that someone would read into it like that, but that's art, I guess."

He smirked at that last bit, and I realized that was the closest he would come to smiling. I was starting to gather that he was a bit baked, his half-closed eyelids and slightly slurred speech being a solid giveaway. Or maybe that's just Drew? I didn't care either way; I liked him.

I explained what I was hoping for. "I'd like to give you artistic freedom to do my portrait with very few guidelines. I can't look submissive or vulnerable. I don't have to look Dominant either, but just not submissive. It should also be obvious that it's me. Someone who knows me should be able to recognize that the face is mine. That's it. I'm fine with nude or not. Whatever inspires you."

"Mmm-hmm... Tell me all about you," he said while glancing at me, then at his knee, maybe not wanting me to feel interrogated. Whatever it was, it worked. I spilled the beans.

I released the most personal details about myself that I could muster on the spot. It was cathartic to be completely raw with a stranger; to expose my weaknesses when I'd asked him to portray me as "not vulnerable."

He listened, looking thoughtful, glancing at me and then back at his lap. He didn't seem surprised or fascinated or anything in particular.

When I finished, silence lingered until he offered, "I'll think about it and… come back with my camera in a couple of days." His process was to take a bunch of photos and use them to create the painting.

He returned a few days later with a clear vision. "Please take off your clothes, and get on the medical table."

I felt self conscious about my breasts—only a couple of weeks old—looking like two over-inflated balloons riding high and hard on my chest. I asked him to paint them as they would be in a while, with more natural sag, but Drew didn't seem to understand; I started wondering if he might be gay. He'd been completely professional, and other than doctors I wasn't used to men being unaffected by my nude body.

He placed the items he'd requested around me: a latex nurse's dress on a chair; my video camera and Louboutin shoes on the floor; a small, framed picture of my mother at nineteen; and a pair of glasses on a table by my feet. He fiddled with the picture and glasses, positioning Mom so that he could see her, glasses pointing at me, picture in between.

"It's like your mother is looking at you…" he murmured.

He carefully positioned the mirror—I was to look at it over my shoulder—and started snapping pictures. He had me adjust my position and facial expression a few times. It didn't take long, and he didn't say much. When it was over, I was left for a moment sitting naked and ignored on the table while he looked at the images on the screen of his camera to ensure he got what he needed.

He hung around for a drink and smoked a joint on my balcony. We chatted about various things, his other jobs, his life. He was excited about this project in a way that was both shy and cocky at the same time. An intense confidence about his work mixed with awkward ambiguity, circling his place in the world like uncertain wolves. It made him seem like a bit of an asshole, but a likeable asshole; the underdog anti-hero in a pulp paperback that rubbed other characters the wrong way but was addictive to the reader.

At his studio, he went to work on the painting, and when I finally got to see it a few weeks later, the result was stunning.

"People will ask you what this or that means, you know?" he said. "It's art. It's, like, for each person to interpret for themselves. I won't answer that for you or anyone else. You know what you told me. You can draw your own conclusions."

As for what it means to me—well, I chose it as the cover for this book. Does that help?

CHAPTER 54

Heroin

—————————

Life went on. I healed from the surgery and got back to work and travelled again as soon as I was able to; I spent some time with long-devoted fans and headed to Florida for Fetcon after that. After a couple of months I was healed enough to return to yoga and, with some trepidation, went back to the yoga studio Donovan and I used to frequent. As I walked up the steps I thought I heard his laughter, and my stomach did a flip-flop. As I entered the room, he turned to look at me and beamed a huge smile at me as he warmly said, "Honeybadger." It was a nickname he had given me "because you don't give a shit about anything," he explained. We were cordial, exchanging pleasantries awkwardly and cautiously. We did yoga in the same room and then went our separate ways.

I ran into Donovan at the yoga studio about once a week when I was in town, but I travelled often. On a trip to New York, Max and I arranged to meet for dinner and a play. Although our first meeting hadn't blown either of us away, we had stayed in touch. I think he found my profession intriguing. The day before we were to meet he wrote to let me know he had just met a woman he was very smitten with. He wanted to be honest and transparent about it and give me a chance to cancel the date if I wanted to. I told him that of course I still wanted to see him and hear all about the new lady. I was surprised he thought I would mind. A man in his position could never be in a relationship with someone like me; it would be scandalous. I had no illusions that whatever was between us would be anything other than casual.

We went to see *The Book of Mormon*, which was completely sold out—but not for people like Max. We went to dinner after, and he told me all about the lady he had met a few days earlier while on vacation. He was enamoured with her, and as he talked about her, his face lit up. He was so much more animated now than in our first meeting that I saw another side of Max. If I had seen that side of him the first time we'd met, would things have turned out differently? I pointed out the difference in his demeanour, and he admitted that he had been stiff and cautious during our first encounter. A little part of me wondered, "What if I missed my *Pretty Woman* moment?"

I also saw the slave who had bought me the video camera and who had paid $1,000 for a snowball. I messaged him from the posh Agent Provocateur lingerie shop telling him he should come pay my bill. I was surprised when he replied he'd be there right away.

When the paypig arrived, he asked if I had time to see his new place. He had recently renovated a swanky penthouse, and he wanted to show it off. We spent the following hours catching up and playing in his ridiculous home. He had covered the walls and ceilings in cream leather. Everything was custom and designed to scream, "Look how rich I am!" I made fun of him for it and talked about how he was compensating for his tiny penis. He loved it. I modelled the lingerie he bought for me, and he jerked off while I talked about wearing it and fucking a big black stud. I would have charged more for my time if it had been a straight cash transaction, but he paid and arranged for a driver for me for the rest of my trip, so I was satisfied.

I went to England again in the fall. Sitting in my room at The FemDom Authority, I got a message from a mutual friend that Donovan wanted me to read a blog he wrote.

It took me a couple of hours to get through it all. Donovan had written a journal about his time in the woods detoxing from heroin. I was shocked; I had no idea he was shooting heroin. The blog explained that he had dabbled in it before we broke up, but he used our breakup as an excuse to go on a bender. I couldn't have known when I'd seen him at the yoga studio, but Donovan was spiralling out of control into full-blown addiction. We only exchanged brief pleasantries, but he displayed no outward sign of being less than fine.

After several months of using, Donovan decided to get himself clean by having someone drop him off deep in the woods with nothing more than a few basic supplies. He wrote the journal I was now reading while on his journey of detoxing. He wrote about his feelings towards me—how he was angry at me for not delivering on things I had never promised him. How he didn't have a right to be angry with me but was nonetheless. I owed and promised him nothing, but he was still disappointed when nothing was what he actually got. He had certainly hoped for more. Donovan was confused by my coldness and detachment, and I had hurt him deeply.

I thought about how he had always asked me to open up to him, how I had kept him at arm's length. How I'd not been capable of doing what he asked, even if I wanted to.

I came out of my room stunned and explained to Audra and Blake what I had just learned. Audra rolled her eyes and said that it was absurd to think I had caused him to become a heroin addict. She had never been supportive of my relationship with Donovan, and this confirmed her low opinion of him.

I didn't think it was absurd, though, and neither did Blake. He had, after all, gone through something similar with me in the last year by developing feelings for me and having me walk away with hardly a second thought. It feels awful apparently, and Blake empathized with Donovan. To different degrees, this pattern had played out over and over in my life. I had a long list of men in my past that would tell a similar story of detachment and confusing heartbreak—I would let them get close enough to fall in love with me, but I never truly let them in. In the end, I always turned away as if they had never meant anything to me at all.

When I gathered myself, I wrote to Donovan and expressed my regret for any part I had played in his addiction and wished him the best in his recovery. I didn't know what else to say.

CHAPTER 55

Black Magic

The next month I went to Mexico for Christmas with a girlfriend. Near the end of the trip I started chatting with a hot black guy named Ben in the pool. One thing led to another, and we ended up back in his room fucking. I was taking a pic of our reflection in the mirror by his bed when Ben said, "We look great together. We should make a video."

I laughed and didn't say anything in the moment; Ben didn't know yet what I did for work. I had brought my video camera "just in case," so I asked him if he was serious about making a video and told him about my business. He was enthusiastic about the idea, and that night I made my first interracial vid. I didn't have good lighting, and it was amateurish, but it was also genuinely real. I knew my fans would eat it up; they'd been begging to see me fuck a black man for years. The sales of that one vid in the first week paid for my whole vacation.

I invited Ben to join me in Vegas at the tail end of my annual porn awards trip to shoot some more scenes. We got along well; he was a gentleman who loved making porn and spent a lot of time working out, so his body was a masterpiece. He was proud to show it off, and he performed like a star.

CHAPTER 56

Money Doesn't Buy Personality

Back in Vancouver, I received a session request from an interesting-sounding client. He claimed that he was a huge fan and would fly to Vancouver in his private jet, get the best suite in the nicest hotel and pay me anything I demanded just to have a session with me. He said discretion was important, but he was forthcoming in telling me who he was and invited me to google him. It turned out he was a high-profile lawyer, so I named an outrageous price. He agreed on the condition that our time together wasn't limited; he wanted the whole afternoon and evening.

I stood in front of the door to a suite in the nicest hotel in Vancouver, gathering myself before knocking. The hotel's decor was luxurious, even in the hallway. I wondered how I had gotten to this place and why obscenely rich men wanted to spend time with me and were willing to pay ridiculous amounts of money for the opportunity. What had it cost to fly a private jet here?

I knocked, and "Harry" opened the door. He was wearing an expensive suit and holding a cut crystal tumbler. I could tell he'd been drinking, and it was only 11 a.m. He reeked of the obnoxious, entitled American vibe that would make many Canadians want to pummel him with a hockey stick.

I entered, and we sat down at the imposing dining room table in a type of hotel suite that I didn't even know existed. It was like a large townhome with multiple rooms and levels: three stories high with floor-to-ceiling windows overlooking the city.

Slurring his words slightly, with bloodshot eyes and glaringly fake-white teeth, Harry started right in asking me personal questions about my love life, my family and, "Has anyone ever paid you this much for a session?"

I wondered how a guy like this didn't get punched in the face every single day of his life.

He tried to get me to come over and sit on his knee. I refused.

He tried to get me to drink with him. I declined.

Eventually, Harry offered to show me the toys he had brought. We went upstairs, and he had dozens of toys, restraints and implements laid out on the bed and dresser. I suggested we get on with things before he became too intoxicated. I changed into boots and fetish lingerie in one of the fancy washrooms and came out to find him standing in the middle of the room naked and grinning foolishly, holding his tumbler of liquor.

We went through the paces of corporal punishment and ass fucking, Harry topping from the bottom and making requests all the while. Even when I put a ball gag on him, he managed to wiggle out of it and keep yammering. Eventually, he started acting sleepy and was asking to cuddle. I explained that I was a Dominatrix: "Cuddling isn't what I do."

He sulked about that but lay down and proceeded to pass out. I tidied up, got dressed in my regular clothes and explored the palatial suite.

I thought about leaving, but he hadn't paid yet. Although it felt tacky to ask up front, I regretted not doing so. Even if I had, it wouldn't have been right to leave this early. I had agreed to spend the afternoon and evening with him.

I sat and read some magazines, took selfies and enjoyed the

view. I could hear Harry's cell phone ringing, but he was out cold. After a couple of hours, he appeared at the top of the stairs looking completely wrecked and asking me again to cuddle with him. I refused, so he came down, and we sat at the table again. He ordered room service to bring him more booze. When I suggested he put something on, he wrapped a plush hotel robe around himself and waited. A demure woman arrived with a tray full of tiny, carefully organized bottles of liquor. It was ridiculous, but apparently there is a law against serving a larger bottle of alcohol to a hotel room.

Harry continued to interrogate me, asking questions that were none of his business. I diplomatically tried to dodge them, but he was skilled at cross-examination. I felt like I was on trial. My desire to ruin his smug face intensified.

Eventually, we went for dinner at a restaurant across the street. It was the most delicious food I'd ever eaten. Harry continued to drink and started feeling unwell near the end of the meal. Slurring his words, talking too loud and saying outrageous things, he was barely fit to be in public. Harry asked, too loudly, what he owed me as he started pulling handfuls of money out of his pocket. I told him the amount, and he counted it out and gave it to me.

Then, in front of the waiter who was refilling our water glasses and as others stared at the spectacle, he started pulling hundred-dollar bills out of his wallet and handing them to me while saying something about getting too drunk. The waiter was diplomatically trying to keep a poker face as our eyes met. Calmly, I took the money; these people were strangers, after all, and I didn't look like a hooker. I had no idea why they might have thought he was handing me money, but I didn't care. It had been a long day of babysitting this drunken man-child, and the least I could do was get well compensated for it.

I went home and counted the money—it was a lot. What the hell just happened? How could a guy like that become so successful? Evidently, Harry was good at his job, but I expected he had far more enemies than friends.

Harry contacted me a few days later begging me to come have a session with him at his place. He said he had a special BDSM apartment he wanted to show me. I told him I didn't want to see him again and that his drinking was unacceptable. He promised he wouldn't drink. I compromised and said that we could meet in Toronto on my way to Nova Scotia to visit family and, if it went well, I would come to see him again on the way back.

Of course this time Harry was on his best behaviour. He put me up in a luxurious hotel suite that we only used for a couple of hours, but I was welcome to spend the night in it. He stayed true to his promise and didn't drink. We had a light session involving boot worship and a golden shower. He paid me well and was pleasant when he wasn't intoxicated, so I agreed to come to his place the next week.

Harry sent a driver to pick me up and take me to my hotel. I had the first night to myself, and we met in the morning for our full-day session do-over. He took me to a discreet apartment that he had cleverly outfitted with secret dungeon equipment and hidden closets, containing everything you could ever imagine. At a glance, the apartment looked perfectly normal, and he assured me that his cleaners would be none the wiser. Everyday-looking chairs converted into spanking benches and bookcases opened up to reveal secret compartments in the walls hiding floggers, canes, crops, gimp hoods and restraints—it was like a funhouse.

Harry requested that he be allowed to have one drink to loosen up and insisted that I join him. I allowed him to pour me a drink, but I only sipped it. He downed his and went for another. I warned him that I would not be okay with him getting intoxicated. He promised he wouldn't. As before, Harry wanted to talk. He loved to hear his own voice, bragging about his success and talking about his fetishes in between asking me personal questions.

We eventually got down to business and put to use a small selection of his extensive collection. I kept him tied up most of the time to keep him from getting drunk. I blindfolded and gagged him, then put a vibrator in his ass so that I could relax. I decided to drink a little more to make the day easier. I usually wouldn't drink, but Harry had stocked the finest champagne—a rare treat. He had paid me earlier in the day, and I kept recounting the massive stack of money while sipping the expensive bubbly and enjoying the opulence of my surroundings.

I wasn't sure if I had made it, or if this was some kind of hell where you use booze and money to mask how miserable you are. No matter how I sliced it, Harry was an abhorrent wretch. The only redeeming quality I found in him was the entertainment value in his outrageous vulgarity. He was a one-man Jerry Springer Show: a human specimen you might want to gawk at briefly but wouldn't want to be in the company of for even five minutes. And after spending so much time with him, I felt the need for a cleanse. Or an exorcism.

CHAPTER 57

Spiritual Gutting

B ack in Vancouver, I discovered that there would be an opportunity to "journey" with ayahuasca a few weeks later with a shaman who was coming from Peru. A friend had been gently encouraging me to try aya for the last year or so. She had been to Peru a couple of times and had journeyed dozens of times there, so she spoke about it with great reverence. It sounded mysterious and risky, but I felt drawn to it.

I did research and learned that it was a psychedelic plant that in some ways is similar to peyote or mushrooms; I had a lot of experience with mushrooms and loved them. Ayahuasca was reportedly life-changing for most people, usually in a good way. It was different for every person, but it helped many people break free from addictions. Others reported altering their lives in a more positive direction afterwards. It sounded crazy, but there was definitely something intangible missing from my life, something deeper I couldn't put my finger on—as cliche as that sounds—so I decided to try it with Candace and Ryan.

After following a specific diet, known as "la dieta," for a week to prepare our bodies for the medicine, the three of us drove to the ceremony together, feeling anxious. We ambled down a narrow dirt road off the highway for a few minutes before coming to a clearing with a round, weather-worn wooden structure in the centre, about thirty feet in diameter. The pitched roof appeared to be made out of cedar slats. I learned this was called a meloka. Tall grass surrounded it, and a little outhouse sat near the entrance. Beyond the tall grass were trees, mostly pine, for as far as I could see. As we approached the covered porch where the entrance was, I noticed stacks of colourful, cheap plastic buckets and about a dozen sets of footwear neatly lined up. We pulled our shoes off and opened the old-fashioned screen door, entering a dimly lit round room in which people were quietly chatting with each other while setting up their mats.

My eyes darted around the room collecting information as I registered the smell of patchouli or something else associated with hippies. I realized there was an altar set up on the far side. I could make out a few candles, crystals and musical instruments. I then noticed an incense stick burning and identified that as the source of the scent.

The people all looked like regular folks wearing mostly comfortable yoga clothing, sweatsuits or warm sweaters. They were demographically similar: white men and women in their mid-twenties to early forties, healthy to average physiques, clean cut—normie conformist types. Everyone was setting up around the circumference of the room, laying out the yoga mats and blankets we were told to bring. More people shuffled in, and we kept squeezing tighter until all the mats were touching and our neighbours were close enough to elbow. I counted twenty-one of us by the time things with the bucket lottery got started.

Someone had brought in all of the buckets and put them in the middle of the room. I heard someone say that everyone should grab a bucket, that there should be enough for everyone, and there was a bit of a rush to the middle of the room. I hung back and got the last one, which was cracked and filthy with dirt and clumped leaves on the inside. The bucket no one else wanted, I guess.

A woman sat down at the altar, and I realized she must be the curandera, the person leading the ceremony. I hadn't noticed her before because she had blended in with the others, and I'm not sure what I was expecting, but it wasn't this.

She was a heavy-set woman, not obese, but she moved with a heaviness that implied she found her weight a burden. A big beige poncho concealed her figure but made her appear voluminous in the dim light. Her wispy, wavy, sandy blonde hair was combed neatly and fell past her shoulders. Milky skin pulled tightly over her round cheeks, and her light eyes gave her a cherub look. She wasn't wearing makeup and struck me as the type of woman who was dead set against such frivolities. Her complexion was flawless and made it difficult to gauge her age, though my guess was maybe late thirties. She explained that she was originally from Alberta and had been living in Peru studying and practicing as a shaman for nearly a decade.

She asked everyone to mentally set an intention for the ceremony, something we hoped to get out of the experience. We were also instructed to honour silence and to stay inside unless we needed to use the latrine. Her helper, a friendly-looking young man wearing what appeared to be white cotton pajamas, smudged each of us with sage. By that I mean he moved a smouldering bundle of dried shrubs the size of a hot dog bun around each of us so that we were anointed with the smoke. This was to cleanse the energy of the space, we were told.

Each of us then took our turn coming up to the altar and drinking our little cup of foul-tasting tea. We sat in the crowded room, lit only by a candle in front of the shaman, waiting for the medicine to kick in.

The shaman started playing one of the string instruments and singing. Her voice was strong, clear and beautiful. The music was what you might expect for a spiritual, holistic experience: soothing, melodic, a near cousin of folk. After about twenty minutes things started happening: I entered a tunnel, a bright kaleidoscope of colours; pastel and bright multi-coloured fractals. I could hear a buzzing in my ears as I moved through this spinning tunnel. It was dazzling and so intense that it terrified me—I did not have the sensation that I was only looking at it; I was in it, of it.

I registered that there was a girl flailing out into the middle of the room, moving toward the candle and yelling for help. I could see her through the tunnel of colour, like when you overlap two photo negatives. I was scared. I wanted to help her, but I couldn't move. I was more in the tunnel than I was in that room. The shaman's helper rushed over to her, and I went back fully into the tunnel, moving through it as the buzzing got louder in my ears, drowning out the music. So bright and beautiful. Ryan crashed into me, but I could not move. He was leaning heavily against my back, and I thought he was throwing up on me, but there was nothing I could do about it and accepted that I would have his vomit on me. I willed myself not to care, but caring was slipping away regardless of my will, like a piece of wet spaghetti sliding thru the tines of a fork.

The glorious-sounding music came and went through the buzzing, a part of me and everything else, colours flowing along with it. I was far, far away, floating, flying and caring less—when suddenly the music changed and became more serious. Things got darker, and the images became scary. Not so easily defined as horrible faces, fangs, hollow eyes, terrifying creatures or monsters, but more of a sense of horror, danger, things unknown, torture, suffering, pain, fear. A consuming, everlasting darkness. Hell. Nausea crept up on me. I grabbed my bucket and vomited. Waves of nausea washed over me as I purged from the deepest part of myself. I was being turned inside out. Everything was dark, and negative images, as well as non-specific memories, consumed me. I was emptying myself into that bucket—it was bottomless eternity, and if it sucked me in, I'd never come back.

I vomited, I purged, I stopped caring about being quiet; I could hear others throwing up too. I let it go, making the worst gut-wrenching noises. I prayed to a god that I did not believe existed that if I could get through this, I would never do ayahuasca again. It went on for hours—hours which stretched to eternity. I fought to stay in the present; I didn't want to go down the tunnel again; I didn't want to get sucked into the bottom of the bucket; I didn't want to give into it. I fought it and fought it. When the effects of the aya started lifting and the ceremony was coming to a close, I felt like I had won but then wondered, *what* had I won? I fought it and suffered greatly the whole time. I felt too weak to walk. What did I win?

Everyone in the group took turns talking about their experience. I couldn't believe that we all had had such different results while in the same room drinking the same thing. I didn't want to talk; I didn't share my experience. No one else experienced anything like I did. Most people described a more pleasant journey, but no two stories were alike.

At the end, the shaman asked me to come up to talk to her personally. I told her that it had been horrible and that I would not be returning for the next two nights even though I had paid for them. She was dismissive and not at all empathetic. I desperately needed to be taken care of, to be nurtured, but she was solid ice. She didn't like me, and therefore I didn't like her.

I went back to Candace and Ryan's to rest, but even though I didn't sleep well, I woke up feeling mysteriously refreshed. I found that very strange—I had retched my guts out for hours the night before and expected to feel physically awful the next day, but I didn't.

The next day I picked up a foster cat from the SPCA and brought him home with me. He had a cold and couldn't be around other cats until he healed. I called him Wheezy because he wheezed when he breathed. He was super cuddly and loving, which was exactly what I needed.

Two days after the ceremony I woke up with Wheezy sleeping nuzzled into my neck. The sun was shining, and I felt better than I had ever felt in my life. An overwhelming sense of joy and gratitude enveloped me—so much that I got misty. I carried that feeling throughout the day and into the next, and the next.

In the following week, I attended social functions where I would usually drink. The thing was, I didn't want the booze. I was able to socialize with people in a way I'd never been able to before. Usually talking with people felt draining, and when others told me their problems I would take them on, but it would weigh me down. Instead I could be present, hear them, empathize, yet not take on their feelings in a way that negatively affected me. I could give them the gift of being heard and then move on. It wasn't my life to live or my problem to solve.

I didn't have anxiety about social situations anymore. Poof—just like that. I didn't understand that I had the anxiety until it was gone; its absence revealed it. I no longer felt compelled to drink to cope. It was a significant shift: I became an emotional superhero.

This lasted for weeks. Six weeks to be exact. That's when I decided to have a drink again. Everything had been going perfectly well, so in a spontaneous moment I decided to have a social drink. I didn't feel like I needed it; I just thought it would enhance the fun I was already having. I was at a party with dear friends, and no one discouraged me from drinking, even the non-drinkers. They thought it was funny that I was making such a big deal of it and that I hadn't drank in six weeks. No one considered me someone with a drinking problem, so it wasn't like an alcoholic falling off the wagon. Plus, I was a fun drunk. That first drink felt amazing, so I had one more. I danced and laughed, and it didn't feel like anything changed about my emotional state that night.

That was the beginning of the busy summer of 2013. I had great beach and party friends. I was consistent with my yoga practice and took trips to meet up with industry peers. Harry flew back into town in his private jet for another session at the swanky hotel. I was able to deal with him better by then. Everything felt easier.

In July I started hanging out with a cute, submissive boy toy. Kenny desperately wanted to become a famous actor, and as a Christian Bale doppelganger, he had the right pretty-boy look. He was a plaything to me, arm candy to accompany me to parties and the beach. He had a foot fetish, and the constant foot rubs were a treat, especially when my feet were sore from kicking him in the balls, which he loved.

Strangely though, something started to shift around the same time he came into my life. I first noticed that I wasn't waking up happy every morning anymore. Some days were good; some days weren't. It was no longer consistently wonderful. Over the following weeks I began to have strange thoughts; darkness was creeping in. The joyous, grateful moments were getting farther apart, and I started to feel as I always had—my old "normal." A few more weeks passed, and the needle slid past "normal" to an even darker place. I began feeling numb, disconnected and slow-moving; I even started to think about killing myself.

CHAPTER 58

Dirty Secret

I told no one how I was feeling and pretended everything was normal. I kept working. I kept partying. I went to industry conventions and put on my best face. The boy toy I was fucking didn't know. David didn't know. None of my family knew. I became obsessed with the idea that death was like before birth: I would be aware of nothing. The calmness of it was so alluring. I felt deep shame and could barely admit to myself that I was suicidal. I was better than that, after all.

I had much to be grateful for: I was incredibly successful, I was attractive and I could fuck nearly anyone I desired. I travelled all over the world, had wonderful friends, and my health was good. I had no reason to be suicidal. The thing is I didn't feel sad; I felt numb—felt nothing—but I didn't want to believe I was depressed. I wanted to go back to how I was the weeks following the aya experience. I just didn't know how to get there.

I was retreating more and more, spending a lot of time alone. Most friends probably thought I was busy with work or spending time with other people. No one realized I was spending so much time alone. One day, desperate to snap myself out of my funk, I spontaneously went to the movie theatre by myself. I randomly chose to see *The Great Gatsby* and loved the visuals, but it was a sad movie overall, and it featured a song with lyrics that haunted me: *Will you still love me when I'm no longer young and beautiful?* It nagged at me. I looked up the song and found it was by Lana Del Ray, who I'd never heard of before. I watched a few of her other videos and was enthralled.

That night I went out to a fetish party with David. I told him nothing about what I was going through, and I felt old and ugly the entire evening. I drank heavily and felt bitter about aging. I knew that the thousands of fans who jerked off to me would move on as I aged. They would find someone younger and more beautiful to worship or lust after. I knew that the ease I had in picking up men at bars would soon end, that I was becoming too old for many men.

I had entered my late thirties. People would say I looked good for my age, implying that I was old and that my expiry date was fast approaching. Who was I without my looks? I'd built an empire based heavily on my physical appearance. No matter how clever I was, I would never have been this successful in the adult film industry without looks—and they were fading. The whole second half of my life would be a downward slide into hideousness and invisibility.

I thought about how Betty Page hadn't allowed any photos to be taken of her after a certain age. I thought about the horrible things they said about Elizabeth Taylor as she aged. I thought about Marilyn Monroe, how she died young—barbiturate suicide—as her looks were starting to go, so as to always be remembered as young and beautiful.

When I got home I listened to Lana Del Ray's song on repeat. I cried. I sobbed. There was no one who would love me when I was no longer young and beautiful. I was alone. All I had was a casual boy toy who wouldn't stick around. I thought about each one of my friends, every one of my family members. Who was worth living for? As much as I cared for some or they cared for me, no one was compelling enough. I started taking pills. I wanted to go to sleep. I didn't care if I woke up.

I held the bottle in my hand wondering if I had enough mixed with alcohol to kill myself. I wanted it—I wanted to die. It felt inescapably alluring. So I took another pill.

Then I thought about David. He had dropped me off only hours before. He had no idea what I'd been going through. I had hid it from him and everyone else. If I killed myself, he would never, ever forgive himself for missing the signs. It would ruin his life, and I couldn't do that to him. It wasn't fair. That mattered more than my release. So I stopped swallowing pills, and I went to bed numb and resentful that I would live. The alcohol and pill mixture did make me sick, and I suffered through the pain, wishing even more that I could die.

I spent the next day in bed but then continued on as if everything was normal. A couple weeks later David and I left for Burning Man, and on the drive down I told him what had happened. It was hard to tell him, and I felt ashamed, overly dramatic and slightly insane. David listened without saying much. He was driving and only glanced at me a few times as I told him the truth. His eyes started to well up at the thought of almost losing me, which made me start to cry too. I didn't want to hurt him.

"Tracey, I need you to tell me if you start to feel that way again," David implored. "Please, don't hide it from me again."

I told him that I couldn't promise, but that I would try.

We went to Burning Man, and I enjoyed it. We didn't talk much more about my suicidal thoughts. On the drive back we took the slow route, stopping by small towns and hot springs. Still, something about that trip revived me, I'm not sure why, and I returned to Vancouver happier than I had been in a while.

CHAPTER 59

Numb

A round that time, out of the blue, I realized that I could fuck any male pornstar I wanted. Thousands of women might lust over them, but I could hire them to do a sex scene with me—then sell the vid and make a profit off of it. It would be for my business. I couldn't believe it hadn't occurred to me before.

I decided to go big right off the bat and reached out to Sean Titanic. He had the biggest black cock in the business, and I figured my fans would go nuts to see us together. But I was a bit concerned about some of his content; he could come across as sort of aggressive and derogatory towards women, and that wouldn't fly in my vids. In my email to him, I explained that I needed to be careful about my FemDom image. Sean didn't have to submit to me—he could be my equal—but he had to come across as respectful to me in the scene. His response was professional and polite: he always performed precisely as he was directed to for a scene, and he would do the same for me.

He told me his rate was $800, which was outrageous. Was I actually going to pay a guy $800 to fuck me? I reminded myself that this was a business decision and I would certainly make that money back from a scene with the famous Sean Titanic.

We set things up, and I planned a trip to LA with Candace. We arrived and went straight to the film studio of the Domme Federation, where I filmed a couple of scenes before dropping our bags off at our hotel and meeting industry friends for dinner.

Candace had been chatting online with a cute goth boy, and he invited us over to his place. Since I wasn't a fan of the music he played, I didn't know who he was, and because he wasn't a fan of the kind of porn I produced, he didn't know who I was, but both of us had thousands of fans who would have loved to trade places with us. His house was part mansion, part haunted house, filled with equally bizarre and beautiful original art. We had a dip in his creepy custom-made hot tub and then retired to his lush, satanic lair for a threesome.

For the now-famous scene I filmed with Sean Titanic, I chose a nice hotel room as a backdrop, and Candace ran camera, which she had never done before. Sean was a perfect gentleman and consummate professional. He had done this hundreds of times. I was extremely nervous, but once the camera was running, it was easy to step into my usual confident character. Sean played with my feet and licked my pussy like I was a tasty dessert. I had no idea how authentically aroused he was by me, but I let myself believe that he found me attractive.

I wasn't abundantly aroused. I was nervous, and my mind was working in director mode as much as performer mode, trying to subtly direct Candace to get the right angles with the camera.

When it was time for penetration, Sean positioned me to enter from behind; in his experience, this would be easier. His cock, fortunately, was not yet fully erect; it still had a bit of sponginess and flexibility. I had known going into it that he had a reputation for not getting rock-hard—and that this was a good thing. His cock was colossal. Horse-like. *At least* as thick as a soda can.

Sean used lube, but nothing could have prepared me for that feeling. The vagina is an amazing thing—babies come out of there, after all—but it does have its limits. And when his cock went in, I felt an alarming ripping sensation inside that shocked me. I was braced for it so didn't scream, but a keen observer would catch the pain in my face before I could correct myself. Thankfully, in a short moment, everything went mostly numb: the body's way of dealing with trauma.

As the scene continued, I looked into the camera and told all kinds of bold-faced lies.

"Look at how his cock completely fills me up, as it should."

The truth is that is never how it "should" be. Sean was an anomaly. No woman needs a cock like that.

"Your little dick is so inadequate. You could never please me like him."

(Realistically, I would've taken anything other than this barrel of horror. There was nothing pleasurable about it except the thought of how much money I would make off this video.)

We wrapped up the scene, and Sean was gone. Although he had been as gentlemanly as possible with me before, during and after the scene, I was shaky; I felt the same feeling I felt after being in car accidents where I was shocked but not hurt. My vagina felt huge, hollowed out and swollen. It felt traumatized, and I didn't know what to do about it. I wished I'd brought some Epsom salts for a bath. Instead, I had a long shower, and then Candace and I got on with our day.

Through it all, Candace was so sweet and nurturing—doting, even. She treated me as if I'd just come out of an operation. "If guys only knew the reality of the videos they thought were so hot," she said as I eased myself into the front seat of the car.

CHAPTER 60

This Exhausted Mind

The next couple of months I kept busy. There was an increased demand for sessions, and I accepted them. I travelled to England for a work trip and did a bunch of filming at The FemDom Authority. My friendship with Audra and Blake remained strong. I opened up to them and came clean about the suicidal thoughts, and they became quiet and serious. Blake's eyes welled up with tears as Audra asked, "Will you promise to tell us if you start to feel that way again?"

"I can't promise that," I replied honestly.

I didn't mean to torture people. Confessing that this had happened was, in a way, my method of shaming myself into not doing it again. It was the best I could do in the moment.

On the heels of the England trip, I went to Peru with Candace, Ryan and Red, one of their close friends. Ryan and Candace were keen to have a more intense ayahuasca experience in the Peruvian jungle. They felt safe with the shaman we had journeyed with before, and she held week-long retreats there. Though I hadn't liked her, I trusted their instincts more than mine. After all, I did end up having a seismic shift as a result of the last journey. Maybe doing it again would provide a more permanent result?

Red was along for the ride. Since she had been such a close friend of Candace and Ryan's for so many years, they wanted her to have the experience too.

By way of a tiny, precarious-looking propeller plane, we flew into Puerto Maldonado on the edge of the Amazon. The sticky, oppressive heat immediately soaked into my clothes, skin and hair—even breathing it in felt like the air was saturating me from the inside. Everything was lush, green, damp and smelled slightly musty, the way the tropics do.

We took a rickety truck taxi to our accommodation, a bunch of basic huts nestled in the jungle. Red and I were sharing one with a couple of single beds, rock-hard pillows and mosquito nets. The toilets were a short walk away, down a dirt path. The sound of the jungle, with its exotic birds, bugs and who knows what else, was glorious.

We soon discovered that there was a clan of tame monkeys, including a tiny baby, that inhabited the same location. They came down from the trees to greet and play with us. I was naturally nervous, as all my encounters with primates in the past had been confrontational and dangerous, but these monkeys were truly sweet, and I soon warmed up to them sitting on my lap and wrapping their tails around my neck.

We only stayed there one night, and I awoke in the morning at first light to the loudest rain I had ever heard. I went outside and was alarmed to see that the dirt pathways were now rivers of muddy water. I had to pee, so I squatted off of the step and went. There was no way I was trudging through the mud and getting soaked to go to the toilet.

I went back to bed, and when I woke up a bit later the rain had stopped and the water had soaked into the dirt. I guess this was life in a rainforest.

We met up with the shaman that day and made our way to the ayahuasca retreat. As soon as I saw Luna, the shaman, I had a feeling in my gut that coming back was a mistake. She looked smug. When we last saw each other, I had told her I wouldn't be back for another night of ayahuasca, and here I was having travelled halfway around the world to journey with her for a week. It was understandable that she would be smug, but you would expect an elevated being to be above that—to project welcoming love or some hippie shit.

She also looked Red up and down like she was rotten roadkill. Red had an extreme look, to be sure—big, red punk-rock hair, loads of piercings and tattoos, ample cleavage on display—but, again, I expected someone in Luna's position to be accepting, not judgmental. We had all paid a lot of money to be there and, if not hippie love, at least some professionalism was in order. Luna was covered from neck to toe with beige, flowing clothing and boots that were overkill for the weather. I would later understand that her style choices stemmed from her body insecurities.

Things had certainly got off on the wrong foot. Red and I eyed each other, both registering the chilly reception from Luna while she immediately started chatting warmly and excitedly to Ryan and Candace like they were old friends.

The retreat was relatively posh, consisting of big bungalows with private bathrooms. This time I had my own space. The grounds were professionally manicured with trimmed grass and pruned trees and shrubs. Lots of exotic birds were around too: colourful and chatty macaws, toucans and others I didn't recognize.

We were fasting the first day, and on the first night we dove right in and had our first journey. As soon as it was dark, our group made its way down a path to the secluded yurt with a barely adequate outhouse. This was similar to the circular wooden building where I had my first ayahuasca journey. This one was a little bigger, and rather than solid wood walls it had screen windows all around the top half. We were all given buckets and a mat. My tummy was doing flip-flops already.

Luna laid out the rules: "Everyone must agree that they will not wander off. If you leave the yurt to go to the washroom, you are to return right away. Everyone is to stay silent during the journey. No singing, shouting or talking to each other. Everyone is to keep their clothes on, and there's no touching or interacting with each other."

I knew these rules from the last time, but Luna still sounded like a hard-ass about everything. I imagined shamans comparing notes of where things went wrong with previous journeys. People getting naked and trying to fuck each other, screaming, wandering off to die in the jungle. I wondered if the shamans laughed their asses off about it. My tummy was now doing somersaults.

The week before, I had done a tutorial with another shaman over Skype who had put on a little workshop at Burning Man on "navigating altered states." She had advised me to ask the ayahuasca to be gentle with me. That was more comforting than anything I was getting from Luna.

After we all got smudged to ward off evil spirits or whatever, we took our places as Luna did a bunch of chanting by candlelight. Then she poured the vile swill into a little cup that she wiped out with the hem of her poncho, and we took our turns kneeling in front of her and taking our drink. It had a horrible taste, and I didn't look forward to tasting it over and over again as I threw it up.

We all sat upright as instructed while Luna played her beautiful music, waiting for the aya to kick in.

After about a half-hour the buzzing started in my ears, and the light show started. A kaleidoscope of bright colours in geometric designs appeared before me—or rather I appeared within a tunnel of colours. Despite being in a dark structure with only a few candles outside to light the way to the outhouse, light was bursting all around me, even below me, as gravity no longer seemed to be a thing. The kaleidoscope of bright light and colour moved around me—or I moved through it—as the humming sound grew louder in my ears. The colours moved in rhythm to the music the shaman was playing, but I was completely transported to another place in every other sense.

My body felt incredibly light—weightless, even—and my skin felt cool in a slightly tingly, vibrating way, though I wasn't cold. I was rushing away, far, far away, and simultaneously feared that I wouldn't come back. I also didn't want to come back. I felt anxious and comforted at the same time. I reminded myself to ask the medicine to be gentle with me, and I felt a little more floaty and happy. I thought I could see smiles, faces and laughing colours.

I was totally fucking high.

I took a moment to ground myself, to feel for my bucket, but I was both here and there. Tugged back by my anxiety, I noticed that the music changed, became a little darker, and I felt a wave of nausea hit. My vision was a hybrid of the dark room and the light show at the edges of my sight. The bucket was a bottomless dark hole, and I emptied my vileness into it. It poured out of me, from deep in my soul—the ugliness, the hatefulness, the evil. I heard myself retching, and I wanted to be louder. I let it out. I wanted the world to hear me. I needed to purge it out of me; it had to get out. *I needed this.*

The music continued. I was back in my tunnel, but the images were a mixture of things I could almost recognize: feathers, leaves, flowers, faces, hands. The sounds of the jungle, the insects, birds and animals making their music produced a grand symphony. My mouth was hanging open in awe. I was grateful for the dark, to be invisible in this vulnerable, awkward state. I sunk into my mat lower and deeper until I was fully reclined. I was supposed to stay sitting up, but I could not.

That first night I kept repeating in my head, "Please be gentle with me," so it was a relatively light, positive experience. I enjoyed the music and was moved to tears with my gratitude for it. Luna was a talented musician and put on a great show.

During the experience when I was feeling good, I heard a voice. I was annoyed because we had all been told not to speak. I didn't understand who was talking and why they were so negative. The voice almost sounded male to me, but it wasn't Ryan. It was aggressive and irritating… and familiar. Finally, I realized it was in my head. It was *my* inner voice. The voice I always hear.

"This is all so stupid. You're not going to get anything out of this because you're not enlightened or any of that shit. You probably look so stupid. None of these people actually like you. You're doing this wrong."

And on and on the harsh voice went. I was touching a cactus— psychospiritual sandpaper—and I recoiled. I was shocked to hear it and realize this is the constant, relentless, critical, negative monologue that goes on in my head. If anyone else talked to me like that, I'd punch them in the face. Why did I put up with it from myself?

At the end, when Luna lit the candle, she played a beautiful song. It was a song featuring a profound poem by Nyoshul Khenpo Rinpoche along with meditative Tibetan chants: Vajra Guru Mantra: Om Ah Hung Benza Guru Pema Siddhi Hung.

Rest in natural great peace
This exhausted mind
Beaten helplessly by karma and neurotic thought
Like the relentless fury of the pounding waves
In the infinite ocean of samsara.
Rest in natural great peace. Rest.

I heard the guru's comforting voice telling me to just let go, to just naturally be. I thought about my exhausted mind, the constant thoughts, and how it never stops, even when I'm sleeping. I wept. The tears poured down my cheeks. I so badly wanted to be able to rest my mind. I had worked it for hours in a way that it had never been worked, and the song was giving me permission to rest.

We quietly wrapped things up and walked back to our cabins. Everyone turned inward, processing their own experiences. I didn't think that I had received any specific "profound lessons," but it was much more positive than my first experience in BC. I was grateful for that. I purged a few times, but I didn't suffer through it. I wasn't tortured by it. The release felt healing. Because I had asked the medicine to be gentle with me, the experience was much lighter; it wasn't full of darkness and fear.

I slept well and awoke early to a toucan on my porch. I took some pics and watched it for a long time. I was close enough to touch its wings, but I didn't. That beak looked like it could take my hand off.

Part of the arrangement was that we would all meet for every meal to connect and talk. So we had breakfast together and all shared our feelings about the previous night. Luna beamed adoration towards Ryan, who was the teacher's pet right from the start. She hung on his every word and praised him like he was the golden child. She was equally loving to Candace, but since Candace was much quieter, Luna didn't have as many opportunities to praise her. She was neutral about me but turned a critical, patronizing eye toward Red. Her questions smacked more of interrogation than curiosity, ready to find the negative in her responses.

Luna asked dismissively, "So, you're a hairdresser?"

"Yes, and I own and run my own hair salon, which is also a venue for local artists to sell their art and jewelry," Red clarified proudly as Luna received the unexpected information with disbelief.

"Why would you get all of those tattoos? Do you not feel comfortable in your own skin?" Luna inquired in a judgmental tone as Red glanced pointedly at Ryan and Candace's full-sleeve tattoos.

After a while Red started to stammer and stumble over her responses. She squirmed in her seat, pinned under the magnifying glass by someone who we had entrusted with our spiritual journey. Was this part of the deal? To break her down to get clarity on some issues, or what? It looked like bullying to me, but Ryan and Candace didn't stick up for Red, so maybe I was reading too much into it?

Luna then turned her attention my way. "And you do video production? What kinds of videos?"

I was still feeling great from the night before—positive, full of gratitude for having had a good experience, wanting to be open and honest, so I proudly explained what my job was, expecting Luna to think that it was great. "I make FemDom fetish adult videos. I run my own successful business that I started from nothing years ago. I perform in the vids and do the editing, marketing and everything else."

The look on Luna's face was unexpected. She looked utterly shocked. I went back over what I'd said in my mind to figure out if I had said something wrong or been unclear. After a moment of awkward silence punctuated only by a small laugh from Red, Luna finally asked what FemDom was, and I was delighted to explain, figuring we were having a minor misunderstanding. As soon as I cleared it up, I figured, she would praise me for being such a clever, creative, fascinating person.

"FemDom means that in all my scenes females, usually me, are Dominant and males are submissive," I explained. "Sometimes there aren't any slaves in the vids, though. Sometimes it's just me talking to the camera, and the guy watching the video is imagining that I'm talking to him."

The blood was now rushing into Luna's face, turning her fair complexion an angry red. A pang struck my gut as I finally registered that something was disturbingly wrong. I glanced across the table at Ryan and Candace, who were smirking at me because of my response. I wasn't sure if they had looked at Luna and figured out that the conversation had taken a nasty turn.

Luna attempted to calm herself and said, slowly, "So you're here to cleanse yourself of this filthy lifestyle and find a new path that better serves the world?"

Taken aback, I laughed and assured her that I was extremely happy with my line of work.

She huffed and exclaimed, "But you have SLAVES?! How can you—"

I interrupted, "No, no, oh no, they're not *real* slaves. That's the term used in the scene for fetishes of BDSM. They're all consenting adults just doing what they're into. No one is doing anything against their will."

"But you're doing things to these men for pornographic purposes? Hurting men?" Luna asked.

"Only if they want to be hurt, but not usually. My content is more about mental or psychological control or Domination. It's just fetish, fantasy stuff. Nothing too crazy." I explained, now on the defensive and starting to sweat profusely.

Luna continued to probe: "But you are making porn and selling it. You're selling your body, your sexuality?"

I stopped explaining at this point, and everyone stayed still as I held her gaze. It was a Mexican standoff. I could feel the pressure of my drumming heart in my ears.

"You lied to me on your application form," Luna accused.

"What?" I replied, confused by the surprise redirection.

"You said on your application for this retreat that you did video production," she said.

"Yes, that's what I do," I reaffirmed.

For some reason, Luna dropped it there—maybe she was too

angry to continue. She got up to leave and asked us all to meet back for lunch at 2 p.m.

After she was out of earshot, we all started to whisper about what had happened. Red was fully on my side, having already gotten a taste of being judged by Luna, but Ryan was playing devil's advocate, saying, "Maybe making porn isn't in line with all this spiritual stuff. And Luna does seem conservative. Whatever, it wasn't a big deal." Ryan caught himself, deciding to move past it, and let it go. Candace looked at me sympathetically but didn't say much.

Since I was dreading lunch, I arrived a few minutes after everyone else. It all went fine, and there was no mention of my work, so I figured it had blown over.

I arrived on time for dinner at 7 p.m. and found Luna sitting by herself. As soon as I sat down, she launched into me with venom: "You lied to me on your application. If you had been honest about your work, I would have called and had a conversation to ensure you were looking for healing, that you wanted to change. If not, I would not have accepted you for this retreat. Any kind of sex work is poisonous to your authentic self. It's destructive to other people—that you would even refer to people as slaves indicates that you've lost touch with—"

Luna didn't have a chance to finish as Red, Ryan and Candace showed up, and she turned on a dime, beaming love out to them with a warm smile as I sat still in shock at the attack, further shocked by how she purposefully was hiding this attack from the rest of our group. *My* friends.

As everyone sat down, Luna announced a noble silence to begin immediately and carry on until the next night's ayahuasca journey. There were to be three nights of journeying over the week, every other day. So this would be about 27 hours of silence. We were not to talk to each other at all. We were encouraged to turn inward, to meditate, to journal, but not to make any sound or have any communication with each other of any kind.

I was furious. I was sure Luna was trying to keep me from telling the others about her attack, masking it as some kind of spiritual shit. I could see that Ryan and Candace were buying into the whole idea and, out of respect for their experience, I decided to honour the instructions for silence. As for Red, I would leave it in her hands. If she broke the silence with me first, I would tell her what happened.

That night and the next day, I wrote furiously in my journal. I was angry that I had spent so much money to have this experience, only to have the person entrusted with guiding me through it tear my tenuous sense of safety to shreds.

It was obvious that Luna had personal issues around sexuality. She was clearly uncomfortable with her body, the way she dressed in this heat covered neck to wrist to toe in draped clothing to hide her body. It wasn't a shamanistic fashion statement; it was conservative dress and broadcasted that she had body image issues—and *she* was supposed to be the elevated one. She should have been able to put her feelings or prejudices aside and do her job, which was to guide me in an ayahuasca retreat for the week. After that, she never needed to see me again. Her lack of professionalism and the attack that came when I needed to feel safe enraged me.

When it was finally time to walk down the path to the yurt, silently this time, I had burned through most of my anger. I had come to a place of understanding that the medicine was the medicine. Luna was only the person who handed out the medicine and played the music. Her shit didn't affect me. My relationship was with the aya, and I would have my experience independent of what was going on with Luna.

Luna made a point of pouring me a generous amount of the vile sludge this time. It was at least double the amount I'd taken the night before. I was scared, but she insisted, so I gulped it down. That night I journeyed hard, and I don't remember a lot of it. I know I purged a few times. I know it was intense, and the theme was certainly forgiveness. Luna had instructed me to sit nearest to her, and I felt she was singing directly to me. I was convinced that she was apologizing, connecting, trying to make right what she had done. I imagined that she felt great remorse for how she had treated me. I recognized she was a flawed person who made mistakes, just like me, just like everyone else, and I forgave her. I forgave myself, and I forgave everyone; seeing the vulnerability and beauty in all beings, I wept and wept with deep forgiveness.

After the ceremony closed, Luna and I hugged warmly. I was bursting with love, acceptance, forgiveness and gratitude: the hippie full-meal deal. Some double-barrel enlightened shit.

When we got back to our cabins, Luna went to hers, and the rest of us went to Ryan and Candace's to talk for the first time in about twenty-seven hours. I was excited to tell them about everything that had happened. Being fully blissed out, they didn't get too worked up about the attack, but they loved the whole forgiveness bit. I went to bed believing everything would be okay.

The next morning at breakfast, recapping with Luna, I started to say that I felt like she was singing directly to me when she dropped the bomb, "So have you had an epiphany about the path you're on? Are you ready to change now?"

I was crushed. All of the good feelings from the night before disappeared. Poof. Instantly, my defenses came up, and the rage returned tenfold. I looked at my friends for some support and got none.

"I am not comfortable having this conversation with you. We're in completely different places, and I don't expect we'll see eye to eye on this topic," I managed to choke out through my rage, on the verge of tears.

Luna reluctantly accepted that and moved on to sweetly suck Ryan's cock. Not literally, but spiritually. She would engage him in conversation and gush over whatever he said. Ryan lapped it up, loving having his ego stroked. Bit by bit, his confidence grew under Luna's heat-lamp gaze of approval. When Luna picked on Red, Ryan said nothing, claiming that Red could fight her own battles. But the game was rigged, and Ryan could have made a difference for us if he had risked his approval rating to defend us.

At one point Luna asked Red if her breasts had been augmented—Red did show a lot of cleavage and had magnificent breasts—and the answer was an unapologetic yes. Luna launched into a rant about how deeply troubled Red must be to do such a thing to herself because only women who hate themselves go to such extreme lengths. I waited for Candace to step up. It was her place to do it, and she eventually did.

"Um, just so you know, Red isn't the only one who's had a boob job here."

Luna was quick to throw an accusatory glare at me before Candace continued, "We all have." And Luna looked at Candace's chest and started to apologize to her. Not to Red, but to Candace. I took Red's hand under the table and gave a squeeze. Solidarity.

The last ceremony for me was all about my parents. I went on a journey of their whole lives. First my dad; then my mom. I saw the difficulties of their childhood. My father wetting the bed and getting beaten and humiliated for it by his mother. Always seeking his father's approval and, despite going to extreme lengths, never getting it.

I saw his pain, his disappointment in so many things not working out as planned. His numerous stumbles and failings at every job and business. His monumental rejection and humiliation in losing by a landslide to an unpopular woman in a municipal election that he was sure he would win. I felt his pain at losing Mom. I saw how he didn't get to do so many things he had dreamed about, like owning and sailing a sailboat. I saw the decades full of hardship, pain and disappointment... and I saw clearly how the best thing in his whole life was me.

I wept at the amount of love he felt for me. How proud he was of me having led the life that I had led; the places I'd travelled to; the things I'd seen, done and experienced; my financial success and how he didn't need to worry about me. That I had grown up to be a strong, independent, healthy woman who made good choices. I saw myself through his eyes; I saw how I was his shining gem in a sea of shit. I wept and I wept, for all his sadness and in awe of how important I am to him.

Before I could catch my breath, my mind turned to my mother and repeated the process. Starting at her childhood, being the oldest of six, having to grow up too fast to help look after the little ones. Her mother, only sixteen years older. A mother who got emotionally stalled at that age, who had the mentality of a teenager, having to compete with her for the attention of boys. Getting pregnant and kicked out at the same age her mother had her. Giving the baby up for adoption, working and living at a nursing home while trying to get through Grade 10. How hard that must have been for her. How abandoned she must have felt. How vulnerable she had been while pretending to be such a tough cookie.

I saw her meeting my dad and seeing an opportunity to elevate herself, going for it, and then struggling, struggling, struggling—a prison of her own design. Trapped up on the mountain with no driver's license, parenting and looking after elderly ladies. And my dad. All the cooking and cleaning, the never-ending laundry and dishes. Each day folding into the next. Only the seasons to break up the monotony. Gardening and lawn work in the summer. Pickling and canning in the fall. A Christmas she looked forward to every year, which she was always, *always* disappointed in. The long winters cooped up in that house. Taking care of everyone, but no one taking care of her. Self-medicating to get her through. Cigarettes, TV and prescription drugs to numb her out.

Her years of cheating on my father, a few good years with Jim before that all turned to shit and he got sick. Back to taking care of someone else and not taking care of herself. All the lives she did not live, all the things she sacrificed... for me. I could see clearly, like with Dad, how I was a gem in a sea of shit. How her whole life was a huge disappointment of pain, but the one beam of sunshine was me. How she had worked so hard to ensure I didn't end up like her... and I didn't. That she tried to motivate me to be financially independent, to not have to rely on a man. That she steered me away from marriage and kids to give me a better chance at life than she had. That I had done exactly what she had hoped I would. That I have become more than she ever dreamed, but certainly what she hoped for. I saw her pride in me, her immense love for me.

I wept with forgiveness for my parents' shortcomings. I forgave them for where they had failed me. I wept, overwhelmed with the feeling of being so loved and so important to these two people, to be the best part of these two people's lives. I wept and I wept until the ceremony ended. I didn't want to share my experience. I wanted to hold it close. To protect it.

Luna asked us to share, and Ryan spoke up enthusiastically,

proclaiming that the message he got was that he needed to live his life for him, that other people couldn't hold him back anymore. He would follow his truth and take care of himself from now on. He was bursting with confidence and bravado. I wanted to punch him in the face. I knew intuitively that Ryan had used this experience to permit himself to be selfish. I saw that it would mean he and Candace would break up. He'd been heading in that direction for a while, and with Luna's stroking, he'd gotten the confidence to say it out loud and pretend it was some ayahuasca epiphany. Hey, maybe he even believed it.

I looked at Candace to see if she was reading the situation the same as me. Her eyes were misty, and she was hugging her knees. I went over to her and put my arms around her. Ryan didn't notice. Luna was egging him on, of course, and I'm sure she was missing how all this was affecting the rest of us.

When it was my turn to share I briefly explained, "My experience tonight was all about forgiving my parents and understanding how much they love me."

Red dreamily mumbled, "It was a great trip for me. Super fun." We all laughed, despite Luna's obvious annoyance.

Candace was still processing what she had experienced and said she would "maybe share in the morning."

The next day we relaxed by the pool. For the first time all week Luna joined us in a full-coverage bathing costume and a wide-brimmed hat. She was visibly uncomfortable as she bobbed around in the water, staying submerged. She chatted about being from Calgary and her life living in Peru the last several years. She mentioned that it was impossible to date there. She was a white Canadian woman, which was intimidating to a lot of the Peruvian men. She felt she had been accepted as a shaman, though, and talked about how much training she had had there. I saw her as a lonely woman who had issues with her body and sexuality, someone who wasn't equipped to deal with people who didn't fit into her narrow worldview. It seemed like she'd spent too much time learning the rituals of being a shaman and not enough time learning the deeper lessons of kindness and how to help people who lived in the real world heal.

After dinner that night, out of the blue, Luna asked me to join her privately. Pumped full of serotonin from the aya, I again optimistically thought she wanted to apologize for how she had treated me. Instead, she launched into another lecture about me lying on my application and how deceived she felt about that. She continued, "I just want to make it clear that you will not be welcome to journey with me again or be a part of any retreats or ceremonies that I'm involved in—"

I interrupted, "Why would you think I would want to? You have been completely unprofessional and judgmental. I've hit a nerve for you, but I haven't done anything wrong. This is your stuff."

I got up and went to Ryan and Candace's cabin. Red was there too. I told them what happened, and they got upset. "I'll have a word with Luna in the morning. This has gone too far," Ryan said firmly.

I thanked him and said, "It would be nice to feel like you have my back."

Since Ryan could do no wrong in Luna's eyes, I thought it might turn the situation around and save it. She might be inclined to see the error of her ways and apologize. I was desperate to forgive since that's what the aya kept telling me all week, but it was hard to forgive without any remorse on her part. I guess I wasn't on the level yet of forgiving even if the other person didn't ask for forgiveness.

The next morning I didn't join them for breakfast. I ate a granola bar instead while packing up to go. We were all to depart together immediately after breakfast. I imagined Ryan having a heart-to-heart with Luna. Her realizing how out of line she'd been and seeking me out to clear the air. I brought my bags down to the dock to wait for the boat. Everyone joined me, but there was no apology from Luna—only more ice. I kept looking at Ryan, expecting him to assure me he had followed through on his promise to defend me, but nothing. Finally on the boat when Red sat down next to me I asked her, and she said there hadn't been an opportunity, that they were rushed through breakfast so fast Ryan didn't have a chance to say anything.

Bullshit. What a cop-out. I understood Red couldn't say anything, and it wouldn't make any difference anyway since Luna had zero respect for her. Candace was quietly emotional with what had happened the night before with Ryan, and she wasn't the confrontational type. But *Ryan*. It would have only taken a moment, a few words, something along the lines of, "Hey, the way you've handled the situation with Tracey was a bit harsh, and we're all feeling kind of uncomfortable with it." Simple.

It was a long boat ride and then a van ride to the airport where we were dropping Luna off. Everyone got out of the van for hugs except me. I had not said a single word to her during the whole trip. She came back into the van and tried to hug me. I glared at her while she said some shit to put on a show for the others—something like, "I wish you the best on your path."

I didn't respond.

Back in the van on the way to our accommodation I asked Ryan, "So you didn't say anything, did you?"

"Oh, yeah, no, didn't get a chance," he replied breezily.

I stewed for hours until I finally told Ryan that I couldn't stand to be around him. That I felt betrayed and wanted to look into moving my flight up to leave right away rather than carrying on with them for another week in Cusco, Machu Picchu and Lima. Ryan was stunned. He was, after all, on his new path of doing whatever he wanted to do for himself, so my feelings about his actions were complicating his new world order. Spiritual bypassing only works when you don't need to witness the consequences of your actions. He didn't stop me from going to a travel agent to make inquiries. Unfortunately, it would cost me a fortune to leave early. I'd have to buy a whole new ticket, and a last-minute one at that. The cost was about triple what I had paid for my original ticket.

I couldn't fly home, but that didn't mean I needed to stay with them. I planned to part ways the next day and go on my own. That night Candace had it out with Ryan; I could hear them talking loudly in their cabin a few yards away. Eventually, Ryan came over and said that he'd had a chance to think about things from my perspective, and that I was right to be upset at Luna and now at him for not defending me like he said he would. He promised to send an email to Luna even though the time had already passed. "It's the right thing to do, and I'm sorry I didn't do it earlier."

He continued, "I hope you'll accept my apology and stay with us for the rest of the trip. We want you with us, and it's not fair to the girls to lose out on your company because I messed up. Stay for them even if you're still mad at me. Please?"

Even if Candace had given him a come-to-Jesus talk, Ryan was sincere, so I stayed, and we continued on to explore more of Peru like regular tourists. We experienced a lot of great things during that trip: the fascinating and eclectic markets where we bought peyote; the ruins of Machu Picchu; the memorable bed and breakfast nestled in the crook of a mountain called The Green House that was run by a charming and ballsy young American woman; paragliding off the cliffs in Lima; and much more. It was a perfectly enjoyable trip, despite the clouds on the horizon. Something had shifted in Ryan. We all saw it, and we all knew what it would mean.

CHAPTER 61

Let's Get Started

For the next six months I went back to my old routine of work and travel. The two were often combined, but not always. A trip to Mexico at Christmas *was* mixed with business: it was a filming trip with the hot American black guy I'd met in Mexico the Christmas before. I found the trip difficult and could never fully relax, always thinking about filming, but filming felt like a chore because it was also like a vacation.

Right after that came the annual Vegas trip for the porn awards and porn convention. It was a great opportunity to meet up with my peers and friends from the biz.

In rapid succession, I made a trip home for my grandmother's eightieth birthday party, another trip to England to film with The FemDom Authority and a spontaneous trip to LA with Candace to see Die Antwoord in concert.

In between trips I watched Candace and Ryan's relationship collapse and spent as much time as I could with my dear friend Gaspman, who was fighting a battle with cancer and losing. It was a difficult time, looking back, and I didn't give myself adequate space to process what was unfolding. I tried to keep busy; my old shtick.

Silently, twilight crept back into my heart; once again I fantasized about escaping it all, of killing myself. I still couldn't manage to verbalize the darkness—I was still ashamed. After all, my life was so good in countless ways. As difficult as it was, I confessed to David, and he said it was time for me to get help. He gave me the name and number of a therapist who had helped him a decade earlier. I reached out and made the appointment.

Then I waited. She was a particularly good therapist, so her waitlist for new patients was long: nearly two months. Luckily I wasn't ready to pack it in; I just wanted to stop thinking about killing myself all the time.

While I waited, I spent time with my friends who were going through much worse. I watched Gaspman fighting for his life, savouring every day that he had, and I wondered whether I'd even bother to fight if I got cancer. Would a terminal illness be a blessing to a suicidal person? I was there for Candace as she processed and mourned the end of her twenty-year relationship, even if it wasn't officially over. She and Ryan still lived together and pretended things were fine most of the time. She cried every day, but he didn't notice. Ryan had moved on emotionally. Ayahuasca had given him permission to be selfish, to do what he wanted to without apologies. I tried not to hate him. I watched Candace suffer and felt guilty for thinking about killing myself. I didn't even have anything to be unhappy about—not the way she or Gaspman did.

I painted on my Mistress T face and filmed scene after scene, pretending to be turned on by pantyhose, pretending to be the cheating wife who loves black cock, pretending to relish kicking guys in the balls, pretending to care if my fans blew their load exactly when I gave them permission to. The work gave me a way to escape and feel productive. My company was my baby. I birthed and raised it, and it was a constant source of pride. Sometimes I'd look at my sales numbers or the money in my bank account to cheer me up. They say money doesn't buy happiness, but it did for me. Financial security was one of my most persuasive motivations, and it was a measure of success.

When the day finally arrived for my first therapy appointment,

I was relieved. I felt beaten down by the unrelenting thoughts of eternal peace. Death flirted with me constantly. I wanted to die.

I entered the dimly lit waiting room tastefully decorated in neutral colours and comfy furniture, plants and forgettable paintings—landscapes, probably. Serene music played, accompanied by the sound of trickling water. I spotted a little fountain of water over smooth black rocks. It was all calming, by design. A dish of chocolates and collection of magazines were displayed on the glass coffee table. *Psychology Today* was an obvious choice, but *Time* and *People* were there for variety.

I was a few minutes early according to the clock on the wall above the water cooler. All of a sudden my throat was dry, so I grabbed a paper cup, filled it and sipped it while leafing through the latest edition of *Psychology Today*.

One headline commanded: "Reinvent yourself, focus on your future self, you'll be surprised at what you can achieve." I wondered, did these articles ever *actually* motivate anyone to change?

The door to Linda's office opened, and she stood there beaming at me. "Tracey? Come on in."

I stepped through the door, and the view of the city was stunning—a big tenth-floor corner office lined entirely in windows. I noted the big pieces of crystal on the fireplace mantel, some hippie-looking paintings, a lot of books and some elephant ornaments.

I took my seat in the obvious place. Linda took hers across from me, and I tried to take her in while feeling her gaze softly holding my eyes. She was beautiful—one of the most beautiful women I'd ever met, in fact. Her beauty wasn't only skin deep; it radiated out of her smile, her eyes, her body language. She looked to be in her early fifties and had a fit build, shoulder-length brown hair and high cheekbones. Expressive, glistening, sharp eyes. Perfectly applied makeup and an elegant business ensemble: floral blouse, long dark skirt, gold earrings and quality low-heeled dress shoes.

"Let's get started," Linda said with a ridiculous, beaming smile. It was ridiculous because she looked at me like I was the most important person in the world, and she had been waiting a long time for me to arrive. It felt like she couldn't have been happier to see anyone else, dead or living. But she didn't even know me.

"As I said in my email, I have constant suicidal thoughts. I have never been depressed. At least I don't think I have. My life is awesome. I don't want to kill myself, but I don't want to think about it all the time either," I explained.

And that's how it started. In our first two sessions, we talked about my ayahuasca experiences. We talked about when the suicidal thoughts started. We talked about my work and my relationships with men. We talked about my feelings, my anxiety and my sense of numbness, and I learned that depression is more about numbness than sadness. We also set some goals for me to work toward:

- Learn to feel my feelings—the full spectrum of my feelings
- Learn to manage my anxiety
- Stop having suicidal thoughts
- Be kinder to myself and less self-critical
- Get to a place where I can love and be loved, to be able to have a healthy intimate relationship

At the end of the second session, I mentioned that my mother was coming to visit the next week, and I asked Linda if she would like to meet her.

Linda inquired, "Would you like me to meet your mother? That's unusual, but if there is a good reason for it, we can discuss that."

"I know we haven't even talked about my mother yet. It's rare for her to come to Vancouver, so there might not be another opportunity. I think after I tell you about my upbringing you might understand," I explained with an uncertain smile.

"Okay, let's talk about your mother next session and decide from there. But it's unlikely that I'll want to meet her," Linda replied. "These sessions are about you and me."

I knew the whole cliché thing in psychology is that everything comes back to your parents. I knew some fucked up stuff had happened with my mom, but we had a great relationship. We talked all the time. We were best friends and could tell each other anything. She was incredibly supportive of my work and anything I wanted to do, except for getting married and having kids, but that just meant that she knew me well enough to know it wasn't the path for me.

The next session I talked about my mother. Linda listened, and as I went through the various stories, her face moved through a range of expressions: shock, anger, outrage, sadness. Linda used words like "abuse," "guilt," "manipulation," "narcissism," and "abandonment" to describe my mother and the things that had happened to me. By the end of the session, the whole tone of my therapy had been set. It all came back to my mother, our relationship and how I was raised—terribly cliché—yet I felt Linda was blowing it out of proportion; what happened back then was water under the bridge. Sort of.

I met up for lunch with David and told him how my therapy sessions were going. I rolled my eyes as I described Linda blaming my mother for everything and painting her as the villain. David looked at me with the hint of a smirk and said, "Ya think?"

He stared at me as my heart started to beat faster. I felt panicky. No, no, no. I loved my mother more than anyone else in the world. I was the most important thing to her. No, no, no—she was *not* the villain in this story.

In our next few sessions, Linda and I went through some of the more memorable situations in detail, including my mother's boyfriend jerking off behind me... "That's called grooming. Pedophiles start with something small and ask if it's okay. He would have escalated given the opportunity, each time going a bit further, and because you had said okay to the last thing it would make it harder for you to say no, to set boundaries," Linda stated matter-of-factly.

When I told her I used to lie to my father for my mother, she explained, "One parent turning a child against another parent is one of the most damaging things that a parent can do to a child."

When I told her how Mom left me to go to the city and then left me again when she moved in with Jim, Linda pointed out, "Being abandoned by a parent sets you up to not be able to truly trust anyone," linking that to my trust issues.

When I told her about Mom not stopping Jim when he kicked me out, she said, "You decided you couldn't make yourself vulnerable to anyone. But if you don't make yourself vulnerable, you can never truly love." Linda tied up everything with a neat little bow.

Bit by bit, I started to understand why I was the way I was, and how all these things that happened in my childhood and teenage years created the adult that I had become. How I had learned to numb out my feelings, especially my disgust, and paint on a happy face while my mother described her sexual adventures. How I learned that my feelings didn't matter and had put them aside to survive. How I had learned that love wasn't safe, that I couldn't truly trust anyone and that making myself vulnerable would end in pain.

I saw how I had put my armour on long ago and never took it off. I could go through the motions of having relationships—I had infatuations and could have decent sex—but I had been incapable of having a healthy, nurturing, two-way intimate relationship with anyone, to deeply love and be loved, to see and be seen, to know someone and have someone truly know me.

I told all of this to David, and he confessed, "I've always seen it, but anytime I tried even to hint that your relationship with your mother was fucked up, you shut down. You wouldn't even hear me. You were so entrenched in the idea that you and your mother have this great relationship that you couldn't see how she'd messed you up."

I was stunned. I didn't remember David ever indicating that there was anything wrong with my relationship with my mother. He had looked at me with an edge of pity when I described some of the events that transpired in my teens. Sure, he might have made a funny face when I mentioned that I sent my mother a vibrator for Christmas because my stepfather couldn't get it up anymore. I figured our relationship was hard for others to understand, but I didn't think there was anything "wrong" with it. I didn't believe that it had damaged me. But hearing David express how obvious it had always been to him shook me to my core. I'd been under a spell and had finally snapped out of it.

I suddenly came to the realization that the last twenty-plus years of my life had been in part—a critically important part—a lie. Who I thought I was, was not who I actually was; I'd been moulded into a lean, mean, money-making man-eater... I'd been conditioned to avoid real relationships, to be anti-marriage and kids... ideas that I had been sure were mine... the feeling of loss... the uncertainty of who I was, even that inner voice I heard in my head all the time, was any of that authentically *me*?

Linda and I agreed on a strategy to get me "in touch with my feelings," which, again, sounded painfully cliché, but it made sense. By doing so, I would hopefully be able to manage my anxiety better and feel less numb, which should eliminate my suicidal thoughts and prepare me to be in a healthy relationship. Part of this was learning to be kind to myself.

Remember that critical inner voice I realized I had during one of my ayahuasca journeys? It was time to rewire that too. So for months I went to therapy every week, and I didn't date or fuck except for when I was filming. I barely had a social life. I hunkered down in my apartment and practiced positive self-talk. I talked out loud to myself, like a sweet grandmother would to her beloved grandchild. I would have sounded like a lunatic to anyone listening:

"Good morning darling! Did you have a nice sleep? Aw, biiiiig stretch! How are you feeling? Shall we do a little body scan together? Wonderful. Would you like some breakfast? Are you hungry? I'll get you something delicious to nourish your beautiful, strong body. Would you like a nice cup of tea? Mmmmm..."

And on and on I went like a complete loon, talking sweetly to myself out loud for months when I was alone—and I tried to be alone as much as possible. I retrained my inner voice. I became more forgiving of others and myself. More understanding, more compassionate, more empathetic. I cut myself a lot more slack. I loved myself more. That part—to fall in love with myself and to generally have a healthy relationship with myself—was critical.

All the while I was going to therapy every week. Linda and I rehashed the events with my mother. We went through exercises to get me in touch with my childhood anger—anger I would have naturally felt but suppressed for survival. We went over my feelings of fear over losing my mother, the things I did to keep her from leaving and my feelings of abandonment when she left me in various ways over and over, despite my best efforts to be someone she would stay for. Little by little, we worked through the anger I felt. *So. Much. Anger.*

I became fragile during this time. The therapy sessions left me raw, stripped of my protective armour, exposed. I didn't feel safe in my world, yet I attempted to continue. I took a trip home at Christmas and tried to act normal with my mother and everyone else. I took a trip to Vegas for the porn awards. After all, the show must go on! Vids needed to be filmed, the business needed to be run and one of my dearest friends, Gaspman, was bravely dying of cancer. I tried to spend as much time with him as possible, but it was difficult for him to have company. I would usually hang out with him in bed watching TV. One of the last times I saw him we both took a bunch of his morphine and listened to Pink Floyd on his high-end surround sound stereo system.

CHAPTER 62

Fuck Me, Fuck Me, Fuck Me

had long ago planned a trip to Mexico, Belize and NYC with some girlfriends, and so I went. A couple of days into our trip, I got word that Gaspman had passed away. I was racked with guilt over not being there at the end, but I knew he would have wanted me to live as he had: to the fullest. Gaspman's death was not the end deserving of the gentleman warrior he was at heart. Though he was surrounded by loved ones, he fought his end; he didn't want to go. It was not graceful. It was not a beautiful death, and although I'm glad I didn't see it, with my vivid imagination, I might as well have been there. Those who were traumatized by it described it to me in such detail that I became physically ill. Being in an unaccustomed state of feeling my feelings, I could hardly cope with the pain.

Maybe it was my reaction to Gaspman's death or maybe it was simply time, but Linda gave me the green light to start dating again if I wanted to. I began to raise my eyes when I walked down the street, to look at men again. I had been careful to cocoon myself off while doing self-work. I didn't want temptations or distractions. I had felt too vulnerable to engage with new people, but now it was time to re-enter the wild.

I quickly took a lover, the wrong kind of lover: easy pickings. He was a fresh divorcee who was interesting and not overly risky. I wanted to break the fast, so to speak. I flirted with another man and went on a couple of dates. He was sexually aggressive, which intrigued me and scared me. I ended it before it got started.

Then I received an invitation from a handsome acquaintance I had flirted with the year before. I hadn't seen him in so long, and I don't know why he thought of me, but out of the blue he asked me to be his date for a private sex party where there would be a Tantra workshop.

I gave him an enthusiastic "YES!"

Travis was a hunk. At 6 foot 4 he towered above the crowd at parties. He was clean-cut, always perfectly groomed, armed with a permanent disarming smile on his face and sweet, dreamy eyes. A fit, active guy, graceful long body, a good dancer and an impressive fucker. I once watched him taking a pretty girl from behind at a sex party and became so aroused that I grabbed the nearest guy and had him right there on the filthy cement floor while people stepped over us.

Travis was also a genuinely good soul. He was well liked, had excellent manners and had his shit together. I was flattered he asked me out. I went out of my way to get extra dolled up for him. He was tall, so I decided to wear my big goth platform boots. I added a skintight black lace dress with a plunging neckline—so plunging, in fact, that the dress barely covered my nipples. I topped the look off with a black, fun, fur vest, big sexy hair and dark, smokey eye makeup. It was a sexy, edgy look that growled self-confidence.

Travis picked me up in his sensible, solid car complete with roof racks. I'm sure he put all kinds of stuff on his roof. Bikes? Kayaks? Shit, being "active" like that wasn't my thing.

"You look beautiful," he said.

"Please don't ask if I bike or kayak," I thought inside my head.

We started out with small talk. "So what have you been up to lately?" Travis asked.

"A lot of work—and yoga, when I get a chance," I answered safely while images of myself lonely and unwashed in my PJs, shuffling around my apartment for months talking to myself like a crazy person and crying in my therapist's office flashed through my mind.

"How about you?" I lobbed an easy ball back into his court. "Get them talking," I heard my mentor's voice say in my head.

Travis proceeded to give up a lot of intimate information in response to my softball question. "I was seeing a married woman for a while. Her husband knew; they were poly. I fell in love with her. It was good, but I finally decided that I wanted a primary relationship. I don't want to be the other guy. I want to have kids, with the right person."

There was an awkward pause. Travis kept driving but glanced over at me to measure my reaction to that last bit. I was poker-faced, so he continued.

"I'm looking for someone to build a life with, to have kids with… do you want kids, Tracey?" He had tossed the ball back at me, but now it felt like a red-hot cannon.

Whether it was my mother's brainwashing or my own truth, there had only ever been one answer to that question, and it was a hard "NO."

"Ya know, Travis, I just turned thirty-nine. I've never wanted kids and, by now, if the ol' biological clock hasn't started ticking, it's not going to. I don't feel called to it, and it would be the end of my career. At this age, my body wouldn't bounce back from pregnancy. I'm not your gal."

Since this wasn't the first time I'd made this speech, it all came out effortlessly.

I softened the rejection and moved things along: "But I think you're super hot, and you're a great guy. I would date you in a heartbeat, but I wouldn't want to waste your time knowing I can't give you what you want. Let's have fun tonight, and any other time you like, but if you see anyone else you're interested in this evening, go for it. We're not attached to each other."

"You too," he said with a broad, easy smile.

It was strange to have such a frank conversation with someone I barely knew, but I appreciated the honesty and clear communication. That's my jam. I wished more people were like that, and I developed a deep respect for Travis… in addition to being excited to fuck him. Yum.

We arrived at a big mansion in a posh part of town. The house was full of swingers, including a few familiar faces. It was a friendly crew but not especially attractive. Mostly average-looking couples around my age or older as I scanned the faces… then I saw *him*.

I somehow registered the black leather pants, long hair and youthful face, smooth olive skin and a unique bone structure. There was something about this man that took my breath away—a barely visible glow—and all of a sudden there was nothing else but him. Everything else blurred, and I thought, "What *are* you?"

He was now looking at me with a smile that stretched from here to infinity… a smile that made his eyes crinkle into pure magic.

I stood there. Staring. Like a complete idiot.

Someone finally introduced us after forever—or maybe just several seconds. He was gently laughing at me, but I simply could not pull myself together. I didn't even catch his name.

It was time for the Tantra talk to start. I realized that my mysterious Magical Beast was on his own. He was, in fact, the only unattached one there except for the guy doing the workshop.

I half-listened to the explanation of Tantra while stealing glances at the Magical Beast on the other side of the room. He didn't look at me. *Fuck.* Heartbreak.

Next, we moved on to an eye-gazing exercise where the men all sat in a ring and the women sat in front of them to eye gaze for a couple of minutes. Then the women moved one guy over for another couple minutes, and so on around the circle until all the women and men had done it. We were supposed to be saying a mantra in our heads. Something like, "The divine within me honours the divine within you" or whatever. I tried to do the exercise the right way, but I was distracted. There were so many men between him and me. When I was finally sitting in front of him and we touched hands, I felt I'd been electrocuted. My whole body was vibrating, and as I held his gaze, my mind screamed, "FUCK ME FUCK ME FUCK

ME." It was a singular, desperate demand. But his face was stark, blank; he wasn't interested. Supreme heartbreak.

The next part of the workshop was a yoni massage demonstration. Another attractive woman cuddled up on the sofa with Mr. Magical Beast, and, even though she was married, my heart continued to break. All the while Travis and I were acting normally, touching a little, cuddling; it was nice, but I was soon distracted once again. I found myself seething with jealousy that this woman would get what I so desperately wanted. A volunteer for the yoni massage was requested, and she threw up her hand. "Oh great, now she's going to seduce him by getting naked in front of him and having an orgasm. Just shoot me," I grimaced in my head.

Moments after the demonstration started, he turned over on the sofa with his back to the action and fell soundly asleep.

What the fuck? *Who the fuck was this guy?* Who naps while a beautiful woman is being brought to orgasm right in front of you???

After her climax, it was announced that it was free-form playtime. There were mattresses all over the floor and a hot tub outside. I suggested to Travis that we hit the hot tub since I wasn't ready to get it on with him. In fact, I was suddenly not all that interested in him.

We were relaxing in the hot tub, looking up at the stars, and it was nice for a few minutes—until the host of the party came out. He owned the house and was clearly tripping on something. He clumsily approached us and sort of bowed as he said, unexpectedly, "It is an honour to have such a Goddess in my hot tub, Mistress—"

I was taken aback but quickly interrupted him before he could go on. "I am not here in that capacity, and I would appreciate discretion."

He blathered an apology and teetered back into the house, the mood left in tatters. Travis knew what I did for work, and he also knew that I kept things separate. It was awkward, but he tried to laugh it off. We soaked for a little while longer and finally started to kiss. He was a startlingly attractive man; maybe I could get into it? I suggested we go shower the chlorine off and join the rest of the party.

We were spraying each other down in the shower and giggling when there was a knock on the bathroom door and the other couple that I knew popped their heads in. I expected they wanted to join in, which was fine, but they started apologizing awkwardly and saying they needed to tell me something.

"While you were in the hot tub, the host started showing porn projected on the wall—" they said.

"Yes, I saw it when I walked through. Good idea. A giant screen of porn during a sex party—" I responded, before they interrupted me.

"He put on one of your vids. I don't know if he didn't realize you were at the party, if it was a coincidence or what..." they explained. "We made him stop as soon as we could, but everyone already saw."

"Oh god, no. Everyone here now knows I'm a porn star? What kind of scene was it?" I asked, feeling sick to my stomach.

"You had a huge strap-on, fucking a guy in the ass. You looked great! It was hot! But yeah, we knew you wouldn't want it being played, so we made him change it as fast as we could," they continued.

"Fuck," I muttered. "The host knows who I am. He's a fan. What an idiot. Oh well, hopefully this crowd will pretend they didn't see it."

We finished rinsing off and went out to the party. I was wearing a teal satin bathrobe. We laid down, and I looked up at the big screen to see one of my famous friends fucking her slave—a guy I also knew well—in the ass with a big strap-on. It wasn't the right fit for this party—a Tantric sex party—but the host clearly had a fetish for FemDom pegging.

I tried to ignore the giant version of my work friend beside me and focused on Travis. It was then I realized my Magical Beast was sitting by himself on the sofa. The room was dimly lit, and he was about twenty feet away, but I could tell that he was bored. Couples were laid out all over the floor in various sexual positions. A few people were standing along the sides chatting annoyingly.

Travis and I started to make out. He gently opened my satin robe, and I felt the air on my skin as he began to explore my body. The light, dim with some movement from the movie on the projection screen, was flattering. Fortunately, the movie's sound wasn't on, but there was some quiet music playing and a fair bit of moaning.

Travis pressed his warm, firm, naked body against me. We were reclined, side by side, and he moved his hand between my thighs as he kissed my lips respectfully. He started to graze my sex, and I peeked an eye open to see if Mr. Magical Beast was watching. It was hard to tell.

Travis started fingering me, and it was slightly uncomfortable. I wasn't feeling it. As I glanced around, I noticed other couples trying out what they'd seen in the demonstration. Women were getting massaged by men who were trying to give yoni massages. But Travis was doing basic fingering; why wasn't he practicing what had been demonstrated?

I glanced over at M.B. again, and this time I was certain his eyes were glued on me. He still looked bored, so I tried to make it more interesting for him by stroking Travis's cock. He was already hard and pressing himself against me. He could tell I wasn't warmed up enough for intercourse yet, so he moved down between my legs and started to lick me. I glanced over his head and saw that we were being watched by the Magical Beast.

I arched my back, and as my head reclined, I caught a glance of my friend on the big screen laughing as she railed against a bound slave with her massive strap-on. Barf. I squeezed my eyes shut and tried to think of something to arouse me. Mmmm, what if M.B. came over and joined in? Mmmm... okay, don't set yourself up for disappointment, time to go to one of your wank-bank places...

In my mind a young blonde cheerleader was getting initiated by the entire football team of black studs in a locker room... that should do it... but no, I had to sneak another peek.

Yes, he was intently watching, looking right into my soul. In fact, his lips were moving. *What the shit?* Surely, I was losing my mind. I snapped my eyes shut again, watched the teen getting fucked in every hole by big, black dicks...

I opened my eyes again and looked over Travis's head. Was the Magical Beast SINGING to me? Was he CHANTING? What the hell? I could barely make it out—some kind of song? Staring into my eyes. I was being pulled across the room by a hook in my chest; I wanted to toss poor Travis out the window.

This wasn't fair to Travis, and I was clearly losing my mind. I gave him the tap and suggested we find a more private spot. We went into a smaller side room, just the two of us, and had sex. It was better when I could focus on him. Travis was a sexy guy and a hot, fun fuck. I'm not sure how long it lasted—half an hour? He climaxed and rolled off me. Travis was starting to take off the condom when who walked in? Mr. Magical Beast and another lady friend I knew he'd not been sexual with. He had the biggest smile and was beaming. He looked so happy to see me.

Without hesitation, I asked Travis, "Do you mind if I invite him in?"

"No problem," he responded... no surprise there; he had just cum.

"Would you like to join us?" I said with a laugh and barely got the invitation out before Mr. Magical Beast started taking off his pants. He was against me. The earth rocked on its axis. Reality shifted, and we melted together. M-E-L-T-E-D together. I knew Travis was there at the start, but I didn't notice when he left.

To say we made love was an understatement. I was already warmed up sexually, so we dove in. He put his fingers inside of me and did a bunch of crazy stuff. I hadn't realized he was a Tantra practitioner as well. He made me cum and squirt, and I gave it all to him. When he penetrated me my entire body responded, as did something deeper. When we finished, we sat up facing each other, my legs wrapped around his hips, him holding me. Travis had wandered back in time to hear him say that he loved me. I pulled back—shocked—and he laughed with abandon, saying, "It's okay, you're not there yet."

I looked at Travis, who was also laughing, and blurted, "I don't even know your name."

He laughed even harder and pointed out that he didn't know mine either.

It was now the wee hours, and Travis was ready to go. On wobbly legs and with a deep smile, I gathered myself and my things. We exchanged contact information and learned each other's names. A rose by any other name, though... he will always be my Magical Beast.

The next day, after pulling that all-nighter, the cold I'd been fighting hit me hard—even though I hadn't had a single drink or done any drugs. I was sniffling away when I got the text from my Magical Beast asking me for a date the next day—dinner at his place.

I didn't want him to think I wasn't interested and I didn't want to blow my chance, so I accepted even though I was feeling sick. I started taking cold meds, which I normally don't do.

I barely slept, giddy with excitement despite feeling like absolute crap. I had committed to lunch with a girlfriend that day, the same day as my dinner date, and I didn't want to flake on her, so I went. I took more cold meds to reduce the symptoms, but I felt quite unwell. The meds made me feel queasy and a little high. I excused myself during lunch and rushed to the washroom. Great, now I had the runs too. On my walk home, I shat myself. Only a little, but let's be honest, no amount of shitting yourself is okay. I panicked. What was I going to do about our date tonight?! I didn't want to bail at the last minute, but I knew we would have sex—and what if I shat myself then? I got home, cleaned myself up and texted David:

"I'm super sick with a cold and the meds I've taken are giving me anal leakage. Jesus, they warn you about those kinds of side effects and we all laugh but I guess it's real. Fuck. I have a hot date tonight that I don't want to jam on. Whaddaya think? Double down and take some Imodium?"

"Cancel the date, freak. Take care of your health," came the rational response.

My heart was racing. It was getting close to the do-or-die time: to either leave to be on time for my date or cancel at the last minute like a jerk.

I raced to the drug store to get the Imodium and took it immediately. I took some more cold meds to stop my runny nose and suppress my cough, then off I went, feeling nauseous and light-headed.

When I arrived at his place, Mr. Magical Beast was wearing sexy white jeans and a sharp, grey, knit V-neck sweater. His hair was pulled back in a neat ponytail. He was beautiful. The kitchen was a disaster, as he was putting the last touches on the meal he'd prepared. He made everything from scratch. Pesto, hummus, pakoras. It looked delicious, but I could barely stand to look at it I felt so gross. I held my breath and took small bites. He picked up a guitar and started playing for me. I didn't think his singing was especially good, but I pretended to be impressed. It was actually incredibly romantic.

But the vibe was not electric. He wasn't that into me—calm, slightly disinterested even. Was he playing it cool?

I was a nervous wreck, trying hard to make a good impression.

The question that I usually dread then came: "So how do you sell your labour?"

"I guess you missed one of my porn vids being screened at the party before it got taken down?" I said with a laugh.

"Oh, that was you? I caught that there was some kind of problem with one of the vids, but I didn't understand it had anything to do with you," he said casually. "You make porn? That's cool. Do you like it?"

I didn't want to talk about my job, but I knew we had to get it out of the way. I tried to answer while giving the impression it wasn't something I was interested in spending much time on. "Sure. I've been doing it for a long time. I make FemDom fetish vids. Kinky stuff where the woman, me, is always in control."

He might have sensed this would normally be awkward and to put me at ease said, "I'm pretty open-minded about that stuff. I was in a relationship with an escort for a while. One of the top independent escorts in the city at the time, actually. She's retired now. I have other friends who do sex work. It's no big deal. If you're happy doing it, that's all that matters."

I was relieved to hear that. We chatted some more, and I could tell that things were moving in the direction of the bedroom; unfortunately, I was more nervous than aroused. I excused myself to the washroom to sit and push to see if I was likely to have an accident in the heat of the moment. All appeared okay in that regard, but I was still slightly lightheaded and queasy; a decidedly unsexy feeling.

Things moved to the bedroom, and we had sex. It was good—adequate—but not great. I was holding back, closed down, attempting to keep myself afloat. It wasn't spectacular for him either, and by the time we were done, I could feel the meds wearing off. My sinuses were starting to loosen up, and a tickle was forming in my throat. My guts were starting to rumble, and I feared the floodgates were ready to open with a river of snot and shit. I hurriedly got dressed and tried to be casual. I tried not to look rushed or panicked as I made movements to evacuate before I had an embarrassing evacuation.

As I passed the kitchen, I remarked, like a perfectly polite Canadian, "Oh, I hate to leave you with all this mess…" expecting him to do the polite Canadian thing and say "no problem"… but he didn't. Unpredictably, he quipped, "So don't."

Eccentric, this one.

I looked back at him. He was picking up his guitar and preparing to play. I had my bag on my shoulder and was at the door. I stuttered, "Pardon?"

He clarified, "If you don't want to leave me with all the mess, I would appreciate some help cleaning up. I hate doing dishes."

I went into a full-blown panic at this point. I *needed* to go; the plug had been pulled from the full tub that was my head; I could feel my sinuses releasing gallons of snot down my nostrils. My guts were rumbling loud enough that I was certain he could hear it fifteen feet away. But I could not walk out at this point. What would I say?! "Oh, shitty for you. I'm not doing your damn dishes after I offered… even though you cooked this amazing meal for me."

Fuck!

So I just dug in as fast as I could. He surely had dirtied every damn dish in the whole kitchen to make that meal and hadn't cleaned up anything along the way. I was sure that I'd never see the end of the dishes, breathing through my mouth and clenching my ass cheeks. He serenaded me romantically as I cleaned the kitchen like a woman on a mission. When it was tidy enough I discreetly bent down and wiped my nose on the bottom of my pant leg, stood, gave him a quick kiss and bolted out the door.

I felt victorious as I rushed down the street without shit in my pants.

Things had cooled between Mr. Magical Beast and me, and I was no longer sure that what I experienced that first night was real. I rested and reflected, trying to recover from my illness in time for our next date a few days later. He had asked me to come to a play.

On the day of the show, I was relaxing in the sun with my other

casual lover and didn't want to leave to get ready for my date, but
I did. I got dolled up and met him at the theatre. He was dressed in
black pleather pants with zippers, a white V-neck t-shirt, black blazer
with pleather sleeves and dressy sneakers. It was an interesting look.
Edgy. Bizarre. A little goth? He was hot but undeniably strange.

Before the play started a cute girl came up to us to say hi. He
introduced me to her and said she was his ex from years before. She
also happened to be in the show. I let that sink in. What kind of guy
brings a new girl to his ex's play? This guy seemed increasingly odd.

After the play, we went to a sex club. It wasn't busy, and the
energy was low, but there was a cute girl back in the dungeon area
getting flogged and fucked by a guy I knew, so we watched for a
little while. Then we started to touch. All of a sudden the passion
was there. I straddled him as he sat on the bench and rode him.
We kissed passionately, and time stopped existing. All those happy
chemicals got released, and I swooned. I could tell it was the same
for him: there was a sparkle in his eye, a big grin, and hunger and
satisfaction at the same time.

CHAPTER 63

This Isn't About a Happy Ending

A big Hollywood director once paid me my hourly rate to interview me about my life. He was trying to create a Dominatrix role for a film and intended to weave together the stories of several real Professional Dommes. I told him a scaled-down version of my story, and he listened as if waiting for something specific. Eventually, he asked me point-blank what traumatic events had shaped my life. This was before ayahuasca and therapy, so I told him there wasn't anything—that I'd had a decent upbringing, had chosen men who weren't abusive, hadn't developed any addictions, and that things had generally gone pretty smoothly.

He was profoundly disappointed. He explained that a good story has to have conflict, trauma, something challenging for the viewer to connect with. I tried to explain that not all sex workers are broken people, but by then he had lost interest. He was so fixated that he offered me more money for the truth. He thought I was holding something back.

And maybe in some ways I was.

My mother had created the perfect storm: a young woman who was ambitious, sexually open-minded and fearless. A good actress. Someone who was willing to do whatever it took to succeed. But all of those things came at a price. I had ambition because I never felt like I was good enough. I was always trying to do better to make her proud, to get her to stay, but she abandoned me over and over anyway—emotionally and literally. I was sexually open because I had been exposed to inappropriate sexual situations as I was hitting puberty, the consequence of having a highly oversexed mother who didn't understand healthy boundaries. One who told me everything about her sex life and normalized me telling her everything too. I was encouraged to be a sexual object from a young age. She liked it when I wore sexy clothes and men looked at me. She dangled me in front of her lovers, proud that she had produced a little sex kitten. I was fearless because she told me I could be and do whatever I wanted. She instilled an almost superhero-like confidence in me. She wanted so badly for me to have a better life than her. But she was doing that as much for me as for herself, living vicariously through me. My desperation for financial security came from growing up poor and knowing that no one was going to take care of me. Financial security represented safety in the deepest sense of the word. Money wasn't about stuff; it was about independence and self-preservation. I was a good actress because I had to be to survive; I had to learn how to lie convincingly to my father, I had to pretend to like Mom's boyfriends, I had to pretend to be interested in hearing about her sexcapades. I got good at pretending, at masking my true feelings, even from myself. I was the victim of a unique kind of abuse from my mother—who I love dearly, despite it—and the evidence of the abuse is both erased and highlighted when you look at what I have become.

But that's not the whole truth.

Having been in the sex industry for over a decade and having experienced it from its core as well as its fringe, I've seen a lot of different perspectives from a lot of different people. There are no easy answers and no tidy endings. You can't say that every sex worker is fucked up, has daddy issues, has been used, abused or broken. Some women assert adamantly that their job in sex work is empowering. Some feminists will even consider self-objectification as powerful, using their sexuality to get what they want. I have objectified myself and allowed men to objectify me. I have felt empowered at times. I've been drunk on power, holding fistfuls of cash with a man begging to give me more, to give me anything, while in the same moment feeling like a two-dimensional thing; the money was for me to play the role of his fantasy, but my own inner world was irrelevant. I've bargained with myself, saying that it was like being an actor. Nothing wrong with that. Play the part. The show must go on. Then I've left feeling empty and given money to a homeless person, just to make a human connection.

The difference with actors in plays and movies is that everyone, including the performer, knows they're acting. Everyone comes in with the clear understanding that this is all pretend. I've dropped the act a number of times in the middle of a scene and watched faces and erections fall. I've seen men thoroughly disappointed in seeing me break character and humanize myself. I can tell you that, in those moments, I felt empowered too… and angry. Angry that seeing me as a real person would be such a boner killer. I have wanted to kill men for it, for putting me in a box labelled "For Sexual Gratification Only." That's how I know that objectification isn't harmless. The rage—which I can finally feel—surges from my core and threatens to burst out of my mouth like a dragon spewing fire.

For years, when I was numb and out of touch with my feelings, I didn't feel that anger. I didn't care. I'd shrug and say, "I may have sold my soul, but at least I got a good price for it." When sex workers, especially Pro Dominatrices, get bitter and jaded, it's because of burnout from the game of smoke and mirrors. It's fatigue from pretending to be what someone else wants us to be: puppets fulfilling fantasies. A persona is projected on us—one we've both allowed and encouraged, but one in which our thoughts and feelings don't matter. It's all an illusion. Men want a woman to take control, but they won't do something they don't want to do. The parameters are set, and a good Domme can pretend to push the boundaries just enough to give the thrill of authentic Domination and control, but the male is still in charge—especially when he's paying for a specific service.

I didn't grow up in a bubble. I had more than my mother's influence to send the message that sex was power; the media made sure my generation was brainwashed with it. During my influential years, Madonna jammed sex and power down our throats with "Like a Virgin," "Like a Prayer" and "Erotica," and I swallowed it up. I still love it. The cosmetics and fashion industries have been thorough in creating a market for women who believe their worth is directly related to their appearance... and that the best appearance is one that attracts men. So, of course, when a woman starts to have money thrown at her by adoring men—a clear sign she has achieved ninja-level sexiness—she is going to feel "empowered." And of course, she is likely to reject the label of "object," as that runs counter to her experience of power... and power is the most commanding drug of all.

Sex workers tend to tighten up their screening process as time goes on because it's one way to regain some control. To refuse service. To choose with whom we engage. That only works at the first stage, though, as refusing service after things have gotten started is a risky move. Most women instinctively know that a horny man can be easily manipulated, but an angry, horny man can be a dangerous beast. Nothing shatters the feeling of empowerment faster than realizing your safety is in jeopardy. Objectification and empowerment are about who is really in control, and when the game is all about control the lines blur. A healthy, balanced woman can understand she is playing a role and embrace that. She can see the client as the interactive audience who she is paid to entertain. In movies or theatre, some performances are meant to be funny, thrilling, endearing, thought-provoking, arousing. The nature of entertainment is to provide an escape from regular life. That's why we watch movies, theatre or sports, go to concerts, play games, gamble, dance, etc. We engage in these things with other people to entertain each other, to make life more interesting. Actors, musicians, athletes, porn stars, magicians—they entertain. If there were less of a stigma attached to sex work, perhaps the sexual objectification aspect would be less of an issue. If we could see it as another form of entertainment, one that is meant to arouse and sexually satisfy and also provide relief from the mundane or stressful, maybe it would be different.

And here's where things get complicated.

How many jobs out there involve taking money from men who see you as an object? Does a waitress care if her customers see her as anything other than a food-delivery vehicle? Does a florist care if her customers see her as anything other than a flower arranger? Does a postal worker care if customers see them as anything other than a mail deliverer? I could go on and on, giving examples of other jobs where people exchange a service for money and demonstrate how their thoughts and feelings don't come into the equation. They do the task they're paid to do, and no one thinks much about it.

Is it different when the service is sexual?

It's unlikely that objectification of florists or postal workers would result in sexual dysfunction, eating disorders, depression or surgical enhancements. Sure, a florist might get cosmetic enhancements to feel better personally, but she isn't going to make more money at her job if she gets bigger tits. The waitress might make more tips if her customers are male. The same goes for a female real estate agent or any woman in a sales job where her clients are men. As long as her breasts aren't too big, right? Then some men might not respect her or take her seriously.

Being attractive is a form of privilege—one that's usually going to result in more money—and that's power. So what happens to a woman who has been attractive, but something changes? She gains weight, starts to age. The world she has been living in starts to shift. I'm now past forty, which is ancient in this industry. Even with MILF being a highly searched term in porn, and even though some men have a preference for older, experienced women, the amount of attention an older woman gets is not in the same ballpark as someone in her twenties. But, hopefully, when a woman gets to that point she has other relationships that are built on genuine connection: friends or family who value her in ways that have nothing to do with her physical appearance. And most importantly, she has an honest relationship with herself that goes beyond her physical-value-for-money power trip.

And that's where I am.

Finally having a healthy relationship with myself is evidence that a combination of ayahuasca and therapy changed my life for the better—ayahuasca for showing me what was possible, and therapy for helping me to integrate the changes needed. And I sometimes think: if I were to sit down now, x years later, with the same Hollywood director, maybe I'd have something different to tell him. Maybe I'd tell him there's more to the story. Maybe I'd tell him that the truth he was trying so hard to find is more complicated than he thought. Maybe I'd say that the stories we tell ourselves and each other have their limits. Maybe we do ourselves a disservice by seeking to portray our messy lives as some kind of cinematic journey, something complete and transformative. Maybe we cheapen the story by casting one another as heroes or villains, or sidekicks, or femme fatales. Maybe the women who choose to pursue a career in sex work are neither entirely empowered nor entirely objectified. Maybe some are drawn to it because they're fucked up, but others aren't. And maybe what's most important is that this industry is a place where women can use those fuckups not just to survive, but to thrive. To succeed not in spite of them, but in part because of them. And maybe that's neither entirely good nor entirely bad.

There's more to the story; there's *always* more to the story. Except that in life, unlike in Hollywood, there are no easy answers, and no happy endings. The show just goes on.

Which means that maybe this story doesn't need an ending at all. Maybe it doesn't matter if I've settled down with the love of my life, moved onto a houseboat in the Caribbean with my best friend or if I'm living alone in a mansion full of cats. Because none of that is really important. This isn't a love story, it's not about my Magical Beast, and it isn't about a happy ending. This is a story about my relationship with myself, and all the factors that contributed to my success in an industry where so few succeed.

Besides, happy endings are for clients, and our session is over.

Printed in the USA
CPSIA information can be obtained
at www.ICGtesting.com
LVHW051023260724
786585LV00008B/250